T0189380

Advances in Information Security

Volume 101

Series Editors
Sushil Jajodia, George Mason University, Fairfax, VA, USA
Pierangela Samarati, Milano, Italy
Javier Lopez, Malaga, Spain
Jaideep Vaidya, East Brunswick, NJ, USA

The purpose of the *Advances in Information Security* book series is to establish the state of the art and set the course for future research in information security. The scope of this series includes not only all aspects of computer, network security, and cryptography, but related areas, such as fault tolerance and software assurance. The series serves as a central source of reference for information security research and developments. The series aims to publish thorough and cohesive overviews on specific topics in Information Security, as well as works that are larger in scope than survey articles and that will contain more detailed background information. The series also provides a single point of coverage of advanced and timely topics and a forum for topics that may not have reached a level of maturity to warrant a comprehensive textbook.

Reza Montasari

Countering Cyberterrorism

The Confluence of Artificial Intelligence,
Cyber Forensics and Digital Policing in US
and UK National Cybersecurity

 Springer

Reza Montasari
Department of Criminology, Sociology and Social Policy
School of Social Sciences
Swansea University
Swansea, UK

ISSN 1568-2633   ISSN 2512-2193   (electronic)
Advances in Information Security
ISBN 978-3-031-21922-1   ISBN 978-3-031-21920-7   (eBook)
https://doi.org/10.1007/978-3-031-21920-7

© The Editor(s) (if applicable) and The Author(s), under exclusive license to Springer Nature
Switzerland AG 2023
This work is subject to copyright. All rights are solely and exclusively licensed by the Publisher, whether
the whole or part of the material is concerned, specifically the rights of translation, reprinting, reuse of
illustrations, recitation, broadcasting, reproduction on microfilms or in any other physical way, and
transmission or information storage and retrieval, electronic adaptation, computer software, or by similar
or dissimilar methodology now known or hereafter developed.
The use of general descriptive names, registered names, trademarks, service marks, etc. in this publication
does not imply, even in the absence of a specific statement, that such names are exempt from the relevant
protective laws and regulations and therefore free for general use.
The publisher, the authors, and the editors are safe to assume that the advice and information in this book
are believed to be true and accurate at the date of publication. Neither the publisher nor the authors or the
editors give a warranty, expressed or implied, with respect to the material contained herein or for any
errors or omissions that may have been made. The publisher remains neutral with regard to jurisdictional
claims in published maps and institutional affiliations.

This Springer imprint is published by the registered company Springer Nature Switzerland AG
The registered company address is: Gewerbestrasse 11, 6330 Cham, Switzerland

To the Heavenly Father
and to my wife:
Anna

Acknowledgment

To my Heavenly Father, who hears and answers prayers, for his abundant love and blessings and to my beautiful wife, Anna, for all her loving support

In writing this book, I was fortunate to have the assistance of my students in different subdisciplines that comprise the field of Social Sciences. The completion of this book would not have been possible without their help. I am grateful to the following individuals for their kind assistance.

Abigail Carolina Boon, Charlotte Alice Dorrington, Sarah Charlin Klingberg, Ellie Moggridge, Megan Wilmot Mcintyre

I am also deeply indebted to Professor Steve Gill and Dr. Fiona Carroll at Cardiff Metropolitan University for their many helpful comments and much constructive feedback.

Contents

List of Abbreviations

ACD	Active Cyber Defence
AgriTech	Agricultural Technology
AI	Artificial Intelligence
ANN	Artificial Neural Networks
APT	Advanced Persistent Threat
AUDREY	Assistant for Understanding Data through Reasoning, Extraction and Synthesis
AuI	Augmented Intelligence
AWS	Amazon Web Services
BDA	Big Data Analytics
BDPA	Big Data Predictive Analytics
BI	Business Intelligence
CAF	Cyber Assessment Framework
CCTV	Closed-Circuit Television
CESG	Communications-Electronics Security Group
CFREU	Charter of Fundamental Rights of the European Union
CLAIRE	Confederation of Laboratories for Artificial Intelligence Research in Europe
CMA	Competition and Markets Authority
CNN	Convolutional Neural Networks
COMPAS	Correctional Offender Management Profiling for Alternative Sanctions
CPD	Chicago Police Department
CPS	Cyber Physical System
CSIS	Center for Strategic and International Studies
CSP	Cloud Service Provider
DARPA	Defense Advanced Research Projects Agency
DF	Digital Forensics
DFR	Digital Forensics Framework
DHS	Department of Homeland Security
DL	Deep Learning
DNAD	Deep Neural Anomaly Detection

DNN	Deep Neural Network
DoD	Department of Defense
DSL	Domain Specific Language
DUR	Dual-Use Research
ECHR	European Convention on Human Rights
ENISA	The European Union Agency for Cybersecurity
EU	European Union
FBI	Federal Bureau of Investigation
FSCC	Financial Sector Cyber Centre
FR	Facial Recognition
FRT	Facial Recognition Technology
GCCC	Government Cyber Coordination Centre
GCHQ	Government Communications Headquarters
GCP	Google Cloud Platform
HMM	Hidden Markov Model
IBM	International Business Machines Corporation
ILP	Intelligence-Led Policing
IoT	Internet of Things
IP	Intellectual Property
IPA	Investigatory Powers Act
IPO	Intellectual Property Office
JPL	Jet Propulsion Laboratory
LAN	Local Area Network
LAPD	Los Angeles Police Department
IARPA	Intelligence Advanced Research Projects Activity
LAWS	Lethal Autonomous Weapon System
LEA	Law Enforcement Agency
MIT	Massachusetts Institute of Technology
ML	Machine Learning
MNIST	Modified National Institute of Standards and Technology
MoD	Ministry of Defence
MP	Member of Parliament
MV	Machine Vision
NASA	National Aeronautics and Space Administration
NATO	The North Atlantic Treaty Organization
NCSC	National Cyber Security Centre
NCSS	National Cyber Security Strategy
NER	Name Entity Recognition
NHS	National Health Service
NIJ	National Institute of Justice
NLP	Natural Language Processing
NLU	Natural Language Understanding
NRR	National Risk Register
NSF	National Science Foundation
NSI	National Security and Investment Act

NSRA	National Security Risk Assessment
NSTC	National Science and Technology Council
NYPD	New York City Police Department
OS	Operating System
OSTP	Office of Science and Technology Policy
PBDP	Predictive Big Data Policing
PBF	Person-Based Forecasting
PCA	Principal Component Analysis
PDNS	Protective Domain Name System
PNC	Police National Computer
SAW	Semi-Autonomous Weapon
SDSR	Strategic Defense and Security Review
SEI	Software Engineering Institute
SERS	Suspicious Email Reporting Service
SME	Small and Medium-Sized Enterprises
SMS	Social Media Site
STEM	Science, Technology, Engineering and Mathematics
SVM	Support Vector Machine
SVR	Russia's Foreign Intelligence Service
TCAV	Testing with Concept Activation Vectors
TCSEW	Telephone-Operated Crime Survey for England and Wales
UAVs	Unmanned Aerial Vehicles
UCAV	Unmanned Combat Air Vehicle
UK	United Kingdom
UKRI	UK Research & Innovation
UN	United Nations
UNCCT	United Nations Counter-Terrorism Centre
UNICRI	United Nations Interregional Crime and Justice Research Institute
US	United States
VBDA	Voice-Based Digital Assistant
VRS	Vulnerability Reporting Service
WAN	Wide Area Network

Chapter 1
Introduction

The Fourth Industrial Revolution, also known as Industry 4.0 or 4IR, could represent the twenty-first century's rapid transformation of technologies, industries, and societal patterns and processes as a result of growing interconnectedness and intelligent automation. In relation to its technological aspect, the 4IR concerns automation and data exchange in various technologies and processes (Schwab, 2018). These consist of Artificial Intelligence (AI); Advanced Robotics; Cyber-Physical Systems; online social and gaming platforms; the Internet of Things (IoT) including the Internet of Military Things and the Industrial Internet of Things; Cloud Computing; Cognitive Computing; and many other technologies. Whilst these technologies have numerous potential "to raise global income levels and enhance the quality of life for populations" globally (Schwab, 2018), they simultaneously present a myriad of challenges that impact businesses, governments and the wider populations. Arguably, even more importantly, this technological revolution could have a significant impact on the national and international security landscape, influencing the likelihood and character of both cyber and conventional warfare.[1] Likewise, as more powerful technologies emerge and become easier to utilise, individuals and groups such as terrorists or organised criminals will gain even more advanced capabilities to cause mass devastation and chaos (Schwab, 2018). Consequently, as cyberspace becomes more complex and ubiquitous, so do the tactics of modern cybercriminals and terrorist groups. The aforementioned technologies combined with anti-forensic tools and methods will all contribute to the offline and online arsenal of state and non-state adversaries and criminals.

These technological developments will have the ability to minimise the extent or effects of cyber threats, for instance, by means of creating new ways of security or

---

[1] For instance, conflicts and international security will be determined by the technological advancements afforded by the 4IR such that future conflicts between states will be completely hybrid based on the combination of classic battlefield strategies and methods formerly linked with the nonstate actors (Schwab, 2018).

© The Author(s), under exclusive license to Springer Nature Switzerland AG 2023
R. Montasari, *Countering Cyberterrorism*, Advances in Information Security
101, https://doi.org/10.1007/978-3-031-21920-7_1

better precision in targeting. One of these technologies is AI, the deployment of which is increasingly becoming of significant value to the western governments' mission to keep their nations safe. AI will be critical to our ability to cope with the growing volume and complexity of data, as well as to build the capabilities required to protect against cyber threats including those enabled by AI, itself. As a general-purpose, dual-use technology, AI can be used for both good and evil. It can be used in support of malicious cyberattacks (attack side) or as a shield to combat cyber threats (defence side). From the attack side, the most dangerous and malicious uses of AI will be likely to include malicious actors being able to train machines to hack or socially engineer victims at human or superhuman levels of performance, resulting in significant threats to our digital, physical, political, economic and social security. Similarly, Machine Learning (ML) and Deep Learning (DL) techniques will be capable of making complex cyberattacks easier to carry out, allowing for more focused, speedier, and destructive attacks. Because of this, the impact of AI on both national and international cybersecurity will broaden the cyber threat landscape, bring new risks, and change the nature of existing threats.

Apart from creating new and powerful avenues for carrying out attacks, AI systems, themselves, will also become more vulnerable to manipulation. At the same time, from the defence side, the utilisation of AI for defensive purposes presents western nations with a wide range of legal, ethical and political challenges. This is highlighted by the European Commission's recently published white paper on AI (European Commission, 2020). The paper outlines policy options for ensuring the safe and trustworthy development of AI (Cohen et al., 2020) and requires the EU countries to regulate AI's high-risk applications and facilitate the responsible use of AI. The US and EU consider it important to work within an internationally recognised legal and regulatory framework that strikes the right balance between the preservation of vital human rights and civil liberties and the safeguarding of our democratic way of life from unprecedented security threats from the likes of Russia and China.

Against this backdrop, it is therefore of paramount importance to understand how AI and associated technologies are adapted and exploited by malicious state and non-state actors in order to carry out or facilitate their activities more effectively. Existing research on AI has mainly focused on its societal benefits in many areas from economics and law to technical subjects such as verification, validity and control. However, few studies have been conducted that encompass both the benefits and the perils of the national and international security uses of AI and related technologies. Filling the gap, this book is intended to provide a comprehensive analysis covering the confluence of AI, Cyber Forensics and Digital Policing in the context of the United Kingdom (UK), United States (US) and European Union (EU) national cybersecurity. More specifically, the book aims to address the following.

With regards to the AI and associated technologies aspect of the book, it explores ways in which the adoption of AI algorithms and its subdomains (such as ML, DL, Natural Language Processing (NLP), and Big Data Predictive Analytics (BDPAs)), transform law enforcement agencies' (LEAs) and intelligence services' practices such as how these technologies might assist them in addressing cyber threats and improving accountability and supervision. To this end, the book explores the role that these technologies play in the manufacture of security, the threats to freedom, and the levels of social control in the surveillance state. More specifically, focusing on the potential of the national and international security uses of AI in the aforementioned western democracies, the book investigates ways in which AI can be deployed to detect and prevent a wide range of malicious activities in both physical and cyber space. As well as its analysis of the beneficial applications of AI in national security, the book also examines the malevolent use of AI and associated technologies by state and non-state actors. Along with this analysis, it also investigates the key legal, political, ethical, privacy and human rights implications of the national security uses of AI in the stated democracies. Accordingly, it offers a set of policy recommendations to help to mitigate these challenges.

In relation to the IoT aspect of the book, it assesses a wide range of AI and Digital Forensic techniques that can be deployed respectively to combat and investigate cyberattacks carried out through or against the IoT platforms. In terms of policing physical and cyber space, the book presents a comprehensive analysis into how new technologies are transforming digital policing in the context of the UK and the US policing. This analysis focuses on both the positive and the negative impact of these technologies when deployed for policing, surveillance and national security purposes. In particular, the book assesses the potential impact of BDPA in policing on individual liberty and the democratic control of policing (Ferguson, 2017), and ways in which an adept balance can be made in covering both the promises and the perils of predictive policing. Similarly, it explores LEAs' automated operations and their negative impact on the minority populations such as being entangled in a web of surveillance and punishment. Furthermore, it is determined how, under the pretence of objectivity, the use of BDPAs to guide policing methods could disguise and strengthen racial bias. Following this analysis, the book, accordingly, offers a number of recommendations with a view to assisting LEAs with conducting predictive policing more effectively whilst, simultaneously, ensuring individuals' human rights and civil liberties.

Last, but not least, the book assesses efforts currently undertaken by the international community to respond to cyber threats, outlining where progress has been made in developing a unified response and highlighting where challenges and ongoing sources of disagreement lie. To this end, it presents a comprehensive analysis of the latest developments associated with the national cybersecurity AI strategies of the US, UK and EU in order to evaluate their strengths, shortcomings and gaps. A comparison is made between the US and the UK AI approaches and those adopted by state adversaries. Along with this comprehensive analysis, the book offers a broad range of potential cybersecurity solutions, policy recommendations and best practices that can be adopted to help mitigate threats against national and international security of the stated democracies. Therefore, what follows in the book aims to provide a comprehensive and useful foundation for understanding how emerging technologies are impacting the national and international security landscape. Hence, the interplay of social, cultural, and technical forces coalesce into a single narrative that is presented as individually distinct chapters within the book which is organised as follows.

Chapter 2 analyses different types of cyber threats, identify the risk they pose to national security, and provides a critical evaluation of cybersecurity policy in the UK. The Chapter will examine how current UK Government policies and practices effectively mitigate the cyber threats to national security, and will explore how these responses can be further developed, with reference to the National Cyber Security Centre, the Active Cyber Defence programme, and the National Cyber Security Strategy 2022–2030.

Chapter 3 analyses AI capabilities in preventing and combatting cyberattacks carried out through or against the IoT platforms. To this end, the Chapter examines ways in which AI can be used both to safeguard and to threaten national security in different ways. Addressing digital security, the Chapter explores how AI could be deployed to combat and prevent cyberattacks on IoT devices by drawing upon recent real-life examples of such attacks. The Chapter also investigates the use of AI and the IoT in military applications along with the risks associated with hacking these technologies when deployed in warfare. Furthermore, the Chapter explores the impact of the misuse of AI on political security, examining how Deepfake technology influences political opinions and how filter bubbles polarise public views. In addition, the Chapter examines the key ethical implications of AI algorithms such as their impact on user privacy or bias against a certain group of individuals. Following the analysis, the Chapter accordingly offers a set of recommendations that can be considered to assist with addressing the stated issues.

Chapter 4 extends the previous Chapter by examining the potential use of AI techniques, such as ML and NLP, in automating certain tasks of the IoT Forensics, such as anomaly and steganography detection. The Chapter also investigates challenges in relation to algorithmic bias and transparency in military AI applications. Accordingly, general policy recommendations are offered in response to increasing transparency and reducing bias in AI algorithms intended for miliary use. Furthermore, the chapter identifies and introduces potential avenues for further research.

Chapter 5 delivers a comprehensive analysis into how new technologies are transforming digital policing in the context of the UK and the US policing. To this end, the Chapter focuses on the analysis of various technologies such as AI, ML, Facial Recognition (FR), NLP and BDPA. At the centre of this analysis is a detailed assessment of both the positive and the negative impact of these technologies when deployed for policing, surveillance and national security purposes. More specifically, an emphasis is placed on examining ways in which the police embrace predictive analytics and innovative surveillance technologies to support an effective crime-preventing strategy, deploy resources more efficiently, identify criminal suspects, conduct investigations, and improve accountability. Following the findings, the Chapter offers a set of recommendations and solutions to the issues raised in the Chapter.

Chapter 6 builds upon the previous Chapter providing an in-depth analysis of some of the negative consequences of the use of the stated technologies to police society. In particular, this chapter specifically seeks to determine the potential impact of BDPA in policing on individual liberty and steps that can be taken to create a smart balance between conducting predictive policing and preserving civil liberties. Additionally, the Chapter seeks to explore how the use of automated operations carried out by LEAs can serve to perpetuate disparities between society and its minority communities and capture them in a web of surveillance and punishment. Following these analyses, the Chapter offers a set of recommendations that serve to mitigate the issues identified as well as directions for further research.

Chapter 7 analyses and critiques the national AI strategies proposed by the US, UK and EU in order to identify their strengths, shortcomings and gaps. Following this analysis, comparisons are made between the aforementioned states' AI approaches with those adopted by state adversaries, namely China and Russia. Accordingly, the chapter presents a set of recommendations that could be implemented by Western governments to ensure that they leverage the beneficial elements of AI, whilst concurrently mitigating its potential risks to their national security.

References

Cohen, I. G., Evgeniou, T., Gerke, S., & Minssen, T. (2020). The European artificial intelligence strategy: Implications and challenges for digital health. *The Lancet Digital Health, 2*(7), e376–e379. https://doi.org/10.1016/S2589-7500(20)30112-6

European Commission. (2020). White paper. On artificial intelligence – A European approach to excellence and trust. Available at: https://ec.europa.eu/info/sites/default/files/commission-white-paper-artificial-intelligence-feb2020_en.pdf. Accessed 21 Aug 2022.

Ferguson, A. G. (2017). *The rise of big data policing: Surveillance, race, and the future of law enforcement*. New York University Press.

Schwab, K. (2018). The fourth industrial revolution: What it means, how to respond. World Economic Forum. Available at: https://www.weforum.org/agenda/2016/01/the-fourth-industrial-revolution-what-it-means-and-how-to-respond/ Accessed 04 July 2022.

Chapter 2
Cyber Threats and the Security Risks They Pose to National Security: An Assessment of Cybersecurity Policy in the United Kingdom

1 Introduction

This chapter will analyse different types of cyber threats, identify the security risks they pose to national security, and provide a critical evaluation of cybersecurity policy in the UK. Due to the interdisciplinary nature and origins of this topic, there are no universally accepted definitions for much of the terminology regarding this subject (Završnik, 2009). Oftentimes, interpretations of these terms will differ depending on "the academic or professional disciplinary origins of the interested parties" (Kiener-Manu, 2019, para. 1). However, this chapter will review cyber threats and cybersecurity within the context of UK Government policy. Therefore, the National Cyber Security Centre (NCSC) glossary, along with other government documents, will be used as the main reference for providing a straightforward set of definitions for commonly used cybersecurity terms. The NCSC is the UK Government's leading technical authority for dealing with cyber threats and is an administrative subdivision of the Government Communications Headquarters (GCHQ), which, as one of the UK's primary intelligence and security agencies, has a strategic focus on cybersecurity (National Cyber Security Centre, 2016).

According to the NCSC, a cyber threat refers to "…any circumstance with the potential to harm an information system through unauthorised access, destruction, disclosure, modification of data, and/or denial of service" (National Cyber Security Centre, 2016, para. 15). By contrast, cybersecurity focuses on reducing the risk of cyber-attacks through the protection of data, devices, services, and networks (National Cyber Security Centre, 2016). In the UK, the current National Security Strategy identifies emerging technologies and the increasing proliferation of cyber capabilities of state and non-state actors as a threat to national security. The concept of national security represents the policy directions whereby national issues are understood and answered (Anwar & Rafique, 2012). As technology becomes an

© The Author(s), under exclusive license to Springer Nature Switzerland AG 2023
R. Montasari, *Countering Cyberterrorism*, Advances in Information Security 101, https://doi.org/10.1007/978-3-031-21920-7_2

increasingly fundamental part of modern life, a better understanding of the cyber threat landscape is needed to properly protect UK interests at home and abroad.

The digitalisation of society and the emergence of new technology has provided numerous opportunities for socio-cultural, economic, and political development in the UK (Trittin-Ulbrich et al., 2020). Considerable technological advancements of recent years have been associated with increased efficiency, better performance, and greater transparency in the public and private sectors (Alcaide Muñoz et al., 2016; Kim & Lee, 2012). However, these new opportunities, guided by digital development, also bring about unprecedented technical, ethical, and legal challenges for law enforcement agencies, government officials, and policymakers in the UK. This technological evolution has also led to the progression of cyber threats, and the continuous development of new types of cyber-attacks, tools, and techniques that pose a major threat to the economy, government administration, and the delivery of vital services that depend on the integrity of cyberspace (Cabinet Office, 2016). As this technological dependency grows, the UK Government must ensure that its approach to cybersecurity evolves to mitigate the dynamic nature of cyber threats and assure the integrity of critical national infrastructure. The COVID-19 Pandemic has also accelerated the digital transformation of organisations and services across the UK and has evolved to be a type of "catalyst" for the deployment and expanding use of digitalisation in workplaces and offices (Amankwah-Amoah et al., 2021). In 2020, Interpol reported an increase in the number of cybercriminals exploiting the pandemic to use ransomware against critical infrastructure and healthcare organisations in charge of the COVID-19 response across Europe (Interpol, 2020). In addition, most of the NCSC's recent work has revolved around the coronavirus outbreak and protecting the services, systems, and staff that support the National Health Service (NHS) (National Cyber Security Centre, 2021a). The exploitation of COVID-19 by cybercriminals, the alarming rate at which new attacks are being developed, and the significant impact of such attacks highlight the relevance of this subject matter in current research.

Although public awareness of cybersecurity-related issues in the UK has increased in recent years, a significant percentage of the general public and Small and Medium-Sized Enterprises (SMEs) underestimate the dangers of cyber threats (Home Office, 2018). Further research is needed in this area to increase awareness and make certain that government organisations have access to reliable and comprehensible information. The fast-changing nature of cyber risks and threats means that future policy and practice must be informed by the most up to date and credible research. This will help ensure that the UK's cyber threat response remains effective while increasing the resilience of the UK's cybersecurity ecosystem as a whole (The Royal Society, 2016). The structure of this chapter will follow three thematic sections in the format of three different research questions. The aim of these research questions is to provide a critical evaluation of cyber threats and the risk they pose to national security, along with a critical evaluation of cybersecurity policy in the UK. These research questions include the following:

RQ1. What are the most prevalent cyber threats to national security, and what risk do they pose?

RQ2. Do current cybersecurity policies and practices in the United Kingdom effectively help mitigate cyber threats to national security?
RQ3. How can current cybersecurity policies and practices be improved to mitigate cyber threats more effectively to national security?

2 The Most Prevalent Cyber Threats

The terms 'cyber threats' and 'cybersecurity' and other related expressions are often widely used but "…mask a range of untested assumptions and unanswered questions, posing a serious difficulty for policy-makers and those responsible for national safety and security" (Cornish et al., 2009, p. 1). Current definitions and discourse regarding these terms in academic literature are often discussed within a traditional policy framework, and encourage a tendency to focus policy-making into something reactive and disproportionate (Carr & Tanczer, 2018). However, the correlation between vulnerability and dependency within the cybersecurity field indicates that it "…is a more challenging problem…one which might not be conductive to a linear analysis based on action and reaction…" (Cornish et al., 2009, p. 2). Focusing on the first research question, this Section analyses the most prevalent cyber threats to national security and the security risks they pose. To this end, the Section provides an overview of cyber threats within the context of national security in the UK in a way that factors in the uncertainty and non-linearity of such a dynamic and constantly evolving issue. This Section will also aim to provide an analysis of current legislation and policy-making in the cybersecurity field.

2.1 The UK Cyber Landscape

The policy challenges presented by the cyberspace are not exclusively technological in nature and require a strategic response that takes into account the complexities of operating in a digital and physical environment (HM Government, 2022, p. 17). The cyberspace "…encompasses all information and communication means in a collection of networks, techniques, users and digital space…" and can be described in terms of three layers: virtual, logical, and physical (Zenon & Trejnis Przemysław, 2017, p. 27; HM Government, 2022). The virtual layer refers to the part of the cyberspace most individuals experience and includes virtual representations such as social media, email, and bank accounts (Cornish et al., 2009). The logical layer is made up of code or data, such as operating systems and databases, while the physical layer is the part of the cyberspace that consists of all the hardware necessary to transmit data such as Wi-Fi, personal devices, and routers (HM Government, 2022). The cyberspace is experienced by a variety of groups, including individuals, businesses, and governments, and it is used by these groups in various ways and for various purposes (HM Government, 2022). Over the past decade, developments in technology have allowed for greater global accessibility of cyberspace. However, increased accessibility also results in more opportunities for the exploitation of the cyberspace by cyber criminals and state-based actors.

2.2 How Cyber Threats Are Identified in the UK

The UK Government uses risk management to "...compare, assess and prioritise all major disruptive risks to national security", and outlines these risks in a public-facing document known as the National Risk Register (JCNSS, 2019). The UK National Risk Register (NRR) (Cabinet Office, 2020) is the unclassified version of the National Security Risk Assessment (NSRA) and provides information on significant risks that could occur within the next 2 years. The aim of the NRR is to "...identify and assess future security risks, generate actions, and offer evidence to enable central and local government to undertake contingency planning" (JCNSS, 2019). The development of the document is led by the Civil Contingencies Secretariat in the Cabinet Office and is informed by intelligence and information across the Government and from a wide range of experts across the UK (Cabinet Office, 2020). Significant risks that have been identified in the NSRA and the NRR are "...represented as 'reasonable worst case scenarios' and indicate the worst plausible manifestation of that particular risk" (Cabinet Office, 2020). The risks are then assessed based on impact and the likelihood of the risk occurring within the next year, and then plotted onto a matrix. Assessed risks are also thematically grouped together on the matrix, and can fall into one of the following six categories as demonstrated in Fig. 2.1.

Fig. 2.1 Categories of the assessed risks as outlined by the UK Government

Cyber-attacks are identified as a significant risk by the NRR 2020 and fall under the Malicious Attacks category on the matrix. In the NRR 2020, cyber-attacks have been given an estimation of 25 to 125 in 500 chances of occurring in the next year, and are considered a level B threat on the indicative impact scale. The indicative impact scale assesses impact across a variety of dimensions, including impact on human welfare, human behaviours, essential services, the economy, the environment, security, and international relations. This assessment places cyber-attacks as having a relatively high likelihood of occurring and causing damage, and groups them in the same risk category as industrial actions, environmental disasters, and organised crime activity, amongst others. The NRR 2020 and the National Cyber Security Strategy 2022–2030 (Cabinet Office, 2022) identify cyber-attacks that threaten national security as attacks that may attempt to access and cause disruption to strategic systems in the UK with "…the purpose of espionage, commercial gain, sabotage and disinformation…" (Cabinet Office, 2022, p.24; Cabinet Office, 2020). The impact of such attacks can often result in a wide variety of consequences such as significant financial loss and risks to critical infrastructure and democratic institutions (HM Government, 2022; Cabinet Office, 2022; Cabinet Office, 2020). The COVID-19 pandemic has also provided new opportunities for exploitation of the cyberspace by malicious state and non-state actors to "…steal vaccine and medical research, and to undermine other nations already hampered by the crisis" (National Cyber Security Centre, 2021a, p.18). So, although pandemics appear to be less likely based on their risk category grouping, their impact is considered much more severe. If the two risk categories are then combined through the complementary effect of the opportunity that the cyberspace provides for those with malicious intent, potentially drawing in the risk of organised crime. For example, the impact generated could be considerably higher than any of these risks on a standalone basis.

2.3   Perpetrators of Cyber Threats

Increased global accessibility of information and communications technologies has transformed the internet "…from an elite research network to a mass communications medium that has altered the global cyberthreat equation dramatically" (Cornish et al., 2009, p. 3; Rudner, 2013). The diverse users and uses of the internet make it increasingly difficult to organise cyber threats into a simple hierarchy. However, challenges related to cybersecurity can often be discussed in terms of four basic cyberthreat domains: state-sponsored cyber-attacks, ideological and political extremism, serious and organised crime, and lower-level/individual crime (Cornish et al., 2009). Large state-sponsored cyber-attacks have the potential to cause significant harm across a variety of critical arenas and will require higher levels of cyber resilience (Tran, 2018). In the National Cyber Strategy 2022, the document highlights the increasing threat of cyber-attacks against the UK and other western targets posed by Russia, China and North Korea (HM Government, 2022). In April 2021, the NCSC and fellow security counterparts in the US revealed that Russia's Foreign

Intelligence Service (SVR) was responsible for carrying out a series of cyber-attacks against US Government agencies and corporations, conducted through a piece of compromised software developed by a company called SolarWinds (FCDO, 2021). These incidents were "...part of a wider pattern of cyber intrusions by the SVR who have previously attempted to gain access to IT networks of NATO members and governments across Europe" (HM Government, 2022, p. 28).

Dominance in the cyberspace will be increasingly held by countries that have a strategic advantage in technology, and it is expected that cyber warfare will become an increasingly crucial aspect in international conflicts in the coming years (Cornish, 2009). The internet has transformed the way in which ideological and political extremists operate, and has created new opportunities for terrorists to communicate at various levels of obscurity (Gordon & Ford, 2002). Cyberterrorism, which refers to "...an act of politically motivated violence involving physical damage or personal injury caused by a remote digital interference with technology systems", enables extremists to commit acts of terror through the exploitation of a global communications infrastructure (Evan et al., 2017, p. 6). One of the first to leverage this new opportunity on a large scale was a young Moroccan man named Younes Tsouli. Considered at one point the world's most wanted cyber-jihadist, Tsouli used virtual terrorist networks to radicalise and advise on carrying out terrorist attacks until his arrest in 2005 and ultimate conviction in 2007, which marked the first instance of internet-based incitement to commit terrorism under British law (Jacobson, 2010). By the time Tsouli was arrested, he and his partner, Tariq al Daour, had managed to charge over $3.5 million using stolen credit cards, and his subsequent conviction provided a vital evidence of how extremists had honed their operational-level planning skills on the Internet (Cornish et al., 2009). It also highlighted that the technological sophistication of the cyberspace was perhaps better understood by the criminals than by the judicial system. Tsouli was arrested only after being geolocated by another Internet user with whom he had been engaging in adversarial online communications. Indeed, at one point in Tsouli's trial, due to the judge's lack of familiarity with the internet, an expert in forensic computing was brought in to explain the fundamental workings of the internet.

The cyberspace has also become a lucrative target not only for criminals looking to perpetrate acts of serious and organised crime, but also for criminals conducting acts at the individual and lower level of severity (Brenner, 2002). Serious organised crime groups, such as the Japanese Yakuza, "...may exploit the cyberspace for a variety of fairly predictable purposes, including money-laundering, drug trafficking, extortion, credit card and ATM fraud [and] software piracy..." (Cornish et al., 2009, p. 9). The migration of organised crime to the cyberspace signals a shift in the way serious and organised crime groups operate and opens up the possibility of a functional relationship between organised crime and extremist groups (Brenner, 2002). However, increased internet literacy and access to hacking guides and software tools mean that even individuals can pose a cyber threat to national security. In

2002, Gary McKinnon was accused of hacking into US Government computers from his flat in the UK, and admitted to plotting attacks in retaliation for what he believed to be US-sponsored post-9/11 terrorism (Cornish et al., 2009, p. 11). His case was ultimately dismissed by the UK Crown Prosecution Service and he faced extradition for trial in the US, which was eventually blocked by Prime Minister Theresa May in 2012. Although McKinnon was acting alone, his actions affected the integrity of the computers' operating systems (OSs) and resulted in over $700,000 in damages (Arnell & Reid, 2009). While the threat from lower-level and individual criminals is often overstated and dramatised, it is clear that the consequences of individual hacking can pose a considerable threat to government services and infrastructure (CISA, 2005). Overall, the four cyberthreat domains identified in this chapter – state-sponsored cyberattacks, ideological and political extremism, serious and organised crime and lower-level and individual crime – present a varied array of interlinked threats that security policy-makers must address (Cornish et al., 2009).

2.4   Types of Cyber-Attacks

Individuals and organisations responsible for cybersecurity breaches and attacks often use various forms of hacking, phishing, and malware to target victims. According to the Cyber Security Breaches Survey 2021 (Department for Digital, Culture, Media and Sport, 2021), 39% of businesses and 26% of charities in the UK reported having cybersecurity breaches or attacks with phishing being the most common type of attack in 2021. Phishing is a type of technique that collects sensitive and personal information using a combination of social engineering and technology by impersonating a legitimate person or business in electronic communication (Basnet et al., 2008, p. 373). Unlike phishing, which relies on individuals voluntarily providing the information that is then used against them for criminal gain, hacking occurs when an individual attempts to gain unauthorised access to a network, system, and/or data by exploiting vulnerabilities in the target's code or programming (Alkhalil et al., 2021). Malware or malicious software is another common type of cyber-attack that is designed to cause harm in a variety of ways, including "…stealing, deleting, or encrypting data from a device or causing a device to become locked or unusable" (National Cyber Security Centre, 2021b, para. 5). Ransomware, which is a form of malware, was the type of attack responsible for the 2017 WannaCry cyber-attack that affected multiple organisations across the world, including the NHS (Ghafur et al., 2019). The cyber-attack impacted over 80 hospital trusts, led to "..disruptions to radiology services; cancelled outpatient appointments, elective admissions, and day-case procedures…", and resulted in an estimated cost of £6 million (Ghafur et al., 2019, para. 1). The attacks raised serious concerns regarding vulnerabilities in healthcare IT systems and highlighted the importance of cybersecurity in protecting various sectors of critical infrastructure in the UK.

3 The UK Cybersecurity Policies and Practices

Focusing on the second research question, this Section aims to assess the effectiveness of the UK cybersecurity policies and practices in mitigating cyber threats to national security.

3.1 Cybersecurity in Government Policies and Strategies

In recent years, the Government has increased efforts to ensure that the UK is "...the safest place in the world to live and work online..." and now regards cybersecurity as a key component in protecting national security (National Crime Agency & National Cyber Security Centre, 2018, para. 2; Carr & Tanczer, 2018). The UK Government's 2022 National Cyber Strategy builds upon almost 20 years' experience of safeguarding government information, systems and networks (NAO, 2013). The importance of protecting the security of data across the government was first recognised by the Communications-Electronics Security Group (CESG) within GCHQ in 2001. They recommended appointing a central sponsor to develop policy for handling and securing government data, and, by 2004, the first national strategy for information assurance was published (NAO, 2013, p. 10). Following two serious losses of data in HM Revenue & Customs (2007) and the Ministry of Defence (2008), the UK Government released its first cybersecurity strategy in 2009, and "...announced an additional £650 million of funding for a 4-year National Cyber Security programme" (NAO, 2013, p. 19).

This was followed by the National Cyber Security Strategy (NCSS) 2011–2016, and the Strategic Defense and Security Review (SDSR) 2015, which committed to developing a more comprehensive strategy to tackle the risk of cyber threats in the UK. In fulfilment of the SDSR 2015, the National Cyber Security Center (NCSC) was launched in 2016 and became the UK's first leading technical authority equipped to handle cyber threats. The Active Cyber Defence (ACD) programme is a key component of the work being carried out by the NCSC, designed to improve cybersecurity in the public sector in the UK. Currently, the NCSS 2022–2030 is the most current piece of legislation regarding cybersecurity issues in the UK. Further discussion on the expected outcomes of the NCSS 2022–3030 is referred to in Sect. 4.

3.2 Current Policies, Strategies, and Practices

The National Risk Register 2020 (Cabinet Office, 2020) identifies the NCSS 2016–2021, the NCSC, and the ACD programmes as the most significant Government responses to mitigating the risk that cyber threats pose to the UK. There are other relevant government documents, groups, and programmes that are responsible for tackling cyber-related issues in the UK such as the National Cyber Strategy 2022. The examination of this body of literature is outside the scope of this study; instead, the analysis focuses on addressing the most significant responses. It is also important to note that since the release of the National Risk Register 2020, the NCSS 2022–2030 has been published, which will replace the NCSS 2016–2021 in this analysis.

3.3   *National Cyber Security Centre*

The NCSC is part of GCHQ and is responsible for protecting critical infrastructure and services "…from cyber-attacks, managing major incidents, and improving the underlying security of the UK internet through technological improvement…" (GCHQ, 2017, para. 2). The NCSC also works alongside citizens and the wider public and private sector to provide support and advice on how to stay digitally protected and secure. Although the aim of the NCSC is to act as a bridge between industry and government and provide greater transparency in the cybersecurity field, not all of its work can be publicly disclosed due to national security concerns (National Cyber Security Centre, 2021a). Most of the NCSC's most recent work has been focused on protecting the individuals and organisations leading the UK's response to the COVID-19 pandemic (National Cyber Security Centre, 2021a). The exploitation of the digitalisation of businesses and government sectors across the country by cybercriminals has generated a significant increase in cybersecurity challenges for the NCSC. In the first 4 months of 2021, "…the NCSC handled the same number of ransomware incidents as for the whole of 2020 – which was itself a number more than three times greater than in 2019" (National Cyber Security Centre, , p. 30). As part of the NCSC's mission to protect the UK, they offer a wide range of free services and programmes, such as the Suspicious Email Reporting Service (SERS) and the Vulnerability Disclosure programmes. The SERS allows the public to report any suspicious emails they receive, and it gathered "…more than 5,427,000 reports in the 12 months up to September 2021 leading to the removal of more than 50,500 scams and 90,100 malicious URLs" (National Cyber Security Centre, 2021a, p. 40). In 2021, the NCSC also launched the Vulnerability Reporting Service (VRS), which aims to encourage greater disclosure of known vulnerabilities in networks and systems, and has helped to remediate over 400 vulnerabilities since its release (National Cyber Security Centre, 2021a). Although the NCSC has not yet been tested by a high-level cyber-attack, the centre has managed to successfully become a leading authority in the industry, and its work on skills and education has laid the groundwork for cybersecurity by defining which aspects of knowledge are critical to this newly recognised scientific field (Hannigan, 2019, p. 21).

3.4 Active Cyber Defence Programme

Under the ACD programme launched in 2016, the NCSC provides eligible organisations with a variety of free cybersecurity tools and services (National Cyber Security Centre, 2021a). The aim of the programme is to help organisations identify and remediate vulnerabilities, assist in managing cyber incidents, and automate the disruption of attacks (National Cyber Security Centre, 2021b) NCSC, 2021. Over the course of 2021, the ACD programmes have enabled the NCSC to "…remove a total of 2.3 million cyber-enabled commodity campaigns, including 13,000 phishing campaigns that were disguised as coming from the UK Government" (National Cyber Security Centre, 2021a, p. 38). Within the ACD programme, there are different services that are offered, including Protective Domain Name System (PDNS) and Exercise in a Box, discussed in more detail below. The aim of the NCSC's PDNS is to prevent users from accessing domains or IP addresses that are known to contain malicious content. By preventing access "…to malware, ransomware, phishing attacks, viruses, malicious sites and spyware at the source it makes the network more secure" (National Cyber Security Centre, 2017, para. 6). In 2021, the number of organisations using PDNS had risen by about 20%, and there was a significant uptake in usage after the NCSC extended PDNS access to healthcare and vaccine development organisations. Unlike PDNS, which is a form of active cyber defence, the ACD's Exercise in a Box programme is proactive in nature and is an online tool that offers organisations training to refine their response to cyber-attacks in a protected environment (National Cyber Security Centre, 2021a). In August 2021, the number of users, with multiple users per organisation, using Exercise in a Box has risen by 56% since September 2020 (National Cyber Security Centre, 2021a, p. 40). Although the NCSC's PDNS and Exercise in a Box programme are just two of the resources accessible to eligible organisations under the ACD programme, they highlight the wide range of measures being implemented by the UK Government to reduce the risk of cyber-attacks. Initial research has shown that the ACD has aided in lowering the prevalence and impact of low-level cybercrime on government institutions and service users since its launch in 2016 (Stevens et al., 2019).

3.5 National Cyber Security Strategy 2022–2030

The final component identified by the NNR 2020 in mitigating the risk posed by cyber threats to national security is the National Cyber Security Strategy. The aim of the NCSS 2022–2030, which builds upon the NCSS 2016–2021, is to ensure that "…core government functions are resilient to cyber-attacks…with all government organisations across the whole public sector being resilient to known vulnerabilities and attack methods no later than 2030" (p. 8). The NCSS 2022–2030 also sets out five main objectives that will "…set the dimensions of cyber resilience…", and include the management of cybersecurity risks, the detection and protection against cyber-attacks, the reduction in the impact of cybersecurity incidents, and the development of cybersecurity skills and knowledge across public and private sectors (p. 9). The UK Government's approach to achieving these aims and objectives will be supported by the introduction of two significant developments: the NCSC's Cyber Assessment Framework (CAF) and the creation of a Government Cyber Coordination Centre (GCCC).

The development of the NCSC'S Cyber Assessment Framework will ensure that the government is evaluating its cyber resilience in a coherent and similar manner to other institutions that provide the UK's essential services" (National Cyber Security Centre, 2021a). The CAF will also be consistent with additional cybersecurity frameworks, such as the ISO 27001, to ensure that the new framework does not conflict with the older risk management structures and processes. The second significant development proposed by the UK Government in the NCSS 2022–2030 is the establishment of a Government Cyber Coordination Centre. The GCCC's mission is to serve as a cyber coordination centre to attune operational cybersecurity efforts throughout government agencies (Cabinet Office, 2022, p. 24). Building upon the success of private sector models, such as the Financial Sector Cyber Centre (FSCC), the GCCC will be designed to ensure that data can be rapidly shared and will improve the UK Government's ability to mitigate cyber threats and incidents. The National Cyber Security Centre, the Active Cyber Defence programmes, and the National Cyber Security Strategy 2022–2030 were all identified in the National Risk Register 2020 (Cabinet Office, 2020), as the most significant and effective Government responses to mitigating the risk posed by cyber threats to national security.

4 Recommendations

Focusing on the third research question, this Section aims to offer a set of recommendations for improving current cybersecurity policies and practices to mitigate cyber threats to national security more effectively.

4.1 Criticisms of the NCSC and Recommendations

The NCSC has rapidly emerged as a key part of the UK Government's strategic answer to cyber threats and has made significant headway in tackling them over the past couple of years (Hannigan, 2019). The introduction and increased uptake of free programmes and services, such as the Vulnerability Disclosure programme and the Suspicious Email Reporting Service, provided by the NCSC, have played a key role in the organisation's success. However, there are multiple areas in which the NCSC will need to develop further in order to remain a key part of the Government's cyber threat response. One of the most significant challenges for the NCSC and the Government includes addressing high-volume cyber-enabled fraud, with local and national law enforcement agencies lacking the staff, skills, and/or technology necessary to meet the increasing demands from public (Hannigan, 2019). Despite the growing threat from large-scale cyber-attacks and increase in volume of cybercrime offences, research has shown that both the general public and businesses underreport cyber incidents and that there is an absence of understanding that certain cyber incidents are in fact crimes (McGuire & Dowling, 2013). The figures from the Telephone-operated Crime Survey for England and Wales (TCSEW) revealed that there were an estimated 1.9 million computer misuse offences in 2021, with a large increase in hacking, yet only a small fraction of these offences were reported to the proper authorities (Elkin, 2022).

While the under-reporting of cybercrimes by the public is likely to occur for a number of reasons, including reporting to other organisations (i.e., Internet service providers, banks, etc.), businesses are more likely to under-report incidents due to concerns about reputational damage and negative publicity (Fafinski & Minassian, 2009). One recommendation that could help reduce the underreporting of cyber incidents, from both the public and the business sector, is increased communication and collaboration between the NCSC and outside organisations. If the NCSC is to keep up with rising expectations and the constantly evolving cyber threat, they must continue to operate in non-traditional ways and increase involvement from the private sector (Hannigan, 2019). The NCSC must show the private sector that the most effective cyber defences are collaborative and transparent in nature, and provide assurance that information will be shared in both directions and that the government will rapidly make information available in order for it to be useful (Hannigan, 2019). This would help ensure that the NCSC has the most accurate information about current cyber threats and vulnerabilities and would help ensure better cyber incident response strategies.

4.2   Criticisms of the ACD and Recommendations

The Active Cyber Defence programme is another crucial component of the UK's cyber threat response. The ACD programme has shown significant potential in helping to improve UK national cybersecurity, but to continue to function effectively, it will need to adapt to shifting sociopolitical and technological environments (Stevens et al., 2019). Up until 2020, the ACD programmes predominantly focused on providing tools and services to the public sector. However, expansion of the ACD programme and increased engagement between the NCSC and the private sector would help develop how the ACD might be deployed throughout UK networks as a means of reducing the risk of large-scale cyber-attacks. While the ACD Broadening project was launched in 2020, with the aim of expanding impact outside the public sector, there is still more work needed to be done to ensure expansion of the programme's tools and services into different areas. The UK Government and the NCSC's partnerships with the private sector will be essential to the success of the programme and must be based on high levels of transparency. This is due to the fact that the NCSC's role is predominantly advisory, assisting organisations in the implementation of ACD as opposed to offering the technology itself (Stevens et al., 2019). Promotion of the ACD model to other countries as a suite of peaceable defensive measures could also help the NCSC gain international influence in the cyberspace and encourage the formation of "industrial partnerships" and trust networks, which results in constructive international cybersecurity solutions (Stevens et al., 2019; Marsden & Goslin, 2022).

4.3 Criticisms of the NCSS 2022–2030 and Recommendations

The final component of the UK's cyber threat response, as identified in the National Risk Register 2020 (Cabinet Office, 2020), is the NCSS 2022–2030. The NCSS 2022–2030, which was released in January 2022, sets out goals for the government's critical functions to become more resilient to cyber threats by 2025, and all public sector organisations to become more resilient by 2030. However, there have been some concerns that the timelines set out in the Strategy are incredibly tight, especially with the increasing threat of large scale cyber-attacks, and growing pressures on government budgets and organisations (Marsden & Goslin, 2022). The Government can support the accelerated delivery of the strategy's outcomes by carefully implementing the strategy across the government to ensure that departments are informed by clear cyber risk management. The success of the NCSS 2022–2030 will be "…determined by the levels of integration achieved across government, regions, with industry partners and specialist organisations" (Marsden & Goslin, 2022, para. 6). There are also some concerns that the NCSS 2022–2030 is predominantly focused on improving the cybersecurity field as it relates to the government's interests, with limited consideration for the private sector (Carr, 2016; Marsden & Goslin, 2022). Although the development of 'cybersecurity skills, knowledge and culture' is one of the key objectives of the strategy, differences in priorities and interests of both sectors may hinder the strategies impact and effectiveness. Typically, the private sector considers cyber-security challenges as financial and reputational risks, rather than a public good, which is how the UK Government views national cybersecurity (Carr, 2016, p. 55). However, the increasing privatisation of critical infrastructural systems, such as utilities and transport, highlights the significance of developing a national cybersecurity strategy that addresses the needs and challenges of both partners.

4.4 Recommendations for the Government's Role

While public and private sector partnerships have often been developed as an effective means to mitigate cybersecurity threats, in the context of national security, this arrangement is uniquely problematic (Carr, 2016, p. 44). In the UK, the unwillingness of politicians to assert authority for the state to enact more stern cybersecurity measures by law, combined with the private sector's reluctance to assuming responsibility raises questions about the extent to which the UK Government can be allowed to yield responsibility for national security (Carr, 2016; Steiger, 2022). However, the increase in 'outsourcing' of national cybersecurity in the UK means that the Government must continue to adapt their strategies, policies and practices to accommodate the needs of its private sector partners (Steiger, 2022). The UK Government can increase the overall sustainability of their cybersecurity goals by placing more emphasis on an 'incentive-accountability structure' within their strategies, that clarifies the specifics of expected roles, responsibilities, incentives, and outcomes (Carr, 2016). In the coming years, the UK Government may need to rethink "…the breadth and depth of security that they can usefully attach to expectations of cybersecurity", as the private sector continues to gain significant control and advantage over critical infrastructure (Carr, 2016, p. 62). The understanding and acknowledgement of these facts by the UK Government is essential to developing a more effective strategy for national security in this information era (Steiger, 2022).

5 Discussion and Conclusion

The aim of this Section is to present the key findings from the previous three thematic sections and critically assess cyber threats and UK cybersecurity policies. With consideration to the key findings, this section will also outline recommendations for further research, as well as recommendations for government cybersecurity policies, practices and programmes. The section will then end with a discussion on the limitations of the chapter and final concluding thoughts.

5.1 Key Findings

The first thematic section explored how relevant cyber threats to national security are identified and categorised in the UK. The NRR 2020, which identifies the most serious risks to UK national security, classifies cyber-attacks as a level B threat and are grouped in the same risk category as environmental disasters, and industrial actions, amongst others. Increased accessibility of the internet and major developments in communication technologies have helped diversify the cyberthreat landscape and provided new opportunities for exploitation of the cyberspace by hostile nation-states, ideological and political extremists, serious and organised crime organisations, and lower-level/individual actors. The type of cyber-attack, such as phishing and malware, can also increase the perceived risk of a cyber threat and can cause major disruptions to government organisations, such as the 2017 WannaCry ransomware attack. This first chapter also explored how the COVID-19 pandemic has accelerated the digitalisation of public and private sector organisations and highlighted the importance of building cyber resilience in various sectors of critical infrastructure across the country to protect national security. In 2021, the NCSC dealt with over 777 cyber incidents (up 7.5% from 723 in 2020), with 20% of reported incidents being linked to the health sector and vaccines (National Cyber Security Centre, 2021a, p. 10).

Overall, the most significant cyber threats perceived by the UK Government to threaten national security are those committed by hostile nations and ideological and political extremists and those targeting critical infrastructure, such as the NHS. The second thematic chapter focused on how current cybersecurity policies and practices in the UK effectively help mitigate cyber threats to national security. As identified by the NRR 2020, the NCSC, the ACD programme and the NCSS 2022–2030 (Cabinet Office, 2022) were selected by the UK Government as its most significant and impactful cyber threat responses. The NCSC, which was launched in 2016, works to mitigate the risk and impact of major cyber threats against critical infrastructure and government organisations by offering a wide range of free advice and services, such as the SERS and the Vulnerability Disclosure programme.

The ACD, another programme offered through the NCSC, aims to provide eligible organisations with the necessary cybersecurity tools and services, such as the PDNS and Exercise in a Box, to help prevent cyber-attacks and mitigate significant vulnerabilities. User organisations of both PDNS and Exercise in a Box have increased in 2021, and initial research has shown that the ACD programme has assisted in lowering the occurrence and consequences of low-level cyberattacks on government organisations (Stevens et al., 2019). The final component identified by the NNR 2020 in mitigating the risk posed by cyber threats to national security is the NCSS 2022–2030. Although a relatively recent addition to the UK's cyber threat response, the strategy aims to increase cyber resilience in the public sector by 2025, and resilience in the private sector by 2030. The Strategy aims to achieve these goals through the development of the NCSC's CAF and the establishment of a GCCC. The CAF and the GCCC will allow for clear cyber risk management and coordination across government organisations and improve the Government's ability to mitigate threats.

The third and final thematic section provided an analysis of how current cybersecurity policies and practices can be improved to mitigate cyber threats to national security more effectively. Although the NCSC, the ACD programme, and the NCSS 2022–2030 have emerged as key parts of the UK Government's strategic answer to cyber threats, there are multiple areas in which these components will need to further develop in order to remain effective. One of the most significant challenges facing the UK Governments' national cybersecurity efforts is the lack of integration on cybersecurity responses throughout the public and private sectors. As national cybersecurity and critical infrastructure become increasingly outsourced, the Government will need to focus on accommodating their response to include the interests and priorities of their private sector partners in order to increase the sustainability of their long-term cybersecurity and national security goals.

5.2 Limitations of the Chapter

This chapter set out to examine types of cyber threats, identify the risk they pose to national security, and provide a critical evaluation of cybersecurity policy in the UK. This literature-based chapter was conducted using a variety of sources, including journal articles, books, newspaper articles, and government reports. While the information gathered from these sources have helped to further develop research in this area, this methodological approach is limited as it does not result in new empirical data. This is important as many cyber incidents go unreported, which makes it difficult for government organisations to form a clear understanding of the cyber threat landscape (McGuire & Dowling, 2013). Therefore, one recommendation for future research is to investigate the factors that contribute to the underreporting of cyber incidents by individuals and businesses.

5.3 Concluding Remarks

In conclusion of the chapter as a whole, it can be asserted that cyber threats and cybersecurity are complex and evolving in nature, and the impact of these issues can have serious implications for the UK Government's policies, practices, and national security. It is clear from this research that hostile nation-states, political and ideological extremists, and serious and organised crime groups pose a significantly increasing threat to national security, with the development of more sophisticated hacking attacks with the potential for serious consequences for national critical infrastructure, including healthcare and vaccine organisations. Going forward, it is paramount that the UK Government bridges the gap between the private and public sectors and increases accessibility to the services provided by the NCSC. This would help to increase visibility in the cyber threat landscape and provide a more reliable insight into current threats, vulnerabilities, and effective responses. While this chapter has helped to further research in this topic area, this topic will need to be continuously researched as threats evolve and as the UK Government becomes more dependent on the integrity of the cyberspace to secure national security.

References

Alcaide Muñoz, L., Rodríguez Bolívar, M. P., & López Hernández, A. M. (2016). Transparency in governments: A meta-analytic review of incentives for digital versus hard-copy public financial disclosures. *The American Review of Public Administration, 47*(5), 550–573. https://doi.org/10.1177/0275074016629008

Alkhalil, Z., Hewage, C., Nawaf, L., & Khan, I. (2021). Phishing attacks: A recent comprehensive study and a new anatomy. *Frontiers in Computer Science, 3.* https://doi.org/10.3389/fcomp.2021.563060

Amankwah-Amoah, J., Khan, Z., Wood, G., & Knight, G. (2021). COVID-19 and digitalization: The great acceleration. *Journal of Business Research, 136*, 602–611. https://doi.org/10.1016/j.jbusres.2021.08.011

Anwar, M. A., & Rafique, Z. (2012). Defense spending and National Security of Pakistan: A policy perspective. *Democracy and Security, 8*(4), 374–399. https://doi.org/10.1080/17419166.2012.739551

Arnell, P., & Reid, A. (2009). Hackers beware: The cautionary story of Gary McKinnon. *Information & Communications Technology Law, 18*(1), 1–12. https://doi.org/10.1080/13600830902727822

Basnet, R., Mukkamala, S., & Sung, A. H. (2008). Detection of phishing attacks: A machine learning approach. In B. Prasad (Ed.), *Soft computing applications in industry. Studies in fuzziness and soft computing* (Vol. 226). Springer. https://doi.org/10.1007/978-3-540-77465-5_19

Brenner, S. (2002). Organised cybercrime? How cyberspace may affect the structure of criminal relationships. *North Carolina Journal of Law & Technology., 4*(1), 1–50.

Cabinet Office. (2016). National Cyber Strategy. https://www.gov.uk/government/publications/national-cyber-strategy-2022/national-cyber-security-strategy-2022#foreword

Cabinet Office. (2020). National Risk Register 2020. UK.Gov. Available at: https://www.gov.uk/government/publications/national-risk-register-2020 (Accessed: 12/12/2022).

Cabinet Office. (2022). Government Cyber Security Strategy 2022–2030. UK.Gov. Available at: https://www.gov.uk/government/publications/government-cyber-security-strategy-2022-to-2030 (Accessed; 12/12/2022).

Carr, M. (2016). Public-private partnerships in national cyber-security strategies. *International Affairs, 92*(1), 43–62. https://doi.org/10.1111/1468-2346.12504

Carr, M., & Tanczer, L. M. (2018). UK cybersecurity industrial policy: An analysis of drivers, market failures and interventions. *Journal of Cyber Policy, 3*(3), 430–444. https://doi.org/10.1080/23738871.2018.1550523

Cornish, P. (2009). *Cyber security and politically, socially and religiously motivated cyber attacks.* Chatham House.

Cornish, P., Hughes, R., & Livingstone, D. (2009). *Cyberspace and the National Security of the United Kingdom: Threats and responses.* Chatham House. https://www.chathamhouse.org/sites/default/files/public/Research/International%20Security/r0309cyberspace.pdf

Cybersecurity and Infrastructure Security Agency. (2005). Cyber Threat Source Descriptions ICISA. CISA.GOV. https://www.cisa.gov/uscert/ics/content/cyber-threat-source-descriptions#:%7E:text=Although%20the%20most%20numerous%20and,damage%20to%20national%2Dlevel%20infrastructures

Department for Digital, Culture, Media and Sport. (2021). Cyber Security Breaches Survey 2021. GOV.UK. https://www.gov.uk/government/statistics/cyber-security-breaches-survey-2021/cyber-security-breaches-survey-202145

Elkin, M. (2022). Crime in England and Wales: year ending September 2021. *Office for National Statistics. Office for National Statistics.* Available at: https://www.ons.gov.uk/peoplepopulationandcommunity/crimeandjustice/bulletins/crimeinenglandandwales/yearendingseptember2021 (Accessed: 12/12/2022).

Evan, T., Leverett, E., Ruffle, S. J., Coburn, A. W., Bourdeau, J., Gunaratna, R., & Ralph, D. (2017). *Cyber Terrorism: Assessment of the Threat to Insurance; Cambridge Risk Framework series; Centre for Risk Studies.* University of Cambridge.

Fafinski, S. & Minassian, N. (2009). UK Cybercrime Report. Garlik–Invenio Research.

Foreign, Commonwealth & Development Office. (2021). Russia: UK and US expose global campaign of malign activity by Russian intelligence services. GOV.UK. https://www.gov.uk/government/news/russia-uk-and-us-expose-global-campaigns-of-malign-activity-by-russian-intelligence-services

Ghafur, S., Kristensen, S., Honeyford, K., Martin, G., Darzi, A., & Aylin, P. (2019). A retrospective impact analysis of the WannaCry cyberattack on the NHS. *NPJ Digital Medicine, 2*(1), 1–7.

Gordon, S., & Ford, R. (2002). Cyberterrorism? *Computers & Security, 21*(7), 636–647. https://doi.org/10.1016/s0167-4048(02)01116-1

Marsden, L. & Goslin, C. (2022). Assessing the aims of the Government Cyber SecurityStrategy. ComputerWeekly.Com. Available at: https://www.computerweekly.com/opinion/Assessing-the-aims-of-the-Government-Cyber-Security-Strategy (Accessed: 12/12/2022).

Government Communication Headquarters. (2017). About the NCSC. GCHQ.GOV.UK. https://www.ncsc.gov.uk/information/about-the-ncsc.

Grewal, A., Kataria, H., & Dhawan, I. (2016). Literature search for research planning and identification of research problem. *Indian Journal of Anaesthesia, 60*(9), 635–639. https://doi.org/10.4103/0019-5049.190618

Hannigan, R. (2019). The future for the NCSC. In *Organising a government for cyber: The creation of the UK's National Cyber Security Centre* (pp. 21–22). Royal United Services Institute (RUSI). http://www.jstor.org/stable/resrep37389.10

HM Government. (2022). National Cyber Strategy 2022: Pioneering a cyber future with the whole of the UK. Available at: https://www.gov.uk/government/publications/national-cyber-strategy-2022/national-cyber-security-strategy-2022 (Accessed: 12/12/2022).

Home Office. (2018). A call to action: The cyber aware perception gap. *The Home Office*. https://assets.publishing.service.gov.uk/government/uploads/system/uploads/attachment_data/file/684609/BT_CYBER_AWARE_V11_280218.pdf.

Interpol. (2020). Covid-19 Cybercrime Analysis Report. file:///C:/Users/aboon/Downloads/COVID-19%20Cybercrime%20Analysis%20Report-%20August%202020%20(1).pdf

Jacobson, M. (2010). Terrorist financing and the internet. *Studies in Conflict & Terrorism, 33*(4), 353–363. https://doi.org/10.1080/10576101003587184

Joint Committee on National Security Strategy. (2019). *The UK's National Security Machinery*. Home Office.

Kiener-Manu, K. (2019). Cybercrime Module 2 Key Issues. *United Nations Office on Drugs and Crime*. https://www.unodc.org/e4j/en/cybercrime/module-2/key-issues/intro.html

Kim, S., & Lee, J. (2012). E-participation, transparency, and trust in local government. *Public Administration Review, 72*(6), 819–828. https://doi.org/10.1111/j.1540-6210.2012.02593.x

McGuire, M., & Dowling, S. (2013). *Cyber crime: A review of the evidence*. Home Office.

National Audit Office. (2013). The UK Cyber Security Strategy: Landscape review.

National Crime Agency & National Cyber Security Centre. (2018). *The cyber threat to UK business: 2017–2018 report*. NCA and NCSC.

National Cyber Security Centre. (2016). NCSC Glossary. https://www.ncsc.gov.uk/information/ncsc-glossary

National Cyber Security Centre. (2017). Protective Domain Name Service (PDNS). Available at: https://www.ncsc.gov.uk/information/pdns (Accessed: 12/12/2022).

National Cyber Security Centre. (2021a). NCSC Annual Review 2021. *NCSC*. https://www.ncsc.gov.uk/collection/ncsc-annual-review-2021. (Accessed: 12/12/2022).

National Cyber Security Centre. (2021b). *Mitigating malware and ransomware attacks*. NCSC. GOV.UK. https://www.ncsc.gov.uk/guidance/mitigating-malware-and-ransomware-attacks#whatismalwareransomware

Rees, J. (2022). The UK National Cyber Strategy 2022: Does It Go Far Enough & What's to Come? – Cyber Security Review. Cybersecurity-Review.Com. https://www.cybersecurity-review.com/the-uk-national-cyber-strategy-2022-does-it-go-far-enough-whats-to-come/.

Rudner, M. (2013). Cyber-threats to critical National Infrastructure: An intelligence challenge. *International Journal of Intelligence and Counter Intelligence, 26*(3), 453–481. https://doi.org/10.1080/08850607.2013.780552

Steiger, S. (2022). Cyber securities and cyber security politics. *Cyber Security Politics*, 141–153. https://doi.org/10.4324/9781003110224-12

Stevens, T., O'Brien, K., Overill, R., Wilkinson, B., Pildegovics, T., & Hill, S. (2019). UK active cyber defence: A public good for the private sector. .

The Royal Society. (2016). Progress and research in cybersecurity supporting a resilient and trustworthy system for the UK. https://royalsociety.org/-/media/policy/projects/cybersecurity-research/cybersecurity-research-report.pdf.

Tran, D. (2018). The law of attribution: Rules for attributing the source of a cyber-attack. *Yale Journal of Law and Technology, 20*, 376–411.

Trittin-Ulbrich, H., Scherer, A. G., Munro, I., & Whelan, G. (2020). Exploring the dark and unexpected sides of digitalization: Toward a critical agenda. *Organization, 28*(1), 8–25. https://doi.org/10.1177/1350508420968184

Webster, J., & Watson, R. T. (2002). Analyzing the past to prepare for the future: Writing a literature review. *MIS Quarterly, 26*(2), xiii–xxiii. http://www.jstor.org/stable/4132319

Wright, R. W., Brand, R. A., Dunn, W., & Spindler, K. P. (2007). How to write a systematic review. *Clinical Orthopaedics and Related Research, 455*, 23–29. https://doi.org/10.1097/BLO.0b013e31802c9098

Završnik, A. (2009). Cybercrime – definitional challenges and criminological particularities. *Masaryk University Journal of Law and Technology, 2*, 1–29.

Zenon, T., & Trejnis Przemysław, Z. (2017). Polityka ochrony cyberprzestrzeni w państwie współczesnym. *Studia Bobolanum, 28*(3), 21–40.

Chapter 3
Internet of Things and Artificial Intelligence in National Security: Applications and Issues

1 Introduction

Attacks on the IoT increased by 600% during the years 2016 and 2017 (Stevens, 2018). This significant increase amplifies the importance of protecting the vast amount of data that is collected from and processed by IoT devices. Moreover, this 'information overload' poses an increasing technical challenge for the global national security community (Babuta et al., 2020). The proliferation of digital data and involvement of IoT technologies require the use of more "...sophisticated analytical tools to effectively manage risk and proactively respond to emerging security threats", such as cyberattacks (Babuta et al., 2020, p. 2). Yet, research has shown that Artificial Intelligence (AI) can offer numerous opportunities for technological development in existing national security processes by improving efficiency and effectiveness (Babuta et al., 2020). The aim of this Chapter is to provide an overview of the beneficial and malicious applications of AI in an IoT context. The chapter also aims to examine the key ethical implications of AI use placing a particular focus on the issues of privacy and discrimination. Following the findings, the study will also offer a set of recommendations both in relation to the algorithmic bias and transparency for the use of AI in military applications.

The remainder of the Chapter is structured as follows. Section 2 provides relevant and necessary background information placing the study in context prior to addressing the core content. Section 3 explores AI and the IoT in the context of national security. To this end, a particular focus will be placed on ways in which they can be used and abused to strengthen and impair national security respectively. Section 4 analyses the privacy implications and other forms of flaws that can result from data processing by AI technology. This analysis will be in line with the existing legal frameworks. Following this analysis, a set of recommendations will be made in relation to addressing key ethical issues associated with AI algorithms. Finally, the chapter will be concluded in Sect. 5.

© The Author(s), under exclusive license to Springer Nature Switzerland AG 2023
R. Montasari, *Countering Cyberterrorism*, Advances in Information Security
101, https://doi.org/10.1007/978-3-031-21920-7_3

2   Background

2.1   Definitions

According to the UK National Cyber Security Centre (NCSC) (2016), cybersecurity describes the protection of networks, services or devices and their information such as data from damage or robbery (NCSC, n.d.). Moreover, cybercrime can be defined as using the internet, computers, or other digital devices to commit crimes such as hacking, theft, homicide (Maras, 2015 as cited in Vincze, 2016) or cyberterrorism (Williams, 2010 as cited in Williams and Wall, 2013). This can be done globally across cultures and time zones (Williams & Wall, 2013), which makes it much faster and more difficult to prosecute (Vincze, 2016). Specifically, according to the NCSC, a cyberattack or cyber incident can be defined based on the Computer Misuse Act (1990) as a breach of a security policy of a system that impedes its integrity. The four main types of breaching a security system are (attempts of) unauthorized access to a system or data, the unauthorized use of systems that process data, changes to systems without the owners' consent or disruption of services (NCSC, 2016).

2.2   National and Domestic Security

National security, as described in 2008 by the then-UK Prime Minister, entails providing security for the country and its citizens by the government. Threats to national security comprise of international terrorism, weapons of mass destruction, conflicts, trans-national crime as well as globalisation. Hereby, cybercrime is included for instance as part of trans-national crimes and globalisation since modern technologies enable new forms of crimes (Cabinet Office, 2008). The security of a nation can be divided into national and domestic security (Osoba & Welser, 2017). National security refers to protecting citizens from external threats or non-state actors such as terrorism or military conflicts, whereas domestic security includes protecting citizens from threats within the nation such as surveillance. Both types of threats are the result of using digital devices, AI and IoT and hence include cyberattacks or cybercrime.

2.3   Definition of Artificial Intelligence

AI seeks to recreate human intelligence in machines, aiming for machines to automatically perform human tasks (Dick, 2019). This involves visual perception, speech recognition, translations of languages, decision-making and problem-solving. AI algorithms can process and make use of massive amounts of data and identify patterns and correlations which would be hidden from a human operator or would require a significant amount of time if done by humans. Although AI is efficient, it is still limited in a variety of ways. Today AI applications still belong to the category of the so-called narrow AI which means the AI algorithm is unable to adapt to the complexity of the world and needs to be programmed very specifically toward a certain task (United Nations Interregional Crime and Justice Research Institute (UNICRI) & United Nations Counter Terrorism Centre (UNCCT), 2021). In contrast, general AI would describe a machine that has the intelligence similar to a human being with the reasoning and adaptability of the human brain but does not require human intervention (Babuta et al., 2020). Moreover, AI algorithms are created by feeding them data and training them for certain tasks (UNICRI & UNCCT, 2021). AI can be used in several contexts such as healthcare, engineering and security which puts it at the centre of the debate among policymakers and ethicists regarding privacy issues and human rights violations (Babuta et al., 2020; Karthikeyan et al., 2021; Nayyar et al., 2020; UNICRI & UNCCT, 2021).

2.4   The Internet of Things

The phrase the "Internet of Things" (IoT) was coined by Kevin Ashton in 1999 to describe the network linking nodes or objects in the physical world to the Internet. The IoT could be defined the networking of distinctively identifiable embedded computing devices. Some IoT appliances are standard objects with built-in Internet connectivity while others are sensing devices designed exclusively for the IoT. The IoT consists of technologies including, but not limited to, autonomous cyber-physical and cyber-biological systems, RFID sensors, wearables, embedded digital items, unmanned aerial vehicles (UAVs), smart swarms, the smart grid, smart buildings and home appliances, machine-to-machine communications and context-aware computing. Each of these technologies has grown into a distinct area on their own merit (Montasari & Hill, 2019).

Often any technology architecture consists of two parts: the key technology components that compose it and the connection between those elements. Components can comprise of hardware, software, or a combination of the two (for instance, a device, an object, a system, or a piece of software that provides a specific technical ability). Currently, there does not exist a standardised architecture on which the IoT is built. Depending upon both the sector in which the IoT is implemented and also its functionality, the IoT architecture can be made up of a number of layers and sublayers in cases of complex architectures. However, a typical architecture could be comprised of a three-stage, four-stage or six-stage layer, based on which an IoT is implemented. Considering the sheer number and the varied implementations of the IoT paradigm, the discussion of the IoT architecture in this Chapter is limited to a four-stage layer. An IoT architecture with a four-stage layer generally contains four components. These include: the Applications and Analytics Component, the Integration Component, the Security and Management Component, and the Infrastructure Component.

IoT devices are employed in a wide range of industries and consumer markets, with the latter constituting approximately 60% of all IoT connected devices by 2020. This share is forecast to remain unaffected over the next 10 years (Vailshery, 2022). Main industries with over 100 million connected IoT devices include gas, electricity and steam; transportation and storage; retail and wholesale; water supply and waste management; and government. As the new types of IoT devices continue to emerge, it is projected that the number of these devices will increase from 8.6 billion in 2019 to 29.4 billion devices in 2030 across all sectors worldwide (Vailshery, 2022). Consumer Internet and media devices such as smartphones are the most common use case for IoT devices in the consumer sector, with the number of IoT devices expected to exceed 17 billion by 2030. Furthermore, by 2030, connected (autonomous) vehicles, IT infrastructure, asset tracking and monitoring, and smart grid will all have more than one billion IoT devices (Vailshery, 2022). Figure 3.1 presents a visual representation of data published by Statista (Vailshery, 2022) covering a forecast of the number in billions of the IoT connected devices worldwide from the period between 2019 and 2030.

The advantages of IoT-connected devices are numerous, both individually and collectively. For instance, interconnected sensors can assist farmers in tracking the health of their herds and monitoring their crops and cattle to increase productivity. Or through wearable technology, intelligent health-connected devices can drastically prolong or save patients' lives (Montasari & Hill, 2019). Nevertheless, IoT-connected devices simultaneously present substantial privacy and security challenges since they collect large volumes of personal information about users. For instance, employers can track where their staff members are inside the building to find out how much time they spend in their offices or the kitchen using the security access cards they provide them with. This presents a privacy concern. Another

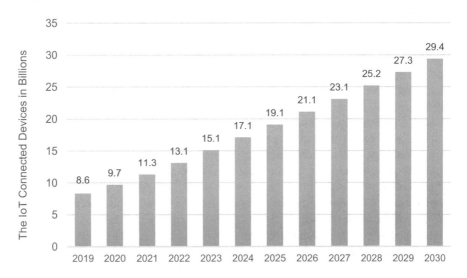

Fig. 3.1 The forecast of the number of IoT connected devices worldwide from 2019 to 2030

illustration involves smart metres, which can identify when a person is at home and what electronics they use. This data is then shared with other devices and stored by the organisations in their databases (Montasari & Hill, 2019).

Concerning the security issues, the IoT poses a greater security attack surface than that presented by the cloud computing. One of the main reasons is due to the ongoing emergence of new and diverse devices with unique OSs as well as different networks and related protocols (Montasari & Hill, 2019). While IoT uses the same monitoring requirements as cloud computing, it presents more security challenges due to issues such as volume, variety, and velocity (discussed in detail in Chap. 4). Furthermore, although IoT device applications are constantly evolving, the security of these devices remains a limitation in their resilience against attacks (Mazhar et al., 2022). Oftentimes, manufacturers of IoT devices are more focused on creating "...new attractive features/functionalities and simplifying the design to make the devices smarter and more cost-effective than making them secure" (Mazhar et al., 2022, p. 2). The increasing exploitation of these vulnerabilities by attackers, coupled with the limitations in memory and processing power of most IoT devices, makes it difficult for investigators to analyse and mitigate serious attacks (Mazhar et al., 2022). Instances of cyberattacks that could be launched against the IoT devices consist of tapping and hacking into cardiac devices such as pacemakers and patient monitoring systems, performing distributed denial of service (DDoS) attacks through breached IoT devices, hacking or intercepting In-Vehicle Infotainment (IVI) systems, and hacking various CCTV and IP cameras. Hence, security is of utmost "importance for the secure and reliable operation of IoT-connected devices" (Montasari & Hill, 2019). Considering the foregoing discussion, the next subsection will analyse a wide range of challenges associated with the digital investigation of cyberattacks carried out against or facilitated by the IoT devices.

2.5 The Internet of Things Forensics

IoT technology has created numerous opportunities for advancements in different fields of academic research, such as healthcare and transportation (Mrdovic, 2021). However, the emergence of these new technologies within the field of IoT has also brought about new opportunities for cybercriminals to target and exploit weaknesses in IoT systems. According to Kaspersky (2022), over 1.5 billion attacks on IoT devices were reported in the first 6 months of 2021, with an estimated 70% of IoT devices being vulnerable to these attacks (Kaspersky, 2022; HP, 2014). Cyberattacks carried out against or facilitated by IoT devices have undoubtedly had a significant impact on a variety of sectors such as government systems, enterprises, ecommerce, online banking, and critical infrastructure. Examples of the challenges arising from advancements in the IoT technology include: "high volume of data, heterogeneous nature of IoT devices, advanced hardware and software technologies, anti-forensic techniques, video and rich media, wireless, virtualisation, live response, distributed evidence, borderless cybercrime, lack of standardised tools and methods, and usability and visualisation" (Caviglione et al., 2017; Lillis et al., 2016; Ruan et al., 2011, 2013; Cameron, 2018; all cited in Montasari & Hill, 2019).

Considering these developments coupled with the ever-growing ubiquity of the IoT technology, there has been a significant increase in cyberattacks within IoT environments as discussed in the previous subsection. As a result, the number of cases necessitating forensic investigations of IoT devices have been on the rise both in criminal investigations and civil litigations (Montasari, 2016a, b). Digital Forensics is a branch of Forensic Science that concerns the acquisition, preservation, analysis, interpretation and presentation of data found on a wide range of digital devices. The term Digital Forensics was originally known as Computer Forensics but has now been extended to include the collection and analysis of data found on all types of devices that can store digital data. Hence, Digital Forensics, itself, now consists of a number of branches with each focusing on a particular area and requiring specialised expertise. Table 3.1 is a graphical representation of the key subdomains of Digital Forensics.

IoT Forensics, a subdomain of Digital Forensics, involves identification and extraction of evidential artefacts from a wide range of IoT devices and objects. These could include: "smart devices and sensors; hardware and software which facilitate communication between smart devices and the external world (such as computers, mobile, IPS, IDS and firewalls); and also hardware and software which are outside of the network being investigated (such as cloud, social networks, ISPs and mobile network providers, virtual online identities and the Internet)" (Montasari & Hill, 2019). Compared to traditional Digital Forensic methods, IoT Forensics poses numerous technical and legal challenges. Some of these challenges concern the different proprietary hardware and software, data formats and protocols, and physical interfaces (Montasari & Hill, 2019). For instance, since IoT devices utilise proprietary formats for data and communication protocols, understanding the links between artifacts in both time and space can be very complex. Other challenges associated with the IoT Forensics are related to the spread of data across multiple devices and platforms, resulting in difficulties to determine where IoT data resides and how this data can be acquired (Montasari & Hill, 2019). For instance, the forensic analysis of IoT devices used in a business or home environment can be challenging in relation to establishing the ownership of the data. This is due to the fact that digital artefacts might be shared or transmitted across multiple devices (Montasari & Hill, 2019). Other challenges associated with the IoT Forensics concern chain of custody issues. "In a civil or criminal trial, collecting evidence in a forensically sound manner and preserving chain of custody are of paramount importance.

Table 3.1 Different branches of digital forensics

Computer forensics	Network forensics	Mobile forensics
Cloud forensics	Social media forensics	Internet forensics
Wireless forensics	Database forensics	Memory forensics
Malware forensics	Email forensics	Multimedia forensics
Unmanned aerial forensics	Internet of Things forensics	Vehicle infotainment forensics

However, ownership and preservation of evidence in an IoT setting could be difficult and can have a negative effect on a court's understanding that the evidence acquired is reliable" (Montasari & Hill, 2019).

Moreover, current Digital Forensic tools and methods for investigating IoT devices were primarily developed for traditional Digital Forensics analysing conventional computing devices such as PCs, laptops, and other storage media, as well as their networks. Instances of existing methods employed to obtain data from IoT devices include: acquiring a flash memory image, capturing a memory dump through Linux dd command or netcat, and obtaining firmware data via JTAG and UART techniques (Montasari & Hill, 2019). In addition, protocols such as Telnet, SSH, Bluetooth and Wi-Fi are used to connect to and interact with IoT devices. Similarly, "tools such as FTK, EnCase, Cellebrite, X-Ways Forensic and WinHex, etc. and internal utilities such as Linux dd command (for IoT devices with OSs such as embedded Linux) are used to extract and analyse data from IoT devices." However, forensic examination of IoT devices requires specialised handling procedures, techniques, and knowledge of various OSs and file systems. Furthermore, using traditional Computer Forensic tools to conduct IoT Forensics would make maintaining a chain of custody regarding the collection of digital evidence extremely unlikely (Montasari & Hill, 2019). Hence, the use of traditional Digital Forensics techniques in IoT investigations are often insufficient due to the unique and complex challenges posed by the IoT (Lutta et al., 2021).

Furthermore, as computing becomes more network centred, it is no longer sufficient for Digital Forensic experts to analyse devices in isolation (Casey, 2011). The dependency of IoT devices on various networks, such as local area networks (LANs) and wide-area networks (WANs), to send and receive data highlights the importance of Network Forensics in conducting investigations into IoT-related incidents (Casey, 2011). Network Forensics refers to the "...monitoring and analysis of computer network traffic for the purposes of information gathering, legal evidence, or intrusion detection" (The European Union Agency for Cybersecurity (ENISA), 2019, p. 10). Unlike other areas of Digital Forensics, Network Forensics deals with volatile and dynamic data and is focused on the prevention and detection of network attacks (Buric & Delija, 2015). Volatile data refers to any type of data that is stored in a system or network and is permanently lost when power is removed from the system or the network's memory (Buric & Delija, 2015). This poses a significant challenge for investigators when collecting evidence in a forensic investigation, as they are often working with systems that cannot be taken offline. While the impact on live systems, such as routers and firewalls, can be minimised using appropriate tools and techniques, it cannot be completely eliminated (Buric & Delija, 2015).

In addition, IoT devices data are often stored in the Cloud considering its scalability and accessibility. Hence, there is a strong correlation between IoT Forensics and Cloud Forensics. Cloud Forensics, a subset of Network Forensics, can be defined as a cross-discipline between cloud computing and digital forensics (Ruan et al., 2011). Cloud computing "...is a model for enabling convenient, on-demand network access to a shared pool of configurable resources that can be rapidly provisioned and released with minimal management effort..." (Ruan et al., 2011, p. 3).

Cloud computing is supported by a global infrastructure of computers, data centres, cables and networks that provide the necessary power to store and transfer mass amounts of data (Maurer & Hinck, 2020). However, complications with conducting forensics in the cloud arise from the fact that cloud service providers (CSPs), such as Amazon Web Services (AWS) and Google Cloud Platform (GCP), can "… fully dictate what happens in the environment, [and] remain in control of the sources of evidence" (Alenezi et al., 2019, para. 3). Their authority over the cloud environment can make the location and acquisition of evidence in a forensic investigation that involves data located in the cloud quite difficult (Alenezi et al., 2019).

Notwithstanding the many challenges discussed in this subsection, there have been modest improvements concerning the forensic analysis process being simplified in the IoT environments. This is mainly owing to the recent developments in the automated detection of cyberattacks on or by IoT devices. Furthermore, the infrastructure that supports cloud services has enabled the growth of IoT in a number of ways by providing the technical framework to support greater connectivity between IoT devices (Kaur et al., 2022). As a result of this continued growth, Cloud Forensics will continue to play an increasingly vital role in the process of investigating IoT-related incidents (MacDermott et al., 2018). However, despite these small-scale improvements, there is still a growing need for multi-pronged approaches in the IoT Forensics for the purposes of locating, extracting and analysing evidential data from various sources in a forensically sound manner.

3   AI and IoT in National and Domestic Security

National security can be divided into three subcategories: digital security, political security, and physical security (Babuta et al., 2020) as presented in Fig. 3.2.

This section explores the implications of AI and IoT in relation to these subcategories. In particular, the section examines how AI can be employed to prevent and

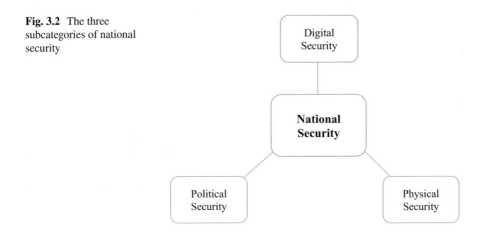

Fig. 3.2 The three subcategories of national security

combat attacks in cyberspace, particularly through or against IoT platforms and devices. Furthermore, the section analyses the relevance of AI and IoT usage in military and national security contexts.

3.1   The Role of AI and IoT in Digital Security

3.1.1   AI for Protecting IoT Devices against Hacking

Being a very valuable tool for the defence of national security, AI can be utilised to secure IoT devices against hackers and cyberattacks as it can be adapted to various applications to advance IoT and performance (Sayler, 2020). The importance of AI in securing IoT devices is highlighted in Wu et al.'s (2020) study, which discusses how ML can be deployed to enhance IoT security. The ML algorithms have been divided into transaction algorithms concerned with data collection and processing, and decision algorithms that work on the previous data. Hence, AI can be trained to manage large volumes of data, point out abnormal patterns, and calculate large data sets in minimal time (Wu et al., 2020). They can also be used simultaneously to evaluate which models to use for decision making and how to increase their effectiveness and precision of an AI algorithm. The overall simplified process of AI solutions for IoT security outlines and connects five steps as shown in Fig. 3.3. These include: data collection, data exploration and pre-processing, model selection and data conversion, model training and testing, and model evaluation and deployment (Wu et al., 2020).

Moreover, in relation to cybersecurity, AI can provide antivirus protection, network detection and user identification whereby it can react in real-time to abnormal network use or malware (Babuta et al., 2020). One of the elements used by AI to

Fig. 3.3 The overall simplified process of AI solutions for IoT security

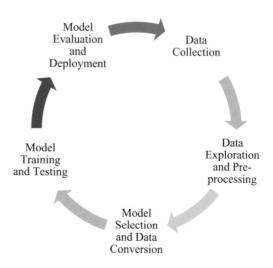

identify those unusual patterns concerns behavioural biometrics (Babuta et al., 2020). For instance, behaviour biometrics can be integrated into smartphones using embedded sensors to measure finger pressure, as well as the area and time of contact (Ellavarason et al., 2020). This can be used to create so-called touch-dynamics based on typing rhythm, swiping speed and the position the device is held in (Bo et al., 2015; Zheng et al., 2014; Xu et al., 2014, all as cited in Ellavarason et al., 2020). When all this information is processed together, a model can be produced that discriminates against users and allows verification processes (Ellavarason et al., 2020).

The importance of AI-focused defence is further demonstrated by DARPA's 2016 Cyber Grand Challenge, developed by The Defense Advanced Research Projects Agency (DARPA). The purpose of this challenge was to build automatic defence systems that could find, prove, and fix software defects in real-time. The challenge required participants to develop AI algorithms that could detect and close vulnerabilities in software before their competitors could target those all within seconds (DARPA, 2016, as cited in Sayler, 2020). This is especially important in the most challenging kind of cyberattack, called Advanced Persistent Threat (APT), through which the attacker is searching for weaknesses in the security system and waiting for mistakes. Previously, this method was labour and resource-intensive, requiring skilled individuals. However, nowadays, with AI technology, this could be achieved through the use of algorithms (Allen & Chan, 2017) more efficiently. Though, different to other warfare technologies, where stolen codes mean the competitor still needs the materials and technologies to copy a new technology, stealing algorithms lead to a zero-cost reproduction. This renders it more essential for countries to secure their research (Allen & Chan, 2017). AI can also be used to recognize unauthorized access and malware as well as to improve the security of IoT systems. Additionally, it can be a valuable tool in protecting devices by authorising the user and only allowing access to certain individuals.

3.1.2 The Malicious Use of AI to Hack IoT Devices

Apart from being a valuable tool for safeguarding IoT devices against being hacked, AI could also be deployed maliciously in the commission of hacking other IoT devices. Here, AI is vital to target the vulnerable spots in a network (Babuta et al., 2020) which can be, for instance, IoT devices. The rapid pace at which AI is being developed and improved has provided the hackers with several means to access and gain private and confidential data (Nayyar et al., 2020). Hilt et al. (2019) investigated cybercrime underground communities that have been matched to the used languages which were Russian, Portuguese, Brazilian, Arabic and English. Findings revealed that most of these focused on monetization by hacking small scale devices, such as routers, to lead to phishing sides and cameras to sell their access. IoT-related cybercrimes have mainly included small scale security violations which appear not to pose a serious threat to national security.

However, several incidences have proved the risk and the possibility of cyberattacks against official or governmental institutions that threaten national security. The Centre for Strategic and International Studies list frequent cyber incidents throughout the world (Center for Strategic and International Studies (CSIS), n.d.). For instance, in January 2022, a cyberattack hit 90 websites and implanted malware into numerous computers in government agencies of Ukraine. Similarly, Chinese hackers gained passwords to access organisation systems and sensitive communications of US defence and technology firms in December 2021. Another example concerns September 2021 cyberattacks against Hungarian polling systems. Two hours after the vote for the Hungarian election opened, the nationwide polling systems were attacked, prolonging the vote for two consecutive days. These cyberattacks on IoT devices demonstrate a risk to political security by potentially changing election outcomes, but also by fuelling international distrust between conflicting countries.

Cyberattacks are also affecting the physical security of nations at an alarming pace. In 2015, the Ukrainian power grid was targeted by a cyberattack leaving Kyiv with no power for many hours (CSIS, n.d.). Likewise, in 2017, the UK National Health Service (NHS) was compromised by the malicious software WannaCry (Stevens, 2018). In both cases, the cyberattacks against IoT devices could have resulted in the loss of many lives caused by, for instance, wrong decisions made by medical professionals due to the missing or unavailable data. Those disastrous consequences become even more amplified when, for instance, botnets target critical infrastructure such as the energy and transport sectors (Pătraşcu, 2021; Stevens, 2018). Until now, there has been no public report of a cyberattack that has directly led to a person's death. Nor has there been a cyberattack that has resulted in the fall of the global financial system. Notwithstanding this, the fear of a cyber-attack triggering political and military action exists among politicians and the NATO (The North Atlantic Treaty Organization) members (Stevens, 2018). In general, AI has the ability to form IoT devices into powerful tools to endanger the domestic and national security of countries worldwide by attacking governmental institutions and critical infrastructure.

3.1.3 The Use of AI in the Military to Hack IoT Devices

AI can also be used in the military to hack and manipulate opponents' IoT devices such as unmanned aerial vehicles (UAVs) or autonomous vehicles. Providing fully automated decision making to AI systems poses a major threat to national security when errors are made (Osoba & Welser, 2017). Specifically, AI weapons without human intervention carry vulnerabilities due to the learning process. Because AI algorithms are only as good as the data they are trained with, this carries the risk of opponents finding ways to feed disinformation to AI systems. As a result, this could bring warfare to a new level. A non-military instance of a manipulated ML algorithm pertains to the Microsoft's chatbot, Tay, which had the ability to learn from and respond to Twitter users. No issues were reported after the chatbot was subjected to a testing phase carried out in a controlled environment. However, when implemented on Twitter, the users were able to manipulate the algorithm. This culminated in offensive statements posted by the chatbot (Lee, 2016, as cited in Osoba & Welser, 2017).

In the same vein, if opponents or non-state actors are able to feed misinformation to AI algorithms that learn to predict behaviours or AI algorithms that select targets, the use of AI for the purposes of national security or for the policing of cyberspace will be rendered ineffective. Therefore, this malicious use of AI could not only have significant repercussions for national security but also undermine the many benefits that AI offers for its security. Overall, AI and IoT devices can not only be used by state actors as weapons but also be subjected to manipulation by opponents. This, in turn, could lead to unwanted outcomes in both domestic and national security.

3.1.4 The Use of AI by Institutions to Safeguard Citizens

Furthermore, AI can indirectly assist with securing national security, for instance, by providing institutions safeguarding the citizens with more robust means to function on a daily basis. In this context, AI has the ability to increase the effectiveness of workers by automating administrative organisation processes (Babuta et al., 2020). This can be achieved through an AI algorithm that is managing human resources, such as filtering job applications and creating work schedules (Babuta et al., 2020). Moreover, AI can be involved in allocating and calculating the finances of the institution's budget and employees' payments (Babuta et al., 2020). Similarly, it can offer a general oversight in managing the diary of several employees and updating their scheduled meetings as well as organising room bookings. Likewise, AI can use IoT devices to secure user authentication, improve network security and flag unusual behaviours (Babuta et al., 2020). Hence, AI has the ability to synchronise and update institutions' IoT devices and perform administrative tasks.

3.2 AI and IoT in Political Security

This subsection explores ways in which the misuse of AI could impact political security.

3.2.1 Deepfake and Mis- and Disinformation

AI can be exploited to create mis- and disinformation with a view to influencing political views. In particular, new Deepfake ML techniques can be applied to change an existing piece of media or even create a new one with only limited resources. Deepfake represents usually high-quality and seemingly realistic videos that can be used legally for entertainment purposes. It can also be deployed illegally to distribute misinformation, propaganda and hate or blackmail individuals (Rana et al., 2022). For instance, Deepfake programs such as Google image search and other social media websites can be utilised to independently create data in order to embed different faces into videos. After the AI system has undergone the training process, no human interaction will be needed, and algorithms will be able to improve themselves (Maras & Alexandrou, 2019).

In the past, the degree to which videos could be manipulated was limited, and doing so would require skills, time and a significant budget. However, this is about to change considering the recent developments in the field of AI Deepfakes. Deepfakes or fake photographs or videos of humans are generated using neural networks. In order to create a fake video of an individual, one would need a significant number of images of that person. However, in 2019, Samsung presented an AI Deepfake system demonstrating how to generate convincing talking heads from as few as a single portrait image (Zakharov, 2019). The Samsung AI initially goes through considerable "meta-learning" by reviewing a vast database of videos. After it has become accustomed to human faces, the system will be able to produce talking heads of previously unseen persons using one or a few images of those individuals. For each image, the AI system will be capable of identifying several features on the face, such as the eyes, nose, mouth, and different lengths and forms (Zakharov, 2019 as cited in Zhang, 2019).

There already exists fake videos such as those belonging to politicians or fake porn celebrities. However, once Deepfake technology starts being used en-masse for social and political leverage, this can create significant damage to national security. There would be substantial volumes of conflicting information online spread at a very rapid pace leading to conflicting information and confusion. Deepfake technologies pose even more challenges when combined with other technologies such as speech editors that take a person's speech and clone it to modify the person's voice and add new phrases. This will bring information warfare to a whole new and dangerous level. Moreover, Deepfake technologies are becoming especially dangerous when considering that video sources can be used as evidence in court. Using this technology, both state and none-state malicious actors would be able to rewrite facts and history. Hence, Deepfake technologies could have serious consequences for political security in a number of ways especially once the technology has been further developed and entered into the mainstream. For instance, in the run up to the 2019 UK general election, a fake social media video in which Boris Johnson and Jeremy Corbyn endorsed each other for prime minister was posted online to demonstrate the ability of Deepfake videos to undermine democracy. The video created by the research organisation Future Advocacy and UK Artist Bill Posters employed AI "and an impressionist to make the candidates' clips appear as real as possible" (BBC, 2019).

Moreover, the internet, especially social media could provide these forms of false information with legitimate power and appear to users' as valid content, influencing their decision making (Babuta et al., 2020). One of the ways in which Deepfakes can be detected is by analysing the biological signals and movements, and phoneme-viseme mismatches (Rana et al., 2022). As demonstrated by Rana et al. (2022) in a review of 112 articles, using deep learning-based methods to authenticate Deepfake, an 89.73% accuracy could be achieved. However, to verify the authenticity of digital evidence, a digital forensic expert would require access to the originality of the source. There are several technologies that can be used to aid decision-making, one of which is AI technology, itself. This creates more challenges since the forensic expert would be required to explain the process involved in their decision making. This could be intricate in cases where an AI algorithm has been used that only provides the output and not the process of the decision making (Maras & Alexandrou, 2019). In summary to this subsection, AI can be used to create Deepfakes that pose a threat to national security by manipulating political opinions. Furthermore, it could have severe repercussions on the legal decision making in courts. This, in turn, could lead to either punishing or exonerating the wrong person, hence impeding the domestic security. On the contrary, AI can also be beneficial to detect Deepfakes.

3.2.2 AI and the Formation of Filter Bubbles

The use of AI in social media algorithms could also pose a number of challenges to national security. Social media sites (SMS) are exploited by terrorist and extremist organisations for the purposes of spreading propaganda, radicalising vulnerable individuals and recruiting new members. They facilitate the creation of political separation within society by creating the so-called filter bubbles. Filter bubbles explain the process of bringing together users with similar preferences and views by using certain AI algorithms to increase users' engagement and advertisement revenue (Eli Pariser, 2011 as cited in Chitra & Musco, 2020). These recommendations can be more direct by suggesting other user profiles on Facebook and Twitter, or more indirect through news feeds (Chitra & Musco, 2020; Evans, 2018). For instance, filter bubbles were blamed for influencing the Brexit referendum and the 2016 US presidential campaign (Jackson, 2017, as cited in Chitra & Musco, 2020). To review Pariser's filter bubble hypothesis, Chitra and Musco (2020) conducted an investigation using mathematical models to try to replicate the filter bubble phenomenon. In their examination, they added the role of a network administrator who could filter social interaction between users. The administrator could also change the algorithm to slightly increase or decrease a user's interaction with certain individuals based on their belief systems. The aim was to connect users to like-minded people and increase their engagement with the social network platform while avoiding the formation of filter bubbles to ensure users were confronted with other perspectives. Findings demonstrated that it was possible for the network administrator to achieve this balance and reduce the polarization (Chitra & Musco, 2020).

However, limited research has been carried out on the extent to which filter bubbles risk an individuals' radicalisation. Filter bubbles have been found to have a slight to moderate negative impact on individuals' political views (Zuiderveen Borgesius et al., 2016 as cited in Baldauf et al., 2019). The majority of the existing research is based on the more or less twofold political party system of the

US. Therefore, it can be argued whether this can be applied to other political systems such as the multi-party system in Germany (Montag, 2019 as cited in Baldauf et al., 2019). Hence, more research is needed to form a sufficient conclusion on the danger of filter bubbles on national security. To conclude this subsection, AI algorithms have been criticised by researchers for forming filter bubbles, and hence amplifying the polarisation of public opinions. However, as demonstrated above, the AI algorithms can be manipulated, for instance, by adding the role of a network administrator to decrease the formation of filter bubbles.

3.2.3 AI and Online Content Moderation

Analogous to filter bubbles, AI can also be used to recognise and delete misinformation or extremist views expressed from social media platforms. In counterterrorism practices, AI can be a valuable tool for flagging and removing extremist or terrorist content from social media platforms by identifying suspicious content and removing it (UNICRI & UNCCT, 2021). This can be done in two ways: deplatforming and shadow banning. Deplatforming is the practice of deleting a user's content, removing the content and limiting the accessibility of content, or completely blocking the user's access to the platform (UNICRI & UNCCT, 2021). For instance, in 2019, Facebook took down videos documenting the Christchurch terrorist attack, which was being live streamed across the platform. In addition to the original video, Facebook's algorithm countered 1.5 million further international attempts in the next 24 h to upload copies of the recording (Facebook, 2019 as cited in UNICRI & UNCCT, 2021).

However, detecting online extremist content has proved challenging considering the fact that AI algorithms are still limited. One of the main reasons for AI's failure to flag extremist content in online posts is due to the variety and diversity of the online content. For instance, it has been reported that Twitter's algorithm is unable to distinguish between offensive language, sarcasm, and friendly fighting (Butler & Parrella, 2021 as cited in UNICRI & UNCCT, 2021). Therefore, AI algorithms must be trained in several languages and formats such as videos, pictures, and text (Fernandez & Alani, 2021; UNICRI & UNCCT, 2021) to address these limitations. Notwithstanding AI's many potentials for online content moderation, the concept of a filtering algorithm has ignited the academic debate on the extent to which such algorithms could undermine human rights and freedom of expression. While reducing hate speech is clearly beneficial for a democratically functioning society, restricting the freedom of opinion is not (Elkin-Koren, 2020).

In summary to this subsection, AI could be implemented to highlight extremist material on social media platforms even though AI algorithms are still limited in their abilities. There is an ongoing academic debate in relation to the potential violation of human rights arising from the use of AI in online content moderation and potential agreements on what content should be restricted in particular.

3.3   AI and IoT in Physical Security

3.3.1   Augmented Intelligence Analysis

AI can be deployed to advance police investigations regarding counterterrorism or homicide cases. As discussed in the previous subsection, AI can be implemented to assist with policing social media platforms by removing extremist content. AI can also function in Augmented Intelligence Analysis. Contrary to AI, which focuses on performing human tasks without human intervention, augmented intelligence (AuI) aims to improve or extend human intelligence by including human interaction. This enables the inclusion of legal, societal, and ethical values in the decision-making process (Gupta et al., 2021; Yau et al., 2021). In this context, it can be used for mimicking human analysis processes in relation to language processing and audio-visual analysis to identify objects and summarise video contents (Babuta et al., 2020).

Traditional practices involve human investigators sifting through media sources that could potentially provide evidential artefacts or hints for solving ongoing investigations and persecuting offenders endangering the society's security. However, viewing certain forms of materials such as rape, murder, or torture can have severe psychological impact on human operators. Seigfried-Spellar (2018) assessed the psychological impacts of child pornography investigations on digital forensic examiners, investigators and individuals who were part of both job categories. Findings revealed that being part of both groups demonstrated significantly higher traumatic stress, feelings of worthlessness and lower concentrations than only being in the digital forensic examiners' category (Seigfried-Spellar, 2018). This illustrates the importance of AuI in relieving pressure from individuals performing both job categories. Hence, AuI could be deployed to filter and prioritise materials as well as perform behavioural analyses of specific individuals which can be overlooked by human operators. It is, however, important to note that the use of AuI does not completely remove the need for human judgement. Nevertheless, it can significantly extend human abilities and, in turn, accelerate investigations whilst, simultaneously, it protects investigators from traumatising content and potential psychological damage (Babuta et al., 2020).

3.3.2   Military Weaponisation of AI and the IoT

Moreover, AI can be implemented in robots and other types of weapons intended for use in military and police applications to shield personnel from physical injury. For instance, a US mass shooting ended when the shooter was killed by a robot-delivered bomb (Murphy, 2016, as cited in Osoba & Welser, 2017). As highlighted, this can provide myriad opportunities to protect police forces and to assist with addressing, for instance, school shootings or terrorist attacks. AI and the IoT are also increasingly being developed and implemented for military applications. For instance, the DARPA of the US Department of Defense (DoD) is funding the creation of a robotic submarine system, which is anticipated to be deployed for a wide range of purposes. This would include detecting underwater mines and engaging with in anti-submarine operations (Singh & Gulhane, 2018). Another example concerns the US Software Engineering Institute (SEI)'s development of a video summarisation pipeline for US military organisations. This tool is intended to inform operators about notable events such as locations of new explosive devices. This tool might be used in the long term to predict such activities (Pitstick, 2018 as cited in Babuta et al., 2020). However, training an AI algorithm to learn to make such predictions can be challenging since most violent attacks by, for example terrorists, take place too infrequent to provide big data for a valid statistical model (Babuta et al., 2020). Furthermore, the US military also deploy AI to support data analysis, logistics, cyber and information operations as well as command and control within military contexts. Likewise, the US have utilised IoT technologies such as autonomous military vehicles for military operations in, for instance, Iraq and Syria (Sayler, 2020). As an illustration, in 2008, there were more US ground robots than British soldiers in Iraq that were used to set explosive devices on the roads (Sharkey, 2008).

Lethal Autonomous Weapon Systems (LAWSs) or Semi-Autonomous Weapons (SAWs) such as the MQ1-Predator Unmanned Combat Air Vehicle (UCAV) have also been effectively deployed in many battle missions to eliminate members of terrorist organisations. Instances of this are illustrated by the many successful attacks on the suspected al-Qaeda and Islamic State of Iraq and the Levant members in Iraq, Syria, Afghanistan and Pakistan. Despite their potentials for military purposes, LAWSs and SAWs, have ignited international outcries given that they have been responsible for multiple errors in killing of innocent civilians. This has evoked an international debate about whether their use is ethical and has a legal basis. The application of AI in military tools might be too dangerous and insufficient to cover all legal and ethical concerns. Hence, AuI might be a more suitable solution to advance warfare and, simultaneously, minimise errors and escalations of conflicts. In summary to this subsection, whilst the use of AI in robots, LAWSs and SAWs for policing and military purposes has been highly criticised, they can have many benefits when used ethically and legally. In the future, AI might be capable of predicting human behaviour and thus become a vital tool for police and military operations. Using AI to predict human behaviour could potentially enable police and military to prevent casualties, violence or suffering both in society and war zones. This, in turn, will lead to a minimised loss of life.

4 Privacy Implications of AI Algorithms

AI algorithms could potentially help to minimise the invasion of user privacy by reducing the amount of data that a human operator is required to view. However, the mere processing and analysis of data by an algorithm can already be viewed as infringing an individual's right to privacy (Babuta et al., 2020). Therefore, the degree of intrusion is of importance regardless of how the data is analysed or reviewed. Considering the foregoing discussion, the remainder of the section will be focused on the impact of the data collection, storage and processing on user privacy.

4.1 Impacts of AI Algorithms on User Privacy

The use of AI for the purposes of data collection, processing and storage presents a number of concerns in relation to user privacy. For instance, AI algorithms can be vulnerable to cyberattacks and biases (discussed later), leading to skewed data selection or impediment to confidentiality (Babuta et al., 2020). Moreover, due to the so-called 'cumulative intrusion risk', involving the interaction of automated systems, the creation of an interconnected network of data collecting systems could result in greater levels of privacy intrusions compared to isolated systems (Babuta et al., 2020). For instance, Google collects various types of data from several applications (Sivarajah et al., 2016) such as information about the browser search from Google search, GPS locations from google maps, and data from Google Assistant through voice recordings (Google, n.d.). All this information can be used to create a much more specific profile about a single individual, hence encroaching on user privacy at a deeper level than the data collection of only the search engine itself (Wachter, 2018).

Voice-Based Digital Assistant (VBDA) IoT devices such as Apple's Siri and Amazon's Alexa are instances of technology using AI to identify queries and requests by processing and responding in spoken language with answers from databases (Maras & Alexandrou, 2019; Vimalkumar et al., 2021). These IoT devices collect and process large volumes of personal data, hence, causing considerable privacy concerns (Vimalkumar et al., 2021). Recent research findings suggest that, compared to the non-users, the users of VBDA have relatively fewer privacy concerns and more trust in the venders of these technologies (Lau et al., 2018). However, the decision-making process in terms of whether one should use, for instance, a smart speaker such as Amazon Echo or Google Home has been found to be based on the balance of perceived privacy risk and the gains from such devices (Lau et al., 2018; Vimalkumar et al., 2021).

IoT devices such as Alexa can store and process users' personal data, hence determining their emotional states and accordingly creating their profiles (Furey & Blue, 2018). There are at least three ways in which profiling can become invasive. Firstly, profiling can make inferences about individuals that can be identified, hence the risk to reveal their private information to other IoT users in cases of a data reach or data processing. Secondly, as noted previously, the IoT devices can work together and combine data in one location to form detailed profiles. As a result, this renders the interaction between datasets even more perilous, particularly when central authentication systems such as SSO have access to data that can be used to authenticate the users. This will be discussed in more detail in the following section. Thirdly, profiling can become invasive when shared data is used by a third party and combines it with other collected data (Wachter, 2018).

Further privacy concerns arise from Emotional AI, which involves human-state measurement to interact with qualitative dimensions of human life. Emotional AI represents technologies that combine affective computing with AI methods to recognise, comprehend, and engage with human emotional life. Considering that Emotional AI is used in most IoT devices and systems, it is now present in almost every aspect of the daily life. It can be found in cars, digital assistants, smart phones, toys, marketing, as well as policing, education and border control. Similarly, Affective Computing concerns the study, design and implementation of digital devices or systems that are capable of distinguishing; explaining the meaning of; processing; and simulating human words and actions as well as information about them. As stated previously, Emotional AI is intended to understand and respond to emotions by means of text, voice, computer vision and biometric sensing. It operates by analysing a user's emotion through the use of soft biometric trait profiling, which could involve gathering data about used words, images, facial expressions, gaze direction, voices, etc. that could be the product of breathing, electrical responses of the skin as well as the heart rate (McStay, 2020). This is accomplished, for instance, by IoT devices such as the Apple Watch, that uses electrocardiogram signals and measures the interruptions in heartbeats for authorisation purposes (Karimian et al., 2016, as cited in Wachter, 2018). Other sensitive data collected for authorisation comprise of vein, fingerprint and iris recognition (Karimian et al., 2016, as cited in Wachter, 2018). Considering the interconnectedness of the IoT devices which can create the accurate profile of a user, this information can be targeted to determine a complete picture of a person's emotional state.

The key challenge within emotional AI is that emotions are being inferred from the output of emotional states such as facial expressions. This could cause issues when similar facial expressions are used to convey different emotions (Barrett et al., 2019, as cited in McStay, 2020). This in turn means that data must be gathered more invasively to increase the accuracy (McStay & Urquuhart, 2019, as cited in McStay, 2020). The output emotional states provided by AI processing can be used to interact with devices or media content to improve a user's experience. Hence, organisations such as Google, Apple, Microsoft and Metaverse are interested in using emotional AI. Moreover, the technology could be used in the public sector to regulate behaviour and mood in, for instance, prisons, or to make decisions in risk assessments for different purposes, such as insurance companies ((McStay, 2020). With regards to national security, this could be implemented at border control or other high-risk locations to determine the risk level of certain individuals and prevent security breaches or even terror attacks.

However, this raises the question about citizens giving consent to the selected data and the right to privacy. Floridi (2016) as cited in McStay (2020) argues that the 'my' in 'my data' is different to the 'my' in other possessions such as a car. Moreover, Floridi (2014) as cited in McStay (2020) states that the right of privacy is not an individual good, but also a common good held by a group, meaning it might be necessary to be collected for the advantage of all. In a 2020 interview with the Financial Times, the former MI5 Director General Sir Andrew Parker stated that he was especially interested in AI "because of our need to be able to make sense of the data lives of thousands of people in as near to real time as we can get to" (Barber & Warrell, 2020). Currently, data collection about daily routine and behaviour is advertised as promoting the user's browsing experience, providing better services, and targeting personal preferences by for instance including the targeted advertisement of products (Schermer, 2011 as cited in Wachter, 2018). However, the ownership of the collected data and data misuse is still a weakness in privacy protection. The challenges attached to data collection can be separated into two categories: first, policies for data collection itself and, second, data anonymization (Zhang et al., 2014). Herein, data collection policies describe the types of data that are to be collected and the legal access to those types of data. Moreover, the amount of data should be restricted considering the fact that large quantities of data are used and collected without the user's awareness, giving them little autonomy (Hon et al., 2016; Wachter, 2018). Data anonymisation inherits the encryption processes whereby data is anonymized. Of important significance is also the concealment of the relationships between the final data and its owner (Zhang et al., 2014). In particular, there are different steps involved in identifying data-individual relationships. One of these include the membership inference, which would not provide the individual's data, itself, but, instead, offer information on whether a particular individual is included in a certain data set (Veale et al., 2018, as cited in Babuta et al., 2020). Of paramount importance is also the need that data cannot be connected to a single individual. Therefore, since the data needs to be shared between IoT devices, it needs to be encrypted in such a way that different types of devices can understand the encryption without enabling outsiders to gain the encryption key (Zhang et al., 2014).

Furthermore, should the users wish to personalise their services in, for instance, online shopping, they will often be required to share their data in a foreign territory. Normally, this data is then stored in the provider's cloud (Meurisch et al., 2020). This culminates in the so-called "personalisation-privacy paradox" (Espato et al., 2019 as cited in Meurisch et al., 2020), which describes the tension between the user providing private data to marketers and the latter who will be allowed to process the data so as to provide the user with personalised services (Lee & Rha, 2016; Sutanto et al., 2013). This poses many privacy concerns as demonstrated in the Facebook–Cambridge Analytica data scandal. In 2010, millions of Facebook users' personal information was obtained by the British consulting company Cambridge Analytica without the users' consents. This data was mainly intended to be used for the purposes of political advertising (Chan, 2019). The data from users' profile was harvested using the "This Is Your Digital Life" app, which would ask users a number of questions to create their psychological profiles. The app also utilised Facebook's Open Graph technology to obtain the personal information of the users' Facebook friends. It is reported that the app gathered up to 87 million Facebook profiles data (Meredith, 2018). The data was used by Cambridge Analytica to support the 2016 Ted Cruz's and Donald Trump's presidential campaigns as well as medalling with the Brexit referendum in the UK (BBC, 2020; Smith, 2018). This scandal illustrates that data provided by users could be used without their consents for purposes different to those originally intended resulting in the infringement of the users' privacy rights. Such data breaches could have severe implications for nation security in that they can be exploited by election candidates to gain full control over voters' decisions. These candidates would normally not be elected due to fascist, racist or discriminating personalities.

4.2   Legal Frameworks for Privacy Relating AI Algorithms

There are several different national and international legal frameworks that can be applied to privacy protection and data collection. To start with, the Universal Declaration of Human Rights as part of the United Nations Charter, adopted in the General Assembly in 1948, is an example of international law. The Human Rights are centred around the protection of an individual's dignity and freedom and applicable respective of an individual's nationality (Dixon et al., 2016). The right to privacy is, for instance, expressed in Article 12 of the Universal Declaration on Human Rights, Article 8 of the Human Rights Act, and Article 17 of the International Covenant on Civil and Political Rights. In particular, it states the right to respect an individual's private and family life, and their home and correspondence (Office of the High Commissioner for Human Rights, n.d.). The representative of these rights in Europe is the European Convention for the Protection of Human Rights and Fundamental Freedoms (ECHR), which was founded in 1953 (Dixon et al., 2016). Hence, some argue that the ECHR must be included in UK national laws since the UK is part of the European Convention (Babuta et al., 2020). Interestingly, Article 8 of the Human Rights Act does also include the restrictions on the right to privacy. As a result, it is allowed to impede someone's privacy if it is proportionate to protect national security, public safety, economy, health, morals, freedoms of other people or prevent crime (Equality and Human Rights Commission, 2021). In this regard, governmental institutions such as the police have the right to use private data.

In general, both, the private and intelligence sector are governed by a combination of legislation, codes of practices and internal policies. However, these frame works can vary contingent upon the type of the sector in which they are deployed, i.e. intelligence sector and the private sector. For instance, the private sector is more governed by data protection frameworks instead of legislation (Babuta et al., 2020). With regard to intelligence services on a national level, the Investigatory Powers Act (IPA) of 2016 encloses the interception of communications and data collection including bulk datasets. Nevertheless, measures taken to infringe on an individual's privacy must be proportionate. Considering this, the UK Supreme Court has created a four-stage test based on the 1988 Human Rights Act to assess whether measures are commensurate. These four steps question whether the situation is sufficiently important, the reduction of the privacy is connected to the aim, there are less intrusive measures available, and whether the right balance between an individual's violation of human rights and the well-being of the community is found (Babuta et al., 2020).

Moreover, there exist acts that provide intelligence services with the rights of privacy, hence enabling them to withhold information that is necessary for them to function (Babuta et al., 2020). Examples of these acts include: the Security Service Act 1989 in relation to the Security Service, and the Intelligence Services Act 1994 with regards to the Secret Intelligence Service and the Government Communications Headquarters (Babuta et al., 2020). There are also several other privacy-related guidelines that are currently being developed such as responsible AI, which concerns the ethical aspects of AI development (Yang, 2021). Other examples of these guidelines comprise of the California Consumer Privacy Act in 2020 in the US and Europe's General Data Protection Regulation (GDPR) 2018, established by the European Union (EU) (Yang, 2021). To provide more in-depth guidance on privacy matters and the European legal situation, the latter will be discussed in more detail in the following.

The GDPR is considered to be one of the world's strictest privacy and security laws. Although it was created and approved by the EU, it requires compliance by all organisations worldwide as long as they target or gather data about individuals residing in the EU (Wolford, n.d.). Organisations found to be in breach of the GDPR will be subjected to high financial penalties. Within the GDPR, personal data is defined as all information related to an individual that can be directly or indirectly identified. This can be web traces, biographical information, biometric data and much more. This definition is further extended to cover the data processing aspects including: the collection, organisation, storage, deletion, and/or usage of data in any way possible (Information Commissioner's Office (ICO.), 2022). The GDPR considers the collection and storage of personal data as a violation of human rights, irrespective of whether these are processed and analysed solely by machines, human operators or a combination of both (Babuta et al., 2020). In view of the fact that the principles of data protection also apply to AI data processing, such processing must be transparent to the user whose data is collected. In addition, data collection needs to have a purpose and be limited to only what is necessary. Data also needs to be accurate and stored only as long as it is needed. Furthermore, the processing is required to be performed in a manner that provides security, integrity and confidentiality. In addition, the accountability for adhering to these principles rests with those who decide how and what data will be used (ICO., 2022).

The invasion of data privacy is independent of the type of operator dealing with the data, whether it be a human or a machine. Additionally, the GDPR provides policies for data collection, the right and responsibilities of data collectors, and the rights of data providers (Wolford, n.d.). Moreover, the anonymisation of data is addressed in relatively broad terms. The two processes that are suggested by the UK GDPR to anonymise data are pseudonymisation and encryption. Pseudonymisation, as defined in the GDPR, is the processing of data so that it cannot be linked to a specific individual (GDPR.EU, n.d.). Encryption describes the process of coding data so that only people knowing the encryption key can access it (Wang et al., 2014). Although the use of these measures is not mandatory, the measures should be considered if seen necessary to maintain the security of data (ICO., 2022).

Due to its flexibility, the GDPR is also capable of providing necessary basic guidelines that can be applied to new (European Commission, 2020). This is of significant importance given that developing suitable regulations often lag behind the rapid technological change (Osoba & Welser, 2017). Although AI is not explicitly stated in the GPDR, many of its regulations are still applicable to AI. This is despite the fact that some of these provisions are undoubtedly challenged by the new means of processing personal data that are facilitated by AI (Sartor & Lagioia, 2020). Likewise, in relation to emotional AI, the GDPR does not directly address the topic, instead requiring these regulations to be interpreted accordingly. Whilst the GDPR contains the strictest data privacy laws worldwide (Wolford, n.d.; McStay, 2020), it lacks explicit regulations concerning emotional intelligence. According to the Article 4 of the GDPR, privacy regulations are subject to protecting personal data including that collected through emotional AI. However, this personal data can be data that is used to identify a single individual. If the data is stored as group data and not raw data, no privacy violation has occurred when collecting and processing these for emotional AI as the GDPR regulations do not apply (McStay, 2020).

Furthermore, in relation to the collection and storage of a single individual's data, the Article 9 of the GDPR forbids the processing of biometric data to identify that person. The same regulations must be applied to VBSD such as Amazon's Alexa. However, exceptions can be made under the following conditions: the individuals have provided explicit consent, it has been collected for the individual's wellbeing without seeking profit, it is private data that already has been made public, the data is related to national security, or it is needed for public research purposes (Intersoft Consulting, n.d.). This circles back to the point made by Floridi (2016), as cited in McStay (2020), that the 'my' in 'my data' is different to the 'my' in other possessions. Although biometric data is often considered sensitive and personal, it is not legally protected as such when it is processed as part of a group (Wachter, 2018, as cited in McStay, 2020).

In summary to this subsection, the main legal guidelines regarding the privacy of data processed by AI can be found in the GDPR as previously discussed. Furthermore, in view of the foregoing discussions, it can be observed that the GDPR is overall capable of addressing most of the privacy concerns analysed in Sect. 4.1.

4.3 Potential Solutions for Privacy Implications

As discussed in Sect. 4.1, there are several perspectives on privacy intrusion. When focussing on the operator, the view that privacy is only violated when data is analysed by human operators can be addressed by improving AI algorithms. This reduces the involvement of human operators in data processing. Moreover, with respect to the legal frameworks, AI data processing is required to be secure and confidential. To ensure these principles, two approaches to data processing will be explored in the following.

The first approach towards privacy-protecting AI is federated learning (FL). The new generation of privacy-preserving computing, which has been developed since the 1970s, has emerged (Pötter et al., 2021; Yang, 2021). Typically, data used to travel to local sites becomes subject to cyberattacks launched from foreign territories with the likelihood to be falsified or used without given consent. In contrast, instead of collecting data from various locations and fusing them at one central location, FL takes the computation to those locations in which data reside in order to protect them. This is carried out by interactions of different parties that communicate their encrypted model details rather than the raw data (Yang, 2021). An analogy provided by Yang (2021) describes it as a sheep and a grass supplier where the former is compared to the collective model and the latter to the data subjects. Instead of the traditional way which involves bringing the grass to the sheep, the sheep is taken to the grass suppliers and raised in the context. In particular, this allows the data to be decentralised while the AI model can be improved. Moreover, this relies on the underlying assumption that it is easier and safer to communicate encrypted model parameters securely than the amount of data (Yang, 2021).

Other propositions concern application areas. Albaseer et al. (2020) suggest a semi-supervised FL method for edge computing called FedSem, that uses unlabelled data in smart cities to train AI. Similarly, Huang et al. (2021) presented a system entitled StarFL, that is claimed to increase the interaction between satellites. Additionally, healthcare systems could benefit from FL technology since medical data consisting of clearly sensitive information is isolated in medical institutions and hence are difficult to harvest (Yang, 2021). For instance, NVIDIA provides a FL platform that enables hospitals and other wellbeing centres to share and combine their information (Yang, 2021; Li et al., 2020). FL can also be deployed differently in the healthcare domain as shown by the University of Pennsylvania, which uses FL to identify brain tumours (Intel, 2021, as cited in Yang, 2021). These examples highlight the potentials of FL for use in intelligence gathering, for instance in the military, with the purpose of protecting national security. Especially, FL could train AI to identify individuals at risk of radicalisation or to determine individuals that are actively engaging in terror.

The second approach presented is based on patching. According to Meurisch et al. (2020), there is no current model that fully protects privacy since data processing in AI algorithms is often beneficial for both parties. Hence, they propose a decentralised privacy platform called PrivAI, which they claim will enable the users to use personalised AI services securely by reducing the inclusion of raw user data. In particular, PrivAI is said to be aimed at dividing AI in cloud-based general training, having local personalisation, and sharing new updates of the AI model within the community. Furthermore, it is stated that PrivAI is able to reduce the personalisation-privacy paradox by granting users more control. Thus, experiments have complemented the effectiveness of the platform to be comparable to current approaches. Unlike FL, this patching method claims to be able to work with every AI algorithm (Meurisch et al., 2020), therefore complementing the first solution that was presented.

5 Conclusion

This Chapter explored ways in which AI and IoT technologies could be used both to protect and to threaten national security. Addressing digital security, it was illustrated how AI could be deployed to prevent cyberattacks and combat such attacks against IoT devices. Furthermore, the Chapter analysed the use of AI and the IoT in military applications and assessed the risks associated with hacking these technologies when deployed in warfare. The Chapter also explored the impact of the misuse of AI on political security, examining how Deepfake technology influenced political opinions and how filter bubbles polarised public views. Additionally, the beneficial applications of AI were examined, focusing on its ability to assess the validity of media contents and detect and remove extremist content from social media. In relation to the physical security, the Chapter also explored police and military uses of AI technology, critically analysing the importance of AI use in processing media content in certain investigations and its use in weapon systems respectively.

The Chapter then proceeded to address the privacy concerns associated with the use of AI, considering the cumulative intrusion risk and emotional AI in relation to profiling individuals. To this end, the Chapter critically examined issues such as the right to privacy and the ownership of data. Furthermore, benefits of national security uses of large data processing were critically analysed in terms of, for instance, improving border control and security measures through the use of AI built with a large set of user data. It was argued that the process of data collection through AI models could present the personalisation-privacy paradox. Next, the Chapter examined the legal frameworks that addressed privacy regulations focusing on the GDPR and its relevance to privacy implications. Likewise, the guiding principles of collecting, storing and analysing data, and the rights of the data subject were investigated. Additionally, the Chapter highlighted the significance of privacy and hence the need for the encryption of user data and prohibition of profiling such data without consent. Finally, a number of recommendations was presented that could be considered to protect user privacy and the implementation of which could assist with preserving privacy and reducing the risk of hacked or manipulated data.

References

Albaseer, A., Ciftler, B. S., Abdallah, M., & Al-Fuqaha, A. (2020). *Exploiting unlabeled data in smart cities using federated edge learning*. In IEEE 2020 International Wireless Communications and Mobile Computing (IWCMC) (pp. 1666–1671).

Alenezi, A., Atlam, H. F., & Wills, G. B. (2019). Experts reviews of a cloud forensic readiness framework for organizations. *Journal of Cloud Computing, 8*(1). https://doi.org/10.1186/s13677-019-0133-z

Allen, G., & Chan, T. (2017). *Artificial intelligence and national security*. Belfer Center for Science and International Affairs.

Babuta, A., Oswald, M., & Janjeva, A. (2020). *Artificial intelligence and UK national security: Policy considerations*. Royal United Services Institute for Defence and Security Studies.

Available at: https://static.rusi.org/ai_national_security_final_web_version.pdf. Accessed 19 Aug 2022.

Baldauf, J., Ebner, J., & Guhl, J. (2019). *Hate speech and radicalisation online*. Institute for Strategic Dialogue.

Barber, L., & Warrell, H. (2020). MI5 chief sees tech as biggest challenge and opportunity. *Financial Times*. Available at: https://www.ft.com/content/f8ef9d84-3542-11ea-a6d3-9a26f8c3cba4. Accessed 27 June 2022.

BBC. (2019). *The fake video where Johnson and Corbyn endorse each other*. Available at: https://www.bbc.co.uk/news/av/technology-50381728. Accessed 22 June 2022.

BBC. (2020). Cambridge Analytica 'not involved' in Brexit referendum, says watchdog. *BBC*. Available at: https://web.archive.org/web/20201009211248/https://www.bbc.com/news/uk-politics-54457407. Accessed 27 June 2022.

Buric, J., & Delija, D. (2015). Challenges in network Forensics. In *2015 38th International convention on information and communication technology, electronics and microelectronics (MIPRO)* (pp. 1382–1386). IEEE. https://doi.org/10.1109/mipro.2015.7160490

Cabinet Office. (2008). *The National security strategy of the United Kingdom* (ID5732621). The Stationery Office.

Casey, E. (2011). *Digital evidence and computer crime: Forensic science, computers and the internet* (3rd ed.). Academic.

Cameron, L. (2018). Future of Digital Forensics Faces Six Security Challenges in Fighting Borderless Cybercrime and Dark Web Tools. Available at: https://publications.computer.org/security-and-privacy/tag/dark-web (Accessed: 12/12/2022).

Center for Strategic and International Studies (CSIS). (n.d.). *Significant cyber incidents*. Available at: https://www.csis.org/programs/strategic-technologies-program/significant-cyber-incidents. Accessed 19 Aug 2022.

Chan, R. (2019). The Cambridge Analytica whistleblower explains how the firm used Facebook data to sway elections. *Insider*. Available at: https://www.businessinsider.com/cambridge-analytica-whistleblower-christopher-wylie-facebook-data-2019-10?r=US&IR=T. Accessed 27 June 2022.

Chitra, U., & Musco, C. (2020). *Analysing the impact of filter bubbles on social network Polarization*. In Proceedings of the 13th international conference on web search and data mining (pp. 115–123). https://doi.org/10.1145/3336191.3371825.

Caviglione, L., Wendzel, S. & Mazurczyk, W. (2017). The Future of digital forensics: challenges and the road ahead. *IEEE Security & Privacy, 6*, 12–17.

Dick, S. (2019). Artificial Intelligence. *Harvard Data Science Review, 1*(1). https://doi.org/10.1162/99608f92.92fe150c30

Dixon, M., McCorquodale, R., & Williams, S. (2016). 6. International human rights law. In M. Dixon, R. McCorquodale, & S. Williams (Eds.), *Cases & materials on international law*. Oxford University Press. https://doi.org/10.1093/he/9780198727644.003.0006

Elkin-Koren, N. (2020). Contesting algorithms: Restoring the public interest in content filtering by artificial intelligence. *Big Data & Society, 7*(2), 2053951720932296. https://doi.org/10.1177/2053951720932296

Ellavarason, E., Guest, R., Deravi, F., Sanchez-Riello, R., & Corsetti, B. (2020). Touchdynamics based behavioural biometrics on Mobile devices—A review from a usability and performance perspective. *ACM Computing Surveys, 53*(6). https://doi.org/10.1145/3394713

Equality and Human Rights Commission. (2021). *Article 8 protects your right to respect for your private and family life*. Available at: https://www.equalityhumanrights.com/en/human-rights-act/article-8-respect-your-private-and-family-life. Accessed 20 Aug 2022.

Evans, B. (2018). The death of the newsfeed. Available at: https://www.ben-evans.com/benedictevans/2018/4/2/the-death-of-the-newsfeed. (Accessed: 12/12/2022).

European Commission. (2020, June 24). *Two years of the GDPR: Questions and answers*. Available at: https://ec.europa.eu/commission/presscorner/detail/en/qanda_20_1166. Accessed 20 Aug 2022.

European Union Agency for Cybersecurity. (2019). *Introduction to network forensics*. ENISA. Available at: https://www.enisa.europa.eu/topics/trainings-for-cybersecurity-specialists/online-training-material/documents/introduction-to-network-forensics-handbook.pdf. Accessed 19 Aug 2022.

Fernandez, M., & Alani, H. (2021). Artificial intelligence and online extremism: Challenges and opportunities. In J. McDaniel & K. Pease (Eds.), *Predictive policing and artificial intelligence* (pp. 132–162). Taylor & Francis.

Furey, E., & Blue, J. (2018). *Alexa, emotions, privacy and GDPR*. In Proceedings of the 32nd international BCS human computer interaction conference (pp. 1–5). https://doi.org/10.14236/ewic/HCI2018.212.

GDPR.EU. (n.d.). *Art. 4 GDPR definitions*. General Data Protection Regulation (GDPR). Available at: https://gdpr.eu/article-4-definitions/31/. Accessed 20 Aug 2022.

Google. (n.d.). *The safer way to search*. Available at: https://safety.google/. Accessed 20 Aug 2022.

Gupta, S., Kamboj, S., & Bag, S. (2021). Role of risks in the development of responsible artificial intelligence in the digital healthcare domain. *Information Systems Frontiers*, 1–18.

Hilt, S., Kropotov, V., Mercês, F., Rosario, M., & Sancho, D. (2019). *The internet of things in the cybercrime underground*. Trend Micro Research.

Hon, W. K., Millard, C., & Singh, J. (2016). Twenty legal considerations for clouds of things. *Queen Mary School of Law Legal Studies Research Paper*, (216).

HP. (2014). *HP study reveals 70 Percent of Internet of Things devices vulnerable to attack*. Available at: https://www.hp.com/us-en/hp-news/press-release.html?id=1744676#.Yv_xKX-bMKbh. Accessed 19 Aug 2022.

Huang, A., Liu, Y., Chen, T., Zhou, Y., Sun, Q., Chai, H., & Yang, Q. (2021). Starfl: Hybrid federated learning architecture for smart urban computing. *ACM Transactions on Intelligent Systems and Technology (TIST), 12*(4), 1–23.

Information Commissioner's Office (ICO). (2022). *Guide to the UK General Data Protection Regulation (UK GDPR)*. Available at: https://ico.org.uk/for-organisations/guide-to-data-protection/guide-to-the-general-data-protection-regulation-gdpr/. Accessed 20 Aug 2022.

Intersoft Consulting. (n.d.). General Data Protection RegulationGDPR. Available at: https://gdpr-info.eu/ (Accessed: 13/12/2022).

Karthikeyan, J., Su Hie, T., & Yu Jin, N. (Eds.). (2021). *Learning outcomes of classroom research*. L Ordine Nuovo Publication.

Kaspersky. (2022). *DDoS attacks hit a record high in Q4 2021*. Kaspersky. Available at: https://www.kaspersky.com/about/press-releases/2022_ddos-attacks-hit-a-record-high-in-q4-2021. Accessed 19 Aug 2022.

Kaur, A., Elarabawy, M. M., Abd-Elnaby, M., Varadarajan, V., & Sharma, S. (2022). *IoT-based technological framework for inhibiting the spread of COVID-19: A pandemic using machine learning and fuzzy-based processes*. Security and Communication Networks.

Lau, J., Zimmerman, B., & Schaub, F. (2018). Alexa, are you listening? Privacy perceptions, concerns and privacy-seeking Behaviors with smart speakers. *Proceedings of the ACM on Human-Computer Interaction, 2*(CSCW), 1–31. https://doi.org/10.1145/3274371

Lee, J.-M., & Rha, J.-Y. (2016). Personalization–privacy paradox and consumer conflict with the use of location-based mobile commerce. *Computers in Human Behavior, 63*, 453–462. https://doi.org/10.1016/j.chb.2016.05.056

Li, T., Sahu, A. K., Talwalkar, A., & Smith, V. (2020). Federated learning: Challenges, methods, and future directions. *IEEE Signal Processing Magazine, 37*(3), 50–60.

Lillis, D., Becker, B., O'Sullivan, T. & Scanlon, M. (2016). Current challenges and future research areas for digital forensic investigation. arXiv preprint arXiv:1604.03850.

Lutta, P., Sedky, M., Hassan, M., Jayawickrama, U., & Bakhtiari Bastaki, B. (2021). The complexity of internet of things forensics: A state-of-the-art review. *Forensic Science International: Digital Investigation, 38*, 301210. https://doi.org/10.1016/j.fsidi.2021.301210

MacDermott, A., Baker, T., & Shi, Q. (2018). *Iot forensics: challenges for the IOA era*. In 9th IFIP international conference on New Technologies, Mobility and Security (NTMS) (pp. 1–5). IEEE. https://doi.org/10.1109/ntms.2018.8328748

Maras, M.-H., & Alexandrou, A. (2019). Determining authenticity of video evidence in the age of artificial intelligence and in the wake of Deepfake videos. *The International Journal of Evidence & Proof, 23*(3), 255–262. https://doi.org/10.1177/1365712718807226

Maurer, T., & Hinck, G. (2020). *Cloud security: A primer for policymakers* (pp. 5–10). Carnegie Endowment for International Peace. http://www.jstor.org/stable/resrep25787

Mazhar, M., Saleem, Y., Almogren, A., Arshad, J., Jaffery, M., Rehman, A., Shafiq, M., & Hamam, H. (2022). Forensic analysis on internet of things (IoT) device using machine-to-machine (M2M) framework. *Electronics, 11*, 1126. https://doi.org/10.3390/electronics11071126

McStay, A. (2020). Emotional AI, soft biometrics and the surveillance of emotional life: An unusual consensus on privacy. *Big Data & Society, 7*(1), 205395172090438. https://doi.org/10.1177/2053951720904386

Meredith, S. (2018). Facebook-Cambridge Analytica: A timeline of the data hijacking scandal. *CNBC*. Available at: https://www.cnbc.com/2018/04/10/facebook-cambridge-analytica-a-timeline-of-the-data-hijacking-scandal.html. Accessed 27 June 2022.

Meurisch, C., Bayrak, B., & Mühlhäuser, M. (2020). *Privacy-preserving AI services through data decentralization*. In Proceedings of the web conference 2020 (pp. 190–200). https://doi.org/10.1145/3366423.3380106

Montasari, R. (2016a). *The Comprehensive Digital Forensic Investigation Process Model (CDFIPM) for digital forensic practice*, PhD thesis.

Montasari, R. (2016b). A comprehensive digital forensic investigation process model. *International Journal of Electronic Security and Digital Forensics, 8*(4), 285–302.

Montasari, R., & Hill, R. (2019). *Next-generation digital forensics: Challenges and future paradigms*. In 2019 IEEE 12th International conference on global security, safety and sustainability (ICGS3) (pp. 205–212).

Mrdovic, S. (2021). IoT forensics. In *Security of ubiquitous computing systems* (pp. 215–229). https://doi.org/10.1007/978-3-030-10591-4_13

National Cyber Security Centre (NCSC). (2016). *What is a cyber incident*. Available at: https://www.ncsc.gov.uk/information/what-cyber-incident. Accessed 19 Aug 2022.

National Cyber Security Centre (NCSC). (n.d.). *NCSC glossary*. Available at: https://www.ncsc.gov.uk/information/ncsc-glossary. Accessed 19 Aug 2022.

Nayyar, A., Rameshwar, R., & Solanki, A. (2020). Internet of things (IoT) and the digital business environment: A standpoint inclusive cyber space, cyber crimes, and cybersecurity. In D. G. Chowdhry, R. Verma, & M. Mathur (Eds.), *The evolution of business in the cyber age* (1st ed., pp. 111–152). Apple Academic Press. https://doi.org/10.1201/9780429276484-6

Office of the High Commissioner for Human Rights (OHCHR). (n.d.). *International standards – Special Rapporteur on the right to privacy*. United Nations Human Rights. Available at: https://www.ohchr.org/en/special-procedures/sr-privacy. Accessed 20 Aug 2022.

Osoba, O., & Welser, W. (2017). *The risks of artificial intelligence to security and the future of work*. RAND Corporation. https://doi.org/10.7249/PE237

Pătrașcu, P. (2021). Emerging technologies and National Security: The impact of IoT in critical infrastructures protection and defence sector. *Land Forces Academy Review, 26*(4), 423–429. https://doi.org/10.2478/raft-2021-0055

Pötter, H., Lee, S., & Mossé, D. (2021, June). *Towards privacy-preserving framework for non-intrusive load monitoring*. In Proceedings of the Twelfth ACM international conference on future energy systems (pp. 259–263).

Rana, M. S., Nobi, M. N., Murali, B., & Sung, A. H. (2022). Deepfake detection: A systematic literature review. *IEEE Access, 10*, 25494–25513. https://doi.org/10.1109/ACCESS.2022.3154404

Ruan, K., Carthy, J., Kechadi, T. & Baggili, I. (2013). Cloud forensics definitions and critical criteria for cloud forensic capability: An overview of survey results. *Digital Investigation, 10*(1), 34–43.

Ruan, K., Carthy, J., Kechadi, T., & Crosbie, M. (2011). *Cloud forensics*. In IFIP international conference on digital forensics (pp. 35–46). Springer.

Sartor, G., & Lagioia, F. (2020). *The impact of the General Data Protection Regulation (GDPR) on artificial intelligence*. Directorate-General for Parliamentary Research Services of the Secretariat of the European Parliament. European Union, 10, 293.

Sayler, K. M. (2020). *Artificial intelligence and national security* (No. R45178). Congressional Research Service. https://crsreports.congress.gov

Seigfried-Spellar, K. C. (2018). Assessing the psychological Well-being and coping mechanisms of law enforcement investigators vs. digital forensic examiners of child pornography investigations. *Journal of Police and Criminal Psychology, 33*(3), 215–226. https://doi.org/10.1007/s11896-017-9248-7

Sharkey, N. (2008). Cassandra or false prophet of doom: AI robots and war. *IEEE Intelligent Systems, 23*(4), 14–17. https://doi.org/10.1109/MIS.2008.60

Singh, T., & Gulhane, A. (2018). *8 Key military applications for artificial intelligence in 2018*. Available at: https://blog.marketresearch.com/8-key-military-applications-for-artificial-intelligence-in-2018. Accessed 23 June 2022.

Sivarajah, U., Kamal, M. M., Irani, Z., & Weerakkody, V. (2016). Critical analysis of big data challenges and analytical methods. *Journal of Business Research, 70*, 263–286. https://doi.org/10.1016/j.jbusres.2016.08.001

Smith, A. (2018). There's an open secret about Cambridge Analytica in the political world: It doesn't have the 'secret sauce' it claims. *Insider*. Available at: https://www.businessinsider.com/cambridge-analytica-facebook-scandal-trump-cruz-operatives-2018-3?r=US&IR=T. Accessed 27 June 2022.

Stevens, T. (2018). Internet of Things: When objects threaten national security. *The Conversation*. Available at: http://theconversation.com/internet-of-things-when-objects-threatennational-security-96962. Accessed 19 Aug 2022.

Sutanto, J., Palme, E., Tan, C.-H., & Phang, C. W. (2013). Addressing the personalization-privacy paradox: An empirical assessment from a field experiment on smartphone users. *MIS Quarterly, 37*(4), 1141–1164.

United Nation Interregional Crime and Justice Research Institute (UNICRI) & United Nations Counter-Terrorism Centre (UNCCT). (2021). *Countering terrorism online with artificial intelligence*. United Nations Office of Counter-Terrorism. Available at: https://www.un.org/counterterrorism/sites/www.un.org.counterterrorism/files/countering-terrorism-online-with-ai-unict-unicri-report-web.pdf. Accessed 19 Aug 2022.

Vailshery, L. S. (2022). *Number of Internet of Things (IoT) connected devices worldwide from 2019 to 2030*. Stat. Available at: https://www.statista.com/statistics/1183457/iot-connected-devices-worldwide/. Accessed 16 June 2022.

Vimalkumar, M., Sharma, S. K., Singh, J. B., & Dwivedi, Y. K. (2021). 'Okay google, what about my privacy?': User's privacy perceptions and acceptance of voice based digital assistants. *Computers in Human Behavior, 120*, 106763. https://doi.org/10.1016/j.chb.2021.106763

Vincze, E. A. (2016). Challenges in digital forensics. *Police Practice and Research, 17*(2), 183–194. https://doi.org/10.1080/15614263.2015.1128163

Wachter, S. (2018). Normative challenges of identification in the Internet of Things: Privacy, profiling, discrimination, and the GDPR. *Computer Law & Security Review, 34*, 436–449. https://doi.org/10.1016/j.clsr.2018.02.002

Wang, X., Zhang, J., Schooler, E. M., & Ion, M. (2014). *Performance evaluation of Attribute-based encryption: Toward data privacy in the IoT*. In 2014 IEEE International Conference on Communications (ICC) (pp. 725–730). https://doi.org/10.1109/ICC.2014.6883405

Williams, M., & Wall, D. (2013). Cybercrime 12. In C. Hale, K. Hayward, A. Wahidin, & E. Wincup (Eds.), *Criminology* (pp. 247–266). Oxford University Press. https://doi.org/10.1093/he/9780199691296.003.0012

Wolford, B. (n.d.). *What is GDPR, the EU's new data protection law?* GDPR.EU. Available at: https://gdpr.eu/what-is-gdpr/. Accessed 20 Aug 2022.

Wu, H., Han, H., Wang, X., & Sun, S. (2020). Research on artificial intelligence enhancing internet of things security: A survey. *IEEE Access, 8*, 153826–153848. https://doi.org/10.1109/ACCESS.2020.3018170

Yang, Q. (2021). Toward responsible AI: An overview of federated learning for Usercentered privacy-preserving computing. *ACM Transactions on Interactive Intelligent Systems, 11*(3–4), 1–22. https://doi.org/10.1145/3485875

Yau, K.-L. A., Lee, H. J., Chong, Y.-W., Ling, M. H., Syed, A. R., Wu, C., & Goh, H. G. (2021). Augmented intelligence: Surveys of literature and expert opinion to understand relations between human intelligence and artificial intelligence. *IEEE Access, 9*, 136744–136761. https://doi.org/10.1109/ACCESS.2021.3115494

Zakharov, E. (2019). Few-shot adversarial learning of realistic neural talking head models [Video]. *YouTube*. Available at: https://www.youtube.com/watch?v=p1b5aiTrGzY. Accessed 22 June 2022.

Zhang, M. (2019). Samsung AI can turn a single portrait into a realistic talking head. *PetaPixel*. Available at: https://petapixel.com/2019/05/24/samsung-ai-can-turn-a-single-portrait-into-a-realistic-talking-head/. Accessed: 22 June 2022.

Zhang, Z. K., Cho, M. C. Y., Wang, C. W., Hsu, C. W., Chen, C. K., & Shieh, S. (2014). *IoT Security: Ongoing challenges and research opportunities*. In IEEE 7th International conference on service-oriented computing and applications (pp. 230–234). IEEE.

Chapter 4
Artificial Intelligence and the Internet of Things Forensics in a National Security Context

1 Introduction

In recent years, there has been an increasing number of cyber-attacks targeting organisations both in the public and private sectors. With an increase in the number of such attacks, combined with the added risks of the Internet of Things (IoT), organisations are finding it increasingly difficult to safeguard their systems against sophisticated and machine-speed attacks. Attackers target systems in sectors such as banking, transportation, law firms, military, academia and hospitals in order to exfiltrate sensitive and confidential data. A successful attack against an organisation can easily lead to reputational damage and subsequent adverse effects such as hefty fines and loss of customers. Organisations that have been breached as a result of a successful cyber-attack will need to understand the attack in its entirety in order to be able to determine what data was compromised. A Digital Forensic investigation can assist with establishing what data was breached. This Chapter analyses how certain Artificial Intelligence (AI) techniques, such as Machine Learning (ML) and Natural Language Processing (NLP), can be used to automate certain tasks of IoT Forensics, such as anomaly and steganography detection. The Chapter also investigates challenges in relation to algorithmic bias and transparency in military AI applications. Accordingly, general policy recommendations are offered in response to increasing transparency and reducing bias in AI algorithms intended for miliary use.

The remainder of the Chapter is structured as follows. Section 2 will initially expand upon information previously covered in Chap. 3 on IoT Forensics. It will then explore the most significant challenges faced by investigators when conducting IoT Forensics. Furthermore, the Section will examine the different types of AI techniques, ways in which these techniques can be used to address the stated challenges, as well as limitations. Section 3 will explore the issue of bias in AI algorithms and will identify the key factors that contribute to inaccurate algorithmic predictions. The Section will also investigate the impact of bias and the lack of accountability

© The Author(s), under exclusive license to Springer Nature Switzerland AG 2023
R. Montasari, *Countering Cyberterrorism*, Advances in Information Security 101, https://doi.org/10.1007/978-3-031-21920-7_4

and transparency in AI algorithms in order to identify factors that can impede transparency. Section 4 will offer a set of recommendations with regards to challenges concerning the use of AI algorithms for national security purposes. To this end, the Section will propose recommendations for reducing AI algorithmic bias as well as suggestions for increasing transparency in AI algorithms. Finally, Sect. 5 will offer concluding remarks and directions for future research.

2   AI Techniques in Automating Tasks of IoT Forensics

The Section aims to investigate the potential use of AI techniques in automating certain tasks of IoT forensics. First, the Section will expand upon information previously covered in Sect. 2 of this chapter on IoT forensics. Then, it will explore the most significant challenges faced by investigators when conducting IoT Forensics. Next, it will examine the different types of AI techniques such as natural language processing (NLP) and machine learning (ML), and how these techniques can be used to address these challenges by automating certain tasks such as anomaly detection and automatic detection of steganography as well as limitations. Finally, the Section will explore the general challenges of AI-enabled IoT Forensics and will offer concluding thoughts.

2.1   A Brief Summary of IoT Forensics from Chap. 3

IoT Forensics is a branch of Digital Forensics that entails finding and collecting digital evidence from a wide range of IoT devices, systems or objects within IoT environments. These could comprise of smart devices and sensors as well as hardware and software. In contrast with conventional Digital Forensic methods, IoT Forensics poses many technical and legal challenges. Some of these challenges concern the varied proprietary hardware and software, data formats and protocols, and physical interfaces. Other challenges concerning the IoT Forensics pertain to the spread of data across multiple devices and platforms, culminating in complexities to establish the location of IoT data and the means by which this data can be extracted. Maintaining chain of custody in IoT Forensics also presents a number of issues. As discussed in Chap. 3, in a civil or criminal trial, collecting evidence in a forensically sound manner and preserving chain of custody are of paramount importance. However, ownership and preservation of evidence in an IoT setting could prove intricate and have a negative effect on a court's understanding that the evidence acquired is reliable. Chapter 3 also identified the management and analysis of the vast amounts of data generated by IoT devices to be a significant challenge faced by investigators when conducting IoT Forensics (Servida & Casey, 2019). The sheer volume of data collected in IoT environments, coupled with the remote multi-cloud nature of IoT devices, "...make it close to impossible to provide an end-to-end analysis of residual evidences…" in IoT Forensic investigations (Conti et al., 2018, p. 4). However, research has shown that AI techniques can be used as an effective tool in increasing efficiency and scalability in big data analytics and IoT Forensics (Mazhar et al., 2022).

2.2 Types of AI Techniques Relevant to IoT Forensics

Continuous developments in technology have led to the increased integration of AI in various fields, including national security and safety (Sayler, 2020). AI refers to a system's capability to accurately interpret external data, to learn from that data, and to apply that learning to accomplish predetermined goals and tasks through adaptable learning (Kaplan & Haenlein, 2019). Within AI, there are a variety of techniques which can be used to enable systems to collect and analyse data with human-like intelligence. However, with regards to IoT Forensics, the most significant and relevant AI techniques include NLP and ML, which will be the focus of the discussions in the following subsections.

2.3 Natural Language Processing

The first AI technique that will be covered in this subsection is NLP, which refers to the branch of AI that aims to assist computers in understanding how humans write and speak (University of York, n.d.). More specifically, Natural Language Understanding (NLU), a sub-branch of NLP, focuses on improving a computer's ability to understand context, which enables computers to improve comprehension rather than focusing purely on understanding literal meanings (University of York, n.d.). NLP is currently used in a number of real-world applications available to the public, including voice-controlled assistants and customer service chatbots (Apple's Siri, Amazon's Alexa, etc). This type of technology uses speech recognition to identify patterns within voice commands and natural language generation to take the appropriate action or offer helpful comments (IBM Cloud Education, 2021; IBM Cloud Education, 2020). However, recent progress in NLP has also resulted in relatively positive implications for law enforcement and security agencies looking to utilise AI to streamline investigations in IoT environments (Blasch et al., 2019). The amount of unstructured text data produced on a daily basis is exponentially growing and presents a variety of challenges for investigators when attempting to categorise, prioritise, and analyse all pertinent data for their particular problem area of concern (Blasch et al., 2019). Yet, research has shown that technological developments in NLP can help to improve the efficiency in Cloud Forensics and Device Forensics (Ukwen & Karabatak, 2021).

Within the field of Cloud and Device Forensics, there is a variety of ways in which NLP techniques can be used to address the big data problem faced by investigators, and a number of new methods and frameworks have been proposed in the existing literature. For instance, at the cloud level, Baror et al. (2020) have proposed a new Digital Forensics Framework (DFR) that they claim to be able to resolve the issue of rapid detection of cybercrime incidents in the public cloud by taking advantage of NLP methods and techniques. Certain aspects of the framework aim to utilise different NLU techniques, such as Name Entity Recognition (NER), to fuse together text summarization and topic modelling to extract valuable information from cybercrime text data. However, the reactive nature of the Digital Forensic investigation process requires the development of a mechanism to link a cybercrime perpetrator to an ongoing cyberattack, as well as the gathering of potential Digital Forensic evidence of cyberattack in public cloud cases (Baror et al., 2020). NLP and NLP-based techniques can also be employed in the Digital Forensic process at the device level to improve efficiency in investigations (Baror et al., 2020). In Anwar and Supriyanto (2019), the authors conducted a study using NLP and data collection techniques to carry out Forensics authentication on WhatsApp Messenger (Ukwen & Karabatak, 2021). The study which was conducted in Indonesia showed how investigators could make use of several techniques utilising Indonesian NLP text matching methods and measurements to carry out investigative processes related to cybercrime and instant messenger applications.

With regards to IoT Forensics as a whole, the application of NLP methods and techniques can be extremely beneficial, particularly when unstructured and large volumes of data must be managed by investigators (Banerveld et al., 2014). However, the effectiveness of using NLP methods in IoT Forensics is limited by a variety of factors, including the structuring of these methods and techniques around low-resource languages. Most of today's NLP research "...focuses on 20 of the 7,000 languages of the world, leaving the vast majority of languages understudied" (Magueresse et al., 2020, para. 1). This poses a significant challenge for investigators seeking to utilise NLP because low-resource languages often lack the necessary data to properly define a problem or task and develop sufficient evaluation procedures within NLP methods. For these reasons, the transferring of tasks from high-resource languages, such as English or Chinese, to low-resource languages, such as Uyghur, also proves challenging for investigators (Magueresse et al., 2020). One approach to mitigating low-resource NLP is to "...use models that are based on linguistic descriptions rather than being data-driven" (Mortensen, n.d., p. 7). However, this approach is dependent on law enforcement agencies (LEAs) having the necessary resources, such as computational linguists, to take advantage of NLP methods to optimise the investigation process.

2.4 Machine Learning

The second AI technique that will be explored in this subsection is ML, which refers to a system's ability to learn from problem-specific training data in order to automate the process of developing analytical models and solving related tasks (Janiesch et al., 2021). Technological advancements in AI have led to the development of Deep Learning (DL), a subset of ML, which utilises the evolution of Artificial Neural Networks (ANNs) to develop increasingly deep neural network infrastructures with improved learning capabilities (Janiesch et al., 2021). Within ML, there are two different approaches that can be used when programming algorithms including supervised and unsupervised learning. The main distinction between these two types of approaches is that supervised ML relies on labelled datasets to train algorithms while unsupervised ML does not (Delua, 2021). With unsupervised ML, the algorithm is tasked with uncovering hidden patterns in unlabelled datasets and does not require human intervention (Delua, 2021). Despite the differences in techniques, both supervised and unsupervised ML have promising benefits for IoT Forensics, and research has shown that ML provides a highly effective approach for mining bigger datasets such as those containing data from a variety of IoT devices (Kebande et al., 2020).

2.5 Machine Learning and Anomaly Detection

Within ML, research has shown that there are several methods that can be applied to different areas of IoT Forensics, which can help mitigate current and future challenges by reducing manual effort and increasing efficiency (Sjöstrand, 2020). ML-based anomaly detection is one type of such methods that can be used to perform forensic analysis in IoT environments. Generally speaking, an anomaly is typically described as a deviation from the norm. Therefore, ML-based anomaly detection refers to the process of using ML to identify outliers in a given dataset (Kotu & Deshpande, 2019). ML is an integral part of anomaly detection considering the fact that current ML algorithms can be refined using different techniques to address a specific problem. Within ML-based anomaly detection, there are different methods that can be used to train algorithms. These consist of supervised, unsupervised, and semi-supervised anomaly detection (Goldstein & Uchida, 2016). Supervised anomaly detection requires the use of a high-quality training dataset to train the algorithm to identify and extract abnormal data points or patterns within the set (Gavrilova, 2021). Alternatively, unsupervised anomaly detection typically relies on the use of ANNs to detect anomalies in unlabelled data and decreases the need for manual work in detecting atypical data points (Gavrilova, 2021).

While supervised learning algorithms are typically more accurate and reliable than unsupervised algorithms, they require upfront intervention to ensure that the data is labelled appropriately. However, labelled datasets enable supervised learning algorithms to avoid computational complexity since they do not require a large training set to generate desired results (Delua, 2021; IBM Cloud Education, 2021; IBM Cloud Education, 2020). The third method that can be used when conducting ML-based anomaly detection is semi-supervised learning. This method combines the benefits of supervised and unsupervised anomaly detection by applying "... unsupervised learning methods to automate feature learning and work with unstructured data" (Gavrilova, 2021, para. 23). However, by utilising human supervision, semi-supervised anomaly detection allows ML engineers to monitor and control the kind of patterns the algorithm learns. This approach usually helps to increase the accuracy of the algorithm's predictions without needing the same level of supervision required by a supervised anomaly detection model.

Within IoT Forensics, ML-based anomaly detection can be utilised to improve precision, sensitivity and specificity in Forensics processes when compared to existing techniques (Venugopal et al., 2022, para. 3). Venugopal et al. (2022) propose a Forensic framework in big data optimisation using Hadoop clustering, convolution-based ADAM optimiser and Deep Neural Anomaly Detection (DNAD), a form of supervised ML. Hadoop clustering is an Apache open-source platform written in Java that uses a group of computers to enable distributed processing of large datasets, and can consist of a single server up to thousands of machines (Venugopal et al., 2022). Once data has been clustered, the framework proposes using a convolution-based ADAM optimiser, which is a stochastic optimisation algorithm for training DL models (Venugopal et al., 2022). The framework also proposes using DNAD to identify and trace cyber-attacks, while also lowering the model's false-negative rate and improving detection accuracy (Venugopal et al., 2022). This is important as the reliability of a Digital Forensic system is dependent on its ability to detect attacks on time while also minimising the security risk associated with IoT devices. Venugopal et al. (2022) claim that the results produced from their research showed that the proposed methodology "...obtains a minimal latency which is 40%-74% less when compared to state-of-art techniques" (para. 19). In this context, latency refers to the delay in processing attacks that have been detected by the model (Venugopal et al., 2022). The main factor contributing to these results is the integration of the convolution-based ADAM optimizer and the Hadoop clustering with the deep neural anomaly detection. This integration enables the model to handle more complex tasks, and identify local and overall abnormal traffic, regardless of the size of the data source (Venugopal et al., 2022). Although the research has demonstrated the effectiveness of the proposed model in performing forensic tasks in IoT environments, the work could be further extended by providing further insight into how the model can be deployed in various real-world IoT networks such as networks for smart health.

In summary to this subsection, ML-based anomaly detection comprises supervised, unsupervised, and semi-supervised techniques and, in recent years, has received considerable attention for its current and potential uses in IoT Forensics. Although there are various anomaly detection techniques, the main technique that was highlighted in this subsection was the use of Deep Neural Networks (DNNs). The use of DNNs for anomaly detection is significant because the introduction of these methods in recent years has proved to perform noticeably better than traditional anomaly detection techniques on tackling challenging detection issues in real-world scenarios (Pang et al., 2022). In particular, DL methods help reduce the need for large-scale labelled data by improving the utilisation of "... labelled normal data or some labelled anomaly data" irrespective of the data type (Pang et al., 2022, p. 5). Subsequently, this results in models that are better informed and more adaptive than traditional methods. However, the use of DNNs for anomaly detection also presents a variety of unique and complex analytical challenges. One of the challenges with using DL methods for anomaly detection is the rarity of anomalies in datasets and class imbalance. Since anomalies tend to be considered rare data instances, it is often difficult for ML engineers to gather a large amount of labelled abnormal data points, and this often results in insufficient large-scale labelled datasets in most applications (Ahmad et al., 2021). Class imbalance is another complex challenge that results from using DL methods for anomaly detection and is because misclassifying anomalies is typically much more expensive than misclassifying normal instances (Pang et al., 2022). Despite these challenges, research has shown that the architecture of DL methods for anomaly detection makes it an ideal methodology to be used in IoT Forensics. This is owing to the mass amounts of data generated by IoT devices and the method's ability to learn intricate features for accurate predictions (Khan et al., 2017; Ahmad et al., 2021).

2.6 Machine Learning and Detection of Steganography

The final ML-based technique that will be addressed in this subsection for use in IoT Forensics is the automatic detection of steganography. This technique refers to concealing data or a secret message inside a cover medium (or carrier), with common covers consisting of videos, audios, text files and images, etc. The analysis of detecting the presence of hidden messages within these covers is known as steganalysis, and it has a variety of real-world applications, including in areas such as Computer Forensic analysis and Cyber Warfare (Prakash et al., 2021). There are two main techniques that can be used when conducting steganalysis, and they consist of signature-based and statistical-based techniques (Kaur & Kaur, 2014). The distinction between the two techniques is "...based on whether the signature of the steganography technique or the statistics of an image is used to identify the presence of concealed messages in images embedded using steganography" (Kaur & Kaur, 2014, p. 1745).

More specifically, signature steganalysis focuses on detecting the existence of a hidden message by identifying repetitive pattern signatures of a steganography tool, while statistical steganalysis analyses the alterations in the statistics of an image due to the embedding of hidden data (Berg et al., 2003). However, statistical steganalysis techniques are often "...more commanding than signature steganalysis, because mathematical techniques are more responsive than visual perception" (Kaur & Kaur, 2014, p. 1746). The use of steganalysis is relevant in IoT Forensics due to the increase in the use of steganography in response to growing concerns regarding privacy and data protection in IoT systems (Koptyra & Ogiela, 2022). However, developments in the sophistication of steganographic algorithms have led to an increase in "...embedding capacity, security and robustness...", which poses major challenges for the use of steganalysis in IoT Forensics investigations (Chutani & Goyal, 2019, para. 2). One of the ways this can be mitigated, with regards to the use of steganography in IoT, is through the use of steganalysis techniques using ML algorithms for the automatic detection of steganography in IoT systems. The automatic detection of steganography refers to the use of ML algorithms to recognise patterns in media files, and automatically identify and differentiate between clean files and files embedded with hidden information (Berg et al., 2003, p. 51).

However, due to the complexities posed by technological developments in steganography techniques, some of the steganalysis techniques that utilise ML algorithms only target specific types of steganography. Hence, Convolutional Neural Networks (CNNs) could be deployed to help address this. For example, Reinel et al. (2021) propose a "...novel CNN [Convolutional Neural Networks] architecture which involves a pre-processing stage using filter banks to enhance steganographic noise, a feature extraction stage using depth wise and separable convolutional layers and skip connections" (p. 14340). The aim of the proposed architecture is to provide a more accurate structure to address the issue of cover and stego image classification and build upon previously proposed AI-based steganalysis procedures and methods (Reinel et al., 2021). According to Reinel et al. (2021), the results achieved by the proposed architecture, known as GBRAS-Net, highlighted the model's ability to detect steganographic images with remarkable accuracy. Reinel et al. report that the proposed model scored the highest accuracy percentage in the classification of cover and stego images "...among eight steganalysis methods against two algorithms" (Reinel et al., 2021, p. 14347). However, further evaluations done by Reinel et al. (2021) demonstrate that "...not all computational elements, such as the absolute value layer, specific activation functions, and several layer configurations, contribute to improving a CNN", and its ability to identify hidden information in images (p. 14348). The authors continue to note that, hence, further research is required to improve the pre-processing stage and the feature extraction stage of the model. It is claimed that this could help strengthen the rating capabilities of CNN architecture for the detection and analysis of steganography in media files (Reinel et al., 2021).

Overall, previous research has demonstrated that the use and potential uses of ML algorithms for the automatic detection of steganography have proved to be helpful in relation to IoT Forensic investigations, especially as the use of steganography techniques to address cybersecurity concerns in IoT systems increases (Djebbar, 2021; Reinel et al., 2021; Chutani & Goyal, 2019). Although there are various ML methods that can be used for the detection of steganography, the main method that was highlighted in this subsection was the use of the Convolutional Neural Network (CNN) method. The use of CNN for the detection of steganography is significant because it allows for the automatic identification of hidden features within a media file without the need for human supervision. Although CNNs "... have achieved state-of-the-art results on a variety of problems...", research indicates that CNNs "...underperform when test data is not exactly distributed as the training data" (Hosseini et al., 2017, p. 1). This could be due to the fact that current training methods for CNNs prioritise the memorisation of inputs and high-quality training data, potentially hindering the model's ability to effectively learn the structures and distinguish between classifications (Hosseini et al., 2017). A better representation of the behaviour and predictions of ML models, such as CNN, for various real-world applications, such as the automatic detection of steganography for IoT related forensic investigations, could be achieved through the use of better training methods and more meaningful performance metrics (Hosseini et al., 2017).

2.7 General Challenges of AI-Enabled IoT Forensics

In previous subsections, the specific challenges and limitations of each proposed AI technique in automating certain tasks in IoT Forensics were identified and addressed. However, there exist two significant challenges faced in particular by AI-based IoT Forensic systems on a more general level that limit efficiency and effectiveness in IoT Forensic processes. The first issue is that the use of AI techniques to automate certain tasks in IoT Forensics is limited by its dependency on experts in AI and forensic investigations to provide oversight. This is primarily because a majority of the AI techniques used in Digital Forensics require the use of supervised or semi-supervised learning models to provide the most accurate and reliable results. Therefore, AI-based techniques are only a valuable asset to forensic investigations if the investigators have been provided with the necessary skills and training to utilise the techniques correctly. Additionally, inexperienced investigators might act on incomplete information because of their complete dependence on the automated systems, raising the likelihood of unsuccessful investigations (James & Gladyshev, 2013; Jarrett & Choo, 2021). The second issue faced in particular by AI-based IoT Forensic systems is the acquisition and analysis of multiple and complicated media formats, such as steganography and other anti-forensic media methods (al Fahdi et al., 2013). This is a result of the widespread adoption and use of IoT devices, which has broadened the spread and flow of diverse media formats. However, it poses significant challenges for investigators utilising AI-based techniques to automate forensic tasks as most learning models are trained to identify and analyse a single media format, as opposed to various formats (al Fahdi et al., 2013). Although AI-based techniques, and more specifically ML-based techniques, have been proven to be more efficient and cost-effective in analysing different types of media in forensic investigations, many law enforcement agencies lack the necessary resources and funding to implement these methods.

3 Sources and Detection of Algorithmic Bias

This Section will explore the issue of bias in AI algorithms and identify the key factors that contribute to inaccurate algorithmic predictions. The Section will also examine the impact of bias and the lack of accountability and transparency in AI algorithms with a view to identify factors that can inhibit transparency.

3.1 Algorithmic Bias

As previously noted, AI is a branch of Computer Science that seeks to re-create human intelligence in machines (Dick, 2019). Within the field of AI, there is a wide variety of techniques that have been developed to mimic specific cognitive qualities and abilities, such as ML, NLP, and Machine Vision (MV) (Delua, 2021; IBM Cloud Education, 2021; IBM Cloud Education, 2020). AI algorithms refer to the set of mathematical instructions that instruct computers how to perform automated tasks, such as data processing and analysis (Elkin-Koren, 2020). Research has shown that the use of AI in various real-world applications has had a positive impact, and AI algorithms are now used in a variety of domains, such as security and health-care settings (Fu et al., 2020). For instance, the U.S. Department of Homeland Security (DHS) has started to implement the use of AI algorithms for facial recognition (FR) in airport security screening (Fu et al., 2020). They have also partnered with NASA's (National Aeronautics and Space Administration) Jet Propulsion Laboratory (JPL) to develop the Assistant for Understanding Data through Reasoning, Extraction and Synthesis (AUDREY), which is a state-of-the-art intelligent reasoning system that aims to "…assist first responders in synthesising high-level data while at the scene of an emergency" (DHS, 2018, para. 2). Yet, the increased reliance on artificial agents also brings about numerous risks, and ML algorithms have increasingly been found to be problematically biased (Fu et al., 2020). Algorithmic bias refers to the "…systematic and repeatable errors in a computer system that create unfair outcomes…" and can also occur when "…an algorithm produces results that are systemically prejudiced due to erroneous assumptions in the ML process" (FSU, 2021, para. 3). If AI systems and algorithms are to continue to become an integral part of the decision-making process in sensitive environments, then it is crucial to ensure that these decisions do not reflect discriminatory behaviours (Mehrabi et al., 2022). However, AI algorithms often contain bias, the sources of which are discussed in the following subsection.

3.2 Sources of Algorithmic Bias

There are three main distinguished causes of bias in AI algorithms, consisting of bias in modelling, bias in training and bias in usage (Ferrer et al., 2021). Bias in modelling, also known as algorithmic processing bias, refers to bias that occurs when the algorithm, itself, is biased in different ways (Danks & London, 2017). Algorithmic processing bias can be caused by a variety of factors, including the use of certain optimisation functions and regularisations, but it is most often generated by the utilisation of a statistically biased estimator (Mehrabi et al., 2022). However, statistically biased estimators in algorithms are often used deliberately in order to mitigate other types of more problematic bias (Danks & London, 2017). For example, the design of an autonomous weapons system might include the use of an ethical module that will stop the system from firing at perceived enemy targets if they are near a protected area of cultural, historical or environmental significance, such as a UNESCO World Heritage Site (Danks & London, 2017; Arkin et al. 2012). An ethical module is a shallow neural network that makes changes in the embedding layers of a pre-trained model to give more representative weight to disadvantaged subgroups (Conti et al., 2021). Therefore, the processing of the algorithm in this example is statistically biased in that its conclusions or decision differ from those of a neutral algorithm (Arkin et al., 2012). Although bias in modelling is often considered negative, the use of ethical modules in algorithms highlights how algorithmic processing bias can be used to produce positive outcomes in real-world applications.

The second type of algorithmic bias, as identified by Ferrer et al. (2021), is bias in training. This type of bias occurs as a result of using biased input data to train algorithms, thereby leading to data bias in the algorithm's output values. Bias in training data can result from various factors, such as the use of a dataset that is incomplete or not completely representative of the context for which the algorithm's use is intended. However, it can often be challenging to identify training data bias in algorithms, as developers often do not disclose the specific data that was used to train certain algorithmic systems. For example, researchers at the Massachusetts Institute for Technology (MIT) found that the algorithms behind three FR software systems, made commercially available to governments and law enforcement agencies by Microsoft, IBM (International Business Machines Corporation), and Face++, were failing to correctly identify individuals with darker-skinned complexions (Buolamwini & Gebru, 2018). More specifically, they revealed that females with darker-skinned complexions were the most impacted by misclassification, with the highest error rates for all gender classifiers ranging from 20.8% to 34.7% (Buolamwini & Gebru, 2018).

The researchers also reported that there was limited information published by all three companies regarding details of their classification methodology, with no mention of what training data was used. However, Lee et al. (2019) note that generally the majority of FR "training data sets are estimated to be more than 75% male and more than 80% white" (p. 16). Although Buolamwini & Gebru (2018) were unable to analyse the training data for all three of the FR software systems, they concluded that the misclassification of females and males with darker-skinned complexions may be highly correlated with a lack of representation of individuals with darker-skinned complexions in the training data of the evaluated classifiers. Although Microsoft and IBM have since stopped the sale of their FR services for police use, Buolamwini and Gebru's (2018) findings highlight the significance and negative implications of bias in training data (Magid, 2020).

Bias in training can also happen as a result of historical human biases in datasets (Lee et al., 2019). Historical human biases in AI algorithms refers to the reflection of embedded prejudices against certain groups in data, which can lead to the reproduction and amplification of such prejudices in learning models (Lee et al., 2019). According to a report released by ProPublica in 2016, the Correctional Offender Management Profiling for Alternative Sanctions (COMPAS) algorithm, which is used as a risk assessment tool in the US criminal legal system, was found to be biased against Black Americans in its assessment (Angwin et al., 2016). More specifically, ProPublica reported that the COMPAS algorithm was "...almost twice as likely to mischaracterise black people as high risk than it was white people" (Angwin et al., 2016; Yeung et al., 2021, p. 4). However, the company responsible for the creation of COMPAS argued that the algorithm was not racially biased in nature, and the discriminatory outputs of algorithm were a natural result of societies in which black individuals are disproportionately imprisoned (Yeung et al., 2021). Moreover, this example highlights the damaging consequences that historical bias, and more specifically, racism and disparities in policing practices, can have on the development and training of AI algorithms.

The third and final type of algorithmic bias, as identified by Ferrer et al. (2021), is bias in usage, and more specifically, transfer context bias and/or interpretation bias. Transfer context bias refers to the issue of employing an algorithm in an environment that deviates from the environment in which the algorithm's use is intended (Ferrer et al., 2021). This can result in the algorithm failing to perform according to appropriate statistical, moral, or legal standards (Ferrer et al., 2021). As an example, the translation of a healthcare algorithm from a research hospital to a rural clinic would have substantial algorithmic bias in comparison to a statistical standard since the transfer context is likely to differ in terms of its characteristics (Ferrer et al., 2021). However, this statistical bias could also translate to a moral bias if the system "...assumed that the same level of resources were available, and so made morally flawed healthcare resource allocation decisions" (Ferrer et al., 2021, p. 4).

Therefore, it is important that users of AI algorithms understand the intended context of operation to avoid inappropriate use and skewed results. Alternatively, interpretation bias can be defined as the misinterpretation of the outputs or predictions of the algorithms based on the internalised biases of the algorithm's user (Ferrer et al., 2021). Although interpretation bias is seemingly simple to understand, i.e., resulting from user error, it is often more complex in nature and can represent a mismatch between the algorithm's outputs and the information requirements of the user (Ferrer et al., 2021). Bias in modelling, training, and interpretation, intended or not, can have significant negative and/or positive consequences depending on the application in which the algorithm is being used. However, regardless of intention, users must ensure that they properly understand the resulting implications of the algorithms results to reduce incidents of harm and discrimination.

3.3 Algorithmic Transparency and Military AI

Another challenge within the field of AI that is closely related to the issue of algorithmic bias is the lack of transparency around algorithmic systems. Although this topic was briefly covered in the previous Sections, the aim of this subsection is to provide further insight into algorithmic transparency and accountability in relation to the use of AI for national security purposes. As previously discussed, the increasing technological developments within the field of AI have potentially significant implications for national security (Allen & Chan, 2017). For example, the US DoD has authorised research for the use of AI within a variety of fields, including cyberspace operations and the use of military autonomous vehicles, with the intention of improving wartime decision-making and accelerating the pace of conflict (Hoadley & Lucas, 2018). China is another leading nation in the development of AI for military purposes, and, similar to US military concepts, aims to use AI to mine vast amounts of intelligence data, deliver a complete picture of the battlespace, and suggest feasible actions to military decision-makers (Hoadley & Lucas, 2018). However, a significant challenge within the field of AI is the unpredictability of results produced by AI algorithms, and the risk posed by these algorithms increases dramatically if they are deployed at scale within a military context (Hoadley & Lucas, 2018). For instance, an AI system that was developed to recognise and understand online text and was primarily trained using formal documents like Wikipedia articles, failed to interpret text in more vernacular settings such as Twitter (Bornstein, 2016).

An algorithm's sensitivity to the training data set is of particular concern in the context of military since it can create issues with domain adaptability (Hoadley & Lucas, 2018). Domain adaptability is associated with transfer learning and refers to the ability of an AI system to adapt to a different, but related, target domain (Hoadley & Lucas, 2018). Insufficiency in the domain adaptability of military AI poses significant risks given the unpredictable nature of warfare and the combat environment. More specifically, lack of a general comprehensive understanding of this phenomenon might lead to a technical debt, "...a term that refers to the effect of fielding AI systems that have minimal risk individually but increase the danger of catastrophe as their collective hazard is compounded by each new addition to the inventory" (Hoadley & Lucas, 2018, p. 30).

Lack of explainability is another challenge that further complicates the issues of predictability within AI systems. Although research has shown that AI systems frequently outperform humans in certain analytical and cognitive tasks, they often produce results without providing the necessary context for human understanding of how the results were derived by the system (Ehsan et al., 2021). As an illustration, in 2012, researchers at Google's X Labs created an artificial neural network of 16,000 processors and allowed the network to analyse random videos uploaded onto YouTube (NPR, 2012). They established that a neuron within the artificial neural network was specifically devoted to identifying cats despite the fact that the learning model had not been explicitly trained to search for cats (NPR, 2012). However, the researchers were unable to determine which physical traits of a cat the system had used to make these identifications, and Google's research highlighted growing concerns regarding dissimilarity between AI and human reasoning and the lack of explainability in AI (NPR, 2012). Another significant issue caused by the lack of explainability in AI systems is that they lack an audit trail that allows the military to verify that a system is compliant with performance standards (Hoadley & Lucas, 2018). This makes it difficult for governments to verify and validate the performance of an AI system before implementing it for use in combat (Hoadley & Lucas, 2018). Overall, recent advancements in military AI have enabled the development of complex systems that can be difficult to comprehend, posing issues of transparency and determining whether the system is functioning as anticipated or planned (Sisson et al., 2019).

3.4   Risks of Increasing Transparency in Military AI

There have been increased calls for greater transparency in the use of AI for military applications. At the same time, growing national security concerns over the dual-use of publicly available information on AI systems and associated data have also increased as a result (Jordan et al., 2020). More, specifically, concerns about trade secrecy have prompted academics to seek a practical compromise between disclosure requirements and genuine commercial interests (Bloch-Wehba, 2021). Currently, the majority of algorithmic systems used by governments and intergovernmental organisations are outsourced to private for-profit companies, who hold a near-monopoly on information regarding the ethical, legal, and political consequences of AI (Robbins, 2018). Yet, increasing demands for transparency in AI systems It can provide a path for those with malicious intent to taint critical data used to inform decisions and introduce bias into AI especially within the context of military AI (Robbins, 2018). As the scale and complexity of military AI applications continue to grow, many leaders within the national security community are becoming increasingly concerned about international competition and, more specifically, a global AI arms race (Clark, 2017; Simonite, 2017).

Legal requirements for governmental transparency in relation to the use of AI could put certain countries at a technological disadvantage, especially since calls for transparency in military AI are representative of a cultural demand for political accountability in western democracies. More specifically, this is highlighted by growing concerns over cyberbiosecurity and the implications of making "...biological and programming components freely available as a consequence of humans striving to be ethical" (Jordan et al., 2020, p. 59). Cyberbiosecurity refers to a relatively new discipline emerging from the integration of the life sciences, information systems, biosecurity, and cybersecurity. It aims to provide a comprehensive understanding of how to mitigate vulnerabilities that develop and occur within the field (Richardson et al., 2019). Until recently, the majority of concerns regarding risk factors for bioterrorism attacks within the biodefense and biosecurity community have primarily revolved around the physical storage and handling of biological agents (Jordan et al., 2020). However, technological advances in cyber capabilities, such as the development of publicly accessible biological data warehouses, emphasises the need for further understanding of how cyberattacks can impact biological processes. Jordan et al. (2020) argue that "...the transparency of AI methods and biological data presents a novel case for national security..." and heightens concerns regarding duality of research in both these areas (p. 60). Within the context of this Chapter, dual-use research (DUR) can be defined as research that is generated for legitimate purposes to further push developments in knowledge and information, while also providing opportunities for exploitation of this information by malicious actors (Jordan et al., 2020). In this regard, two threat scenarios have been proposed (Jordan et al., 2020). One of these highlights how increased transparency in AI and biosecurity can be utilised by private companies to commit acts of espionage using information that is publicly available on the US National Library of Medicine's clinical trials website. However, it should be noted that open access to biological data and information regarding AI systems has played a significant role in the rapid advancements of both fields in a relatively short period.

4 Recommendations

The aim of this Section is to offer a set of recommendations in relation to challenges associated with the use of AI algorithms for national security purposes. To this end, the section will propose recommendations for reducing AI algorithmic bias as well as suggestions for increasing transparency in AI algorithms. Finally, the Section will offer concluding remarks and directions for future research.

4.1 Recommendations for Detecting Algorithmic Bias

The growing technical complexity and opacity of AI algorithms can make it increasingly difficult to investigate and detect algorithmic bias (Ayres, 2010). Despite these challenges, there is a variety of techniques and programmes that are currently utilised, such as regression analysis and Google's Testing with Concept Activation Vectors (TCAV), to test for bias in algorithms (Ayres, 2010). Regression analysis is typically used to predict the likelihood of favourable or unfavourable decisions within groups based on sensitive characteristics (Fu et al., 2020). In this type of analysis, certain variables are controlled to identify underlying risk and sensitive attributes are used to predict selective likelihood (Fu et al., 2020). The result of a "... significant, non-zero coefficient for the protected attributes is viewed as the presence of discrimination…" in the analysis (Fu et al., 2020, p. 16). However, the use of sensitive attributes in this context, such as race and gender, for regression analysis is immutable, which can make it difficult to fully recognise and understand their effect on decisions (Greiner & Rubin, 2011). Despite this, regression analysis is still often used to find initial evidence of bias and discrimination in algorithms (Fu et al., 2020). Another technique that can be used to identify bias, including race, gender and location bias, in ML algorithms is Google's TCAV. This tool uses "...directional derivatives to estimate the degree to which a user-defined concept is important to the results of the classification task at hand" (Cerrato et al., 2022, p. 6). The use of concept activation vectors in the tool can help detect biases in algorithms by uncovering unexpected word or concept associations that might indicate an inequity (Cerrato et al., 2022). The development of Google's TCAV tool, and other tools such as IBM's AI Fairness 360, highlight the push for more transparency around algorithmic bias in the field of AI (Cerrato et al., 2022).

4.2   Recommendations for Reducing Bias in Algorithms

Currently, steps to identify and reduce bias in AI algorithms are "...being taken by various stakeholders - spanning companies, academia, government, multilateral institutions, [and] non-governmental organisations (NGOs)..." (Smith & Rustagi, 2020, p. 8). The aim of this subsection is to provide recommendations for reducing bias in AI algorithms. More specifically, this subsection will focus on recommendations in response to the three distinguished causes of algorithmic bias, as identified by Ferrer et al. (2021), which includes bias in modelling, bias in training and bias in usage.

The first cause of bias in AI algorithms that was addressed in the previous Section was bias in modelling, also referred to as algorithmic processing bias. As previously mentioned, algorithmic processing bias can occur as a result of a variety of factors, but often transpires from the use of statistically biased estimators in an algorithm (Ferrer et al., 2021). Although bias in modelling is often considered negative, the previous Section highlighted how the use of ethical modules in algorithms can be used to produce positive outcomes in real-world applications. However, the establishment of policies and practices that enable responsible algorithm development is the main recommendation for reducing the occurrence of problematic algorithmic processing bias (Smith & Rustagi, 2020). Although policies and practices will need to be developed in response to concerns regarding the intended use of each specific algorithm, general recommendations can be made regarding the implementation of ethical frameworks for AI developers. The role of these proposed ethical frameworks in the development of AI algorithms is to equip developers with the necessary guidelines and resources to allow for the prioritisation of equity in the algorithms' objectives and ensure that certain variables do not disadvantage one group over another (Smith & Rustagi, 2020).

Policies encouraging the audit of algorithms by internal and external auditors could also help reduce bias in algorithmic processing. While the external auditing of AI algorithms is typically conducted after the deployment of the model, it can still be used to identify risks and serve as an accountability measure that can help reduce bias in the future development of the model (Smith & Rustagi, 2020). However, the external auditing of AI systems is typically conducted through a third-party company, and therefore is limited by a lack of access to internal processes, such as intermediate models and/or training data (Raji et al., 2020). Alternatively, internal auditors often have direct access to the internal processes of the relevant AI system, thus, extending conventional external auditing models by including additional data usually absent for external assessments to uncover previously unknown risks (Raji et al., 2020). As a result, the internal auditing of AI algorithms can be used as a more effective mechanism to check that the engineering processes involved in the development of the algorithm meet ethical expectations and standards (Smith & Rustagi, 2020, p. 33).

The second cause of bias in AI algorithms addressed in the previous Section was bias in training, also referred to as training data bias. As noted, training data bias occurs as a result of using biased input data to train algorithms, thereby culminating in data bias in the algorithm's output values (Ferrer et al., 2021). Training data bias can result from various factors, such as the lack of diversity and historical human biases in training datasets. Two recommendations for reducing bias in algorithm training are the establishment of policies and practices regarding responsible dataset development and the pre-processing of data (Smith & Rustagi, 2020). Responsible dataset development can be achieved through the implementation of standard checks and balances that encourage developers to intentionally gather inclusive data and fully understand who benefits from the data collected (Smith & Rustagi, 2020). By ensuring the evaluation of the quality of the data gathered for the training of learning models, developers can assess whether the training data sufficiently and accurately represents different subgroups within the population (Smith & Rustagi, 2020). Another recommendation for reducing training data bias is the pre-processing of the datasets. The aim of pre-processing methods is to transform the training dataset such that it smoothes out any discriminatory biases it might contain (Edizel et al., 2019). Therefore, the use of pre-processing methods to reduce bias in training data will arguably result in the hampering of biased decisions generated by the learning model (Edizel et al., 2019).

The third cause of bias in AI algorithms that was addressed in the previous Section was bias in usage, also referred to as transfer context bias and interpretation bias. As previously mentioned, transfer context bias is the issue of operating an algorithm outside of its intended environment, while interpretation bias is the misinterpretation of the algorithm's outputs by the user (Ferrer et al., 2021). One recommendation for reducing bias in algorithms is to increase the requirements for disclosure of an algorithm's classification methodology. Oftentimes, AI developers are unwilling to disclose information about an algorithm's classification methodology over concerns that it will provide their competitors with an unfair advantage in AI research and development (Smith & Rustagi, 2020). However, increased requirements for classification disclosure and, more specifically, information regarding the training data used would help to ensure that existing algorithms and datasets are being used appropriately. That would then decrease the risk of transfer context bias and interpretation bias in AI algorithms.

4.3 Recommendation for Algorithmic Transparency in Military AI Applications

Recent technological advancements have led to the increased integration of AI into a range of military applications, such as cyberspace operations and the use of military autonomous vehicles, with the aim of improving wartime decision-making and helping to provide a better understanding of the battlespace. However, the steady increase in the integration of AI in military systems raises multiple ethical concerns, including lack of accountability and transparency (Hoadley & Lucas, 2018).

Therefore, the aim of this subsection is to provide recommendations for increasing algorithmic transparency within the field of military AI. The first two recommendations will focus on the implementation of general policies and practices that can help increase transparency in military AI, while the third recommendation will address some of the concerns discussed in the previous Section in relation to the risks of increasing transparency in DUR fields, as highlighted by Jordan et al. (2020).

As previously discussed, two factors that can hinder transparency in AI systems intended for use in military applications is lack of predictability and explainability. Unpredictability in AI can be defined as the inability of the system's user to "… precisely and consistently predict what specific actions an intelligent system will take to achieve its objectives…", even if the user knows the terminal end goals of the algorithm (Yampolskiy, 2019, p. 2). Furthermore, issues around explainability in AI systems often refer to the lack of context provided by the system to allow for human understanding of how the algorithm's outputs were derived (Ehsan et al., 2021). Although the development of explainable AI is an emerging area of research with promising implications for military AI, changes in governmental policies and frameworks may have more immediate impact. Therefore, the implementation of policies and practices that focus on increasing the level of skill and understanding among technical experts regarding "…the traceability of the processes and decisions of AI systems at both development and deployment stages…" is one recommendation for promoting transparency (Taddeo et al., 2021, p. 1718). Traceability is an important aspect of establishing transparency because AI systems are often designed and developed by different individuals to the ones who implement them (Taddeo et al., 2021). Therefore, encouraging policies that support traceability can help ensure that the "…chain of events leading to possible unwanted outcomes is not lost in the distributed and dynamic nature of…AI" (Taddeo et al. 2021, p. 1722).

Another recommendation for increasing transparency in military AI applications is the implementation of practices that encourage international cooperation and policy alignment between countries regarding the development and employment of military AI. Policy alignment can help improve transparency by increasing interoperability in guidelines and technical frameworks (Stanley-Lockman, 2021a). Policy alignment can also help to ensure that "…accountability and ethical principles enter into the design, development, deployment, and diffusion of AI" for military applications (Stanley-Lockman, 2021b, p. 1). Alternatively, lack of collaboration among allied militaries could result in discrepancies in responsibilities, and ethical and legal guidelines regarding joint military AI operations. By encouraging international coherence, allied countries can work together to identify responsible and ethical approaches to military AI that encourage transparency, while simultaneously developing their own unique AI technique (Stanley-Lockman, 2021a, b).

However, as also noted by Jordan et al. (2020), there are growing national security concerns regarding the risk of too much transparency in AI and, more specifically, the implications of increased transparency in relation to biological and programming components. One recommendation for mitigating some of the consequences that come with increasing transparency in military AI is the development of a risk assessment to raise awareness of the increase of dual-use potential for topics such as AI (Jordan et al., 2020). As previously noted, DUR refers to research that is generated for legitimate purposes to further push developments in knowledge and information, while also providing opportunities for exploitation by malicious actors (Jordan et al., 2020). A risk assessment for the dual-use potential of AI applications would help reduce the possibility for exploitation by highlighting information or data that may potentially threaten national security, if published. However, the development process for a risk assessment of this type must take into consideration the potential harm posed by risks stemming from unforeseen interactions, as opposed to explainable risks (Jordan et al., 2020). This will help expand understanding regarding the risks posed by dual-use AI applications in military and governmental organisations, while also increasing transparency in a way that does not threaten national security.

5 Conclusion

The aim of this Chapter was to investigate the potential use of AI techniques in automating certain tasks of IoT Forensics. First, the Chapter provided a brief summary of IoT Forensics and identified the management and analysis of the vast amounts of data generated by IoT devices as one of the most significant challenges faced in IoT Forensic investigations (Servida & Casey, 2019). Next, the Chapter explored how different types of AI techniques, such as NLP and ML, can be used to automate IoT Forensic tasks. NLP can be used in a variety of ways to improve efficiency in investigations, such as enabling the extraction of valuable information from text data. However, most of the NLP research is focused on high resource languages, leaving a vast majority of the world's languages understudied and underutilised (Magueresse et al., 2020). The Chapter also examined how ML could be employed to detect anomalies and steganography in data. Within IoT Forensics, ML-based DNAD can be used to detect atypical data points which can help indicate signs of a cyberattack on a system or device (Venugopal et al., 2022). Yet, it can often be difficult for ML engineers to gather enough labelled abnormal data points. This results in a lack of high-quality large-scale datasets to properly train learning models for most real-world applications (Pang et al., 2022). Similar to anomaly detection, ML-based techniques, such as CNNs, can also be used for the automatic detection of steganography in certain types of data, such as video, image, audio, and/or text data (Prakash et al., 2021). However, current training methods prioritise the memorisation of inputs and high-quality training data, which does not provide an accurate representation of the behaviour and predictions of ML models for various real-world applications (Hosseini et al., 2017). Furthermore, the general challenges of AI-enabled IoT Forensics were reviewed, and the lack of necessary resources, funding and training were identified as significant limitations in the use and implementation of AI-based techniques for IoT Forensics across LEAs.

The research has shown that the use of AI applications, such as ML- and NLP-based learning models, can help to improve efficiency and cost-effectiveness in IoT

Forensics. More specifically, AI techniques can be used to mitigate challenges posed by Big Data Analytics in IoT devices and systems. However, current academic literature on the use of these techniques to automate certain tasks in IoT Forensics is limited, and further research is required to fully understand the potential uses and impacts of these techniques. As previously stated, Forensic investigators are often tasked with the collection and analysis of data from live systems, which can pose significant technical challenges. Therefore, one proposed area of study for further research is the potential role of supervised ML and NLP techniques in performing live Forensics across various IoT ecosystems (Kebande et al., 2020). Further research is also needed to "...ensure that Digital Forensic capabilities keep pace with emerging technologies, as well as designing AI-based approaches to facilitate digital forensics and real-time incident detection..." (Kebande et al., 2020). Within the broader context of this Chapter, the use of AI-based techniques for the automation of IoT Forensics also has positive implications for national security-related issues. However, the academic literature on the combination of these three topics was extremely limited, and, therefore, parts of this Chapter provided a general overview of AI-based techniques and IoT Forensics. Yet, as AI techniques and applications grow in sophistication, "...they are likely to become more and more prevalent in the national security space." (Blasch et al., 2019, p. 2).

The Chapter also identified two significant concerns within the field of AI which included the challenges regarding algorithmic bias and the lack of transparency in AI systems intended for use in military and governmental AI applications. Research indicates that ML algorithms have increasingly been found to be problematically biased, which holds significant implications for governments seeking to utilise military AI. Algorithmic bias, which typically results from bias in modelling, training and/or usage, can have significant negative repercussions, as evidenced by Buolamwini and Gebru (2018) and Yeung et al. (2021). Although recent advancements in AI technology have led to better bias detection techniques and tools, such as Google's TCAV tool, there are still further developments that can be made. Overall, recommendations in relation to the implementation of internal and external auditing at all stages of AI development and deployment were identified as the most impactful. The Chapter then proceeded to investigate how issues related to lack of predictability and explainability in AI systems could hinder algorithmic transparency in military applications of AI. Technological developments in military AI have allowed for the construction of intelligent and complex systems that can be utilised in various environments. However, the increasing technical complexities of algorithmic processing make it difficult for the users to ascertain a comprehensive understanding of how the output of a system has been derived. Therefore, the most significant recommendation proposed by this Chapter in response to the lack of transparency is to focus on the implementation of policies and guidelines that focus on the traceability of the development and deployment stages of military AI.

References

Ahmad, Z., Shahid Khan, A., Nisar, K., Haider, I., Hassan, R., Haque, M. R., Tarmizi, S., & Rodrigues, J. (2021). Anomaly detection using deep neural network for IoT architecture. *Applied Sciences, 11*(15), 7050.

al Fahdi, M., Clarke, N., & Furnell, S. (2013). Challenges to digital Forensics: Challenges to digital forensics: A survey of researchers & practitioners attitudes and opinions. *2013 Information Security for South Africa.* https://doi.org/10.1109/issa.2013.6641058.

Allen, G., & Chan, T. (2017). *Artificial intelligence and national security.* Belfer Center for Science and International Affairs.

Angwin, J., Larson, J., Mattu, S., & Kirchner, L. (2016). Machine bias. *ProPublica.* Available at: https://www.propublica.org/article/machine-bias-risk-assessments-in-criminal-sentencing. Accessed 18 Aug 2022.

Anwar, N., & Supriyanto. (2019). Forensic authentication of WhatsApp messenger using the information retrieval approach. *International Journal of Cyber-Security and Digital Forensics, 8*(3), 206–213.

Arkin, R. C., Ulam, P., & Wagner, A. R. (2012). Moral decision making in autonomous systems: Enforcement, moral emotions, dignity, trust, and deception. *Proceedings of the IEEE, 100*(3), 571–589. https://doi.org/10.1109/jproc.2011.2173265

Ayres, I. (2010). *Testing for discrimination and the problem of "included variable bias".* mimeo/ Yale Law School.

Banerveld, M. V., Le-Khac, N. A., & Kechadi, M. (2014). *Performance evaluation of a natural language processing approach applied in White collar crime investigation.* In International conference on future data and security engineering (pp. 29–43). Springer.

Baror, S. O., Venter, H. S., & Adeyemi, R. (2020). A natural human language framework for digital forensic readiness in the public cloud. *Australian Journal of Forensic Sciences, 53*(5), 566–591. https://doi.org/10.1080/00450618.2020.1789742

Berg, G., Davidson, I., Duan, M. Y., & Paul, G. (2003, August). *Searching for hidden messages: Automatic detection of steganography* (pp. 51–56). American Association for Artificial Intelligence.

Blasch, E., Sung, J., Nguyen, T., Daniel, C. P., & Mason, A. P. (2019). *Artificial intelligence strategies for national security and safety standards.* arXiv preprint arXiv:1911.05727.

Bloch-Wehba, H. (2021). *Transparency's AI problem. Knight first amendment institute and law and political economy project's data & democracy essay series.* Texas A&M University School of Law. https://scholarship.law.tamu.edu/facscholar/1477

Bornstein, A. M. (2016). Is artificial intelligence permanently inscrutable? *Nautilus.* Available at: https://nautil.us/is-artificial-intelligence-permanently-inscrutable-5116/. Accessed 22 Aug 2022.

Buolamwini, J., & Gebru, T. (2018, January). *Gender shades: Intersectional accuracy disparities in commercial gender classification.* In Conference on fairness, accountability and transparency (pp. 77–91). PMLR.

Cerrato, P., Halamka, J., & Pencina, M. (2022). A proposal for developing a platform that evaluates algorithmic equity and accuracy. *BMJ Health & Care Informatics, 29*(1), e100423. https://doi.org/10.1136/bmjhci-2021-100423

Chutani, S., & Goyal, A. (2019). A review of forensic approaches to digital image steganalysis. *Multimedia Tools and Applications, 78*(13), 18169–18204. https://doi.org/10.1007/s11042-019-7217-0

Clark, C. (2017). Our artificial intelligence 'sputnik moment' is now: Eric Schmidt & Bob work. *Breaking Defense.* Available at: https://breakingdefense.com/2017/11/our-artificial-intelligence-sputnik-moment-is-now-eric-schmidt-bob-work/?_ga=2.65416942.1702442390.1509614577-220094446.1509614577. Accessed 22 Aug 2022.

Conti, M., Dehghantanha, A., Franke, K., & Watson, S. (2018). Internet of things security and forensics: Challenges and opportunities. *Future Generation Computer Systems, 78*, 544–546. https://doi.org/10.1016/j.future.2017.07.060

Conti, J. R., Noiry, N., Clemencon, S., Despiegel, V., & Gentric, S. (2021). *Learning an ethical module for bias mitigation of pre-trained models*. In ICLR 2022 conference paper2812.

Danks, D., & London, A. J. (2017). *Algorithmic bias in autonomous systems*. In Proceedings of the twenty-sixth international joint conference on artificial intelligence. https://doi.org/10.24963/ijcai.2017/654.

Delua, J. (2021). *Supervised vs. unsupervised learning: What's the difference?* Available at: https://www.ibm.com/cloud/blog/supervised-vs-unsupervised-learning#:%7E:text=To%20put%20it% Accessed 22 Aug 2022.

Department for Homeland Security. (2018). *Snapshot: Public safety agencies pilot artificial intelligence to aid in first response | Homeland security*. https://www.dhs.gov/science-and-technology/news/2018/10/16/snapshot-public-safety-agencies-pilot-artificial-intelligence

Dick, S. (2019). Artificial Intelligence. *Harvard Data Science Review, 1*(1). https://doi.org/10.1162/99608f92.92fe150c30

Djebbar, F. (2021). Securing IoT data using steganography: A practical implementation approach. *Electronics, 10*, 2707. https://doi.org/10.3390/electronics10212707

Edizel, B., Bonchi, F., Hajian, S., Panisson, A., & Tassa, T. (2019). FaiRecSys: Mitigating algorithmic bias in recommender systems. *International Journal of Data Science and Analytics, 9*(2), 197–213. https://doi.org/10.1007/s41060-019-00181-5

Ehsan, U., Liao, Q. V., Muller, M., Riedl, M. O., & Weisz, J. D. (2021). *Expanding explainability: Towards social transparency in AI systems*. In Proceedings of the 2021 CHI conference on human factors in computing systems, (pp. 1–19). https://doi.org/10.1145/3411764.3445188.

Elkin-Koren, N. (2020). Contesting algorithms: Restoring the public interest in content filtering by artificial intelligence. *Big Data & Society, 7*(2), 2053951720932296. https://doi.org/10.1177/2053951720932296

Ferrer, X., Nuenen, T. V., Such, J. M., Cote, M., & Criado, N. (2021). Bias and discrimination in AI: A cross-disciplinary perspective. *IEEE Technology and Society Magazine, 40*(2), 72–80. https://doi.org/10.1109/mts.2021.3056293

Florida State University. (2021). *Research guides: Algorithm bias: Home*. Florida State University Libraries. https://guides.lib.fsu.edu/algorithm

Fu, R., Huang, Y., & Singh, P. V. (2020). AI and algorithmic bias: Source, detection, mitigation and implications. *SSRN Electronic Journal*. https://doi.org/10.2139/ssrn.3681517.

Gavrilova, Y. (2021). *What is anomaly detection in machine learning?* Serokell Software Development. https://serokell.io/blog/anomaly-detection-in-machine-learning

Goldstein, M., & Uchida, S. (2016). A comparative evaluation of unsupervised anomaly detection algorithms for multivariate data. *PLoS One, 11*(4), e0152173. https://doi.org/10.1371/journal.pone.0152173

Greiner, D. J., & Rubin, D. B. (2011). Causal effects of perceived immutable characteristics. *Review of Economics and Statistics, 93*(3), 775–785.

Hoadley, D., & Lucas, N. (2018). *Artificial intelligence and national security*. Congressional research service report.

Hosseini, H., Xiao, B., Jaiswal, M., & Poovendran, R. (2017). *On the limitation of convolutional neural networks in recognising negative images*. Network Security Lab (NSL), Department of Electrical Engineering, University of Washington.

IBM Cloud Education. (2020). *Unsupervised learning*. IBM. Available at: https://www.ibm.com/cloud/learn/unsupervised-learning. Accessed 22 Aug 2022.

IBM Cloud Education. (2021). *Natural Language Processing (NLP)*. IBM. Available at: https://www.ibm.com/cloud/learn/natural-language-processing. Accessed 22 Aug 2022.

James, J., & Gladyshev, P. (2013). *Challenges with automation in digital forensic investigations*. arXiv.Org. https://arxiv.org/abs/1303.4498

Janiesch, C., Zschech, P., & Heinrich, K. (2021). Machine learning and deep learning. *Electronic Markets, 31*(3), 685–695. https://doi.org/10.1007/s12525-021-00475-2

Jarrett, A., & Choo, K. R. (2021). The impact of automation and artificial intelligence on digital forensics. *WIREs Forensic Science, 3*(6). https://doi.org/10.1002/wfs2.1418

Jordan, S. B., Fenn, S. L., & Shannon, B. B. (2020). Transparency as threat at the intersection of artificial intelligence and cyberbiosecurity. *Computer, 53*(10), 59–68. https://doi.org/10.1109/mc.2020.2995578

Kaplan, A., & Haenlein, M. (2019). Siri, Siri, in my hand: Who's the fairest in the land? On the interpretations, illustrations, and implications of artificial intelligence. *Business Horizons, 62*(1), 15–25.

Kaur, M., & Kaur, G. (2014). Review of various Steganalysis techniques. *International Journal of Computer Science and Information Technologies, 5*(2), 1744–1747.

Kebande, V. R., Mudau, P. P., Ikuesan, R. A., Venter, H., & Choo, K. K. R. (2020). Holistic digital forensic readiness framework for IoT-enabled organizations. *Forensic Science International: Reports, 2*, 100117. https://doi.org/10.1016/j.fsir.2020.100117

Khan, N., Abdullah, J., & Khan, A. S. (2017). Defending malicious script attacks using machine learning classifiers. *Wireless Communications and Mobile Computing, 2017*.

Koptyra, K., & Ogiela, M. R. (2022). Steganography in IoT: Information hiding with APDS-9960 proximity and gestures sensor. *Sensors, 22*(7), 2612. https://doi.org/10.3390/s22072612

Kotu, V., & Deshpande, B. (2019). Anomaly detection. *Data Science*, 447–465. https://doi.org/10.1016/b978-0-12-814761-0.00013-7

Lee, N. T., Resnick, P., & Barton, G. (2019). *Algorithmic bias detection and mitigation: Best practices and policies to reduce consumer harms*. Brookings Institute.

Magid, L. (2020). IBM, Microsoft And Amazon not letting police use their facial recognition technology. *Forbes, Forbes Magazine*, 13. https://www.forbes.com/sites/larrymagid/2020/06/12/ibm-microsoft-and-amazon-not-letting-police-use-their-facial-recognition-technology/

Magueresse, A., Carles, V., & Heetderks, E. (2020). Low-resource languages: A review of past work and future challenges. *ArXiv, abs/2006.07264*.

Mazhar, M., Saleem, Y., Almogren, A., Arshad, J., Jaffery, M., Rehman, A., Shafiq, M., & Hamam, H. (2022). Forensic analysis on internet of things (IoT) device using machine-to-machine (M2M) framework. *Electronics, 11*, 1126. https://doi.org/10.3390/electronics11071126

Mehrabi, N., Morstatter, F., Saxena, N., Lerman, K., & Galstyan, A. (2022). *A survey on bias and fairness in machine learning*. USC, Information Sciences Institute.

Mortensen, D. (n.d.). *Algorithms for natural language processing*. Carnegie Mellon University's School of Computer Science.

NPR. (2012). *NPR cookie consent and choices*. National Public Radio. Available at: https://www.npr.org/2012/06/26/155792609/a-massive-google-network-learns-to-identify?t=1660853174759. Accessed 22 Aug 2022.

Pang, G., Shen, C., Cao, L., & Hengel, A. V. D. (2022). Deep learning for anomaly detection. *ACM Computing Surveys, 54*(2), 1–38. https://doi.org/10.1145/3439950

Prakash, V., Williams, A., Garg, L., Savaglio, C., & Bawa, S. (2021). Cloud and edge computing-based computer forensics: Challenges and open problems. *Electronics, 10*(11), 1229. https://doi.org/10.3390/electronics10111229

Raji, D., Smart, A., White, R. Mitchell, M., Gebru, T., Hutchinson, B., Smith-Loud, J., Theron, D., & Barnes, P. (2020). *Closing the AI accountability gap: Defining an end-to-end framework for internal algorithmic auditing*. In Proceedings of the 2020 conference on fairness, accountability and transparency (pp. 33–44).

Reinel, T. S., Brayan, A. A. H., Alejandro, B. O. M., Alejandro, M. R., Daniel, A. G., Alejandro, A. G. J., Buenaventura, B. J. A., Simon, O. A., Gustavo, I., & Raul, R. P. (2021). GBRAS-net: A convolutional neural network architecture for spatial image Steganalysis. *IEEE Access, 9*, 14340–14350. https://doi.org/10.1109/access.2021.3052494

Richardson, L. C., Connell, N. D., Lewis, S. M., Pauwels, E., & Murch, R. S. (2019). Cyberbiosecurity: A call for cooperation in a new threat landscape. *Frontiers in Bioengineering and Biotechnology, 7.* https://doi.org/10.3389/fbioe.2019.00099

Robbins, M. (2018). The case against transparency in government AI. *Policy Options.* Available at: https://policyoptions.irpp.org/fr/magazines/may-2018/the-case-against-transparency-in-government-ai/. Accessed 22 Aug 2022.

Sayler, K. M. (2020). *Artificial intelligence and national security* (No. R45178). Congressional Research Service. https://crsreports.congress.gov

Servida, F., & Casey, E. (2019). IoT forensic challenges and opportunities for digital traces. *Digital Investigation, 28,* S22–S29. https://doi.org/10.1016/j.diin.2019.01.012

Simonite, T. (2017). For superpowers, artificial intelligence fuels new global arms race. *Wired.* Available at: https://www.wired.com/story/for-superpowers-artificial-intelligence-fuels-new-global-arms-race/. Accessed 22 Aug 2022.

Sisson, M., Spindel, J., Scharre, P., & Kozyulin, V. (2019). *The militarization of artificial intelligence.* Stanley Center for Peace and Security/United Nations.

Sjöstrand, M. (2020). *Combatting the data volume issue in digital forensics: A structured literature review.* The University of Skövde.

Smith, G., & Rustagi, I. (2020). *Mitigating bias in artificial intelligence: An equity fluent leadership playbook.* Berkeley Haas Center for Equity. Available at: https://haas.berkeley.edu/wp-content/uploads/UCB_Playbook_R10_V2_spreads2.pdf. Accessed 19 Aug 2022.

Stanley-Lockman, Z. (2021a). From closed to open systems: How the US military services pursue innovation. *Journal of Strategic Studies, 44*(4), 480–514.

Stanley-Lockman, Z. (2021b). *Responsible and ethical military AI.* Centre for Security and Emerging Technology.

Taddeo, M., McNeish, D., Blanchard, A., & Edgar, E. (2021). Ethical principles for artificial intelligence in National Defence. *Philosophy & Technology, 34*(4), 1707–1729. https://doi.org/10.1007/s13347-021-00482-3

Ukwen, D. O., & Karabatak, M. (2021). *Review of NLP-based systems in digital forensics and cybersecurity.* In 2021 9th International symposium on digital forensics and security (ISDFS) (pp. 1–9). https://doi.org/10.1109/isdfs52919.2021.9486354.

University of York. (n.d.). *The role of natural language processing in AI.* Available at: https://online.york.ac.uk/the-role-of-natural-language-processing-in-ai/. Accessed 18 Aug 2022.

Venugopal, S., Rengaswamy, R., & Winster Sathianesan, G. (2022). IoT based cyber forensics in big data optimization and privacy using deep neural anomaly detection with Hadoop clustering and convolution-based Adam optimizer. *Concurrency and Computation: Practice and Experience, 34*(11). https://doi.org/10.1002/cpe.6881

Yampolskiy, R. (2019). Unpredictability of AI. *arXiv preprint arXiv:1905.13053.*

Yeung, D., Khan, I., Kalra, N., & Osoba, O. (2021). *Identifying systemic bias in the acquisition of machine learning decision aids for law enforcement applications.* RAND. Available at: https://www.jstor.org/stable/resrep29576#metadata_info_tab_contents. Accessed 18 Aug 2022.

Chapter 5
The Application of Big Data Predictive Analytics and Surveillance Technologies in the Field of Policing

1 Introduction

This chapter aims to address the emerging technologies surrounding digital policing by critically analysing its potentiality to assist law enforcement agencies (LEAs) in solving crime. More specifically, the chapter will examine technologies such as Machine Learning (ML), Facial Recognition (FR), Natural Language Processing (NLP) and Big Data Predictive Analytics (BDPA), all of which are considered to be branches of Artificial Intelligence (AI). The world of AI is forever expanding and, as a result, has become an integral part of various industries such as information technology, marketing, healthcare, cybersecurity, art and the military (Nadikattu, 2016). Whilst AI plays a crucial role in all sectors of society, its deployment in policing differs from that in other fields. AI provides law enforcement with additional capabilities to arrest, detain and assert a degree of power in appropriate circumstances, and with such power, concerns and criticisms are raised (Joh, 2016). It is due to these differences that this chapter focuses on the impacts that AI has specifically in the field of policing. This research is important in order to strengthen policing capabilities, and the ability to question new technology is vital to maintain confidence and integrity in policing (Joh, 2016).

Considering the foregoing discussions, this chapter aims to provide a critical analysis of predictive analytics and innovative technologies deployed in policing and ways in which such technologies can assist police in resolving crime and improving accountability. Therefore, to accomplish the research aim, this chapter seeks to address the following two research questions that have been identified:

RQ1. How do law enforcement agencies adopt AI and surveillance technologies to deploy resources efficiently, identify criminal suspects and carry out investigations?

RQ2. How might the adoption of BDPA assist police in resolving crimes and improving accountability?

© The Author(s), under exclusive license to Springer Nature Switzerland AG 2023
R. Montasari, *Countering Cyberterrorism*, Advances in Information Security 101, https://doi.org/10.1007/978-3-031-21920-7_5

The stated issues will be explored and evidenced in policing practise to provide a justified and well-rounded response to the use of predictive policing and surveillance technologies. In particular, this response will be focused on the positive and negative implications of these technologies such as raising issues concerning accountability. To address the proposed research aim and questions, both primary and secondary sources will be utilised and critically analysed. To this end, the chapter will adopt a mixed method approach to attain both qualitative and quantitative findings to allow for an integration of different ideas and theories.

The remainder of the chapter is structured as follows. Section 2 provides an overview of AI's key concepts and history. Section 3 examines law enforcements' use of BDPA and various other technologies of predictive policing with a view to assessing the efficiency and effectiveness of these technologies. Section 4 offers a set of appropriate and justified solutions to assist with adopting a more efficient and well-equipped policing strategy that deploys AI technologies into everyday policing with limited harm to the public. Finally, the Chapter is concluded in Sect. 5, which provides an overall review of the research problem, theorising main findings and contributions that this body of work makes to existing field of Digital Policing and AI.

2   Key Concepts and History of AI

Predictive policing and AI continue to grow in prominence. To fully address the role of AI in digital policing, it is important to consider the history and broader context of what it consists of. AI is a technological innovation that works to replace human manual work in various fields. Broadly speaking, AI is a field of computing that focuses on "the transmission of anthropomorphic intelligence and thinking into machines" that can assist humans in day to day life. This growth in interest to examine and study this field has the potential for bigger breakthroughs and change. There are two branches that divide development and research of AI including applied and generalised AI (Nadikattu, 2016). Applied AI incorporates principles of technology for 'stimulation of human thought processes in regards to carrying through specific tasks' whereas generalised AI instead develops machine intelligence systems that can be 'used in any responsibility, much like that of a real person' (Nadikattu, 2016;909). The primary understanding is that machinery can acquire intelligence. It can be said that there is little agreement on an accepted definition of AI, with one perception claiming, "artificial intelligence becomes nothing more than a means to tackle certain kinds of challenging empirical exercises that are easy for humans and represent activities that seem to be distinctly human as speech" (Berk, 2021, p.211). Although the term is also commonly associated with robotics, the concept incorporates "broader technology ranges, from search engines to speech recognition, to learning/gaming structures and speech recognition (Nadimpalli, 2017). These will be discussed in detail at a later stage in the chapter.

The lack of accepted views of what artificial intelligence entails has repercussions such as the nations' inability to establish the success of their own AI strategies and, therefore, there is a large divide over how much of each nation's resources should be invested into such technologies (Filimowicz, 2022). AI, when integrated into police work, can increase police efficiency and its capacity to detect and investigate crime. With its combination of Computer Science and Mathematics, it works to effectively process data, predict likely suspects and point to effective evidence (McDaniel & Pease, 2021). Similarly, this is referred to as "smart policing" in the sense that it is a more efficient manner of policing, with fewer resources utilised and better results (McDaniel & Pease, 2021).

2.1   Predictive Policing

Predictive policing is not a new phenomenon; it has always been part of policing strategy. However, there has been a shift/advancing in the tools utilised (Ferguson, 2017). Predictive policing is closely linked to a variety of other law enforcement approaches such as intelligence-led policing, data driven policing, risk-based policing, 'hot spot' policing, evidenced-based policing and pre-emptive policing. The concept involves applying analytical techniques to data for the purposes of generating statistical predictions. Such predictions are made to assist in policing in a variety of ways, such as to identify crime hotspots and criminal targets. Arguably predictive policing is never a 'fully automated process'. Instead, some argue that it is a 'multi-dimensional, iterative and socio- technical practice'.

Moreover, various predictive police strategies demonstrated in practice include the use of algorithms to predict when and where future crimes will occur, the use of network models to predict an individual's likely involvement in gun violence and risk models that have the ability to identify law enforcement officers that are most likely to engage in at risk behaviours (Brayne, 2017). Predictive policing is comprised of two key features. The first characteristic is its 'broad variety of sorts of data'. Furthermore, this depicts a shared consensus of predictive policing being made up of 'descriptive analytics', which aim to comprehend and anticipate crime trends through the synthesis of (un)structured data (Meijer & Wessels, 2019). The second feature is 'pre-emptive policing', which consists of acting on criminal activity before it becomes a crime (Meijer & Wessels, 2019). This proposes the idea of upstream prevention being used to prevent criminal behaviour (Meijer & Wessels, 2019). Hence, pre-emptive policing refers to actions "taken prior to an event occurring, where it is believed an event would otherwise occur " (Bennett Moses & Chan, 2018, p. 808). Similarly, upstream prevention implies municipal council collaboration and organised global laws that make cross-border offenders easier to target and arrest. Pre-emptive policing is distinct from predictive policing in that it is not dependent on data-driven forecasting (Bennett Moses & Chan, 2018).

2.2 History of AI

The very first introduction into AI can be traced back to the 1940's, more specifically, 1943, when American Science Fiction writer Isaac Asimov published his short story "the round around", which inspired generations of scientists in the field of robotics and later artificial intelligence (Haenlein & Kaplan, 2019). During the same time period, Alan Turning discovered the "enigma code", which led to his seminal article "Computing Machinery and Intelligence". The article provided an introduction insight into the intelligence of an artificial system and how to design and test intelligence machines (Haenlein & Kaplan, 2019). Few years later, in 1955, McCarthy, as cited in (Anderson, 2002), coined the term "Artificial Intelligence" in a published essay and research (Andresen, 2002). Additional papers[1] by McCarthy focused on the idea of building machines that could reason intelligently. The project was approved and consisted of a 2-month, ten-man study of AI, that attempted to explore how computers could be programmed to use a language, "neural nets, computational complexity, self-improvement, randomness and creativity" (Rajaraman, 2014, p.202). McCarthy, known as the 'Father of Artificial Intelligence', was the director of Stanford's AI laboratory from 1965 until 1980. He also founded two AI laboratories in 1957 and 1963, namely the Massachusetts Institute of Technology (MIT) Laboratory and the Stanford Laboratory respectively (Andresen, 2002).

Later, in the 1960s, Joseph Weizenbaum produced the Natural Language Processing programme "ELIZA", which was thought to be the first programme to successfully pass the "Turing test", a process proposed by Alan Turing to assess whether a computer demonstrated intelligence (Lawrence, 2020). ELIZA functions to imitate a "non directive psychoanalyst" by selecting keywords and "printing out" changes of a supply of common phrases (Pruijt, 2006, p.517). Furthermore, ELIZA's programming enables human-machine interaction through text-based communications and serves as the foundation for today's interactive talking machines, such as Apple's Siri, Microsoft's Cortana, and Everfriend's spoony character (Shah et al., 2016). However, reactions to the development of "ELIZA" demonstrated a tendency to treat "responsive computer programmes as more intelligent than they really are", with Weizenbaum, himself, reporting that users thought that the software could truly understand information entered into the machine (Pruijt, 2006). This was referred to as the ElIZA effect. Social Theorist Sherry Turkle describes the system ELIZA as a "very small amount of interactivity that causes us to project our complexity onto the underserving object" (Switzky, 2020). Furthermore, Turkle contends that the impacts of this model demonstrate an erosion of "relational authenticity" since its users seek love and consolidation in virtual companions who are incapable of reciprocating such sentiments (Switzky, 2020).

In 1976, AI additionally made its first medical appearance at the Academy of Ophthalmology convention in Las Vegas, Nevada (Kaul et al., 2020). This was a consultation programme for glaucoma that was utilised in the construction of the

---

[1] Titled "A Proposal for the Dartmouth Summer Research Project on Artificial Intelligence

'CASNET' model, which can best be described as a "casual-associational network" consisting of model building, consultation, and database models (Kaul et al., 2020). More specifically, these three main components were "observations of a patient, pathophysiological states and disease classifications" (Weiss et al., 1978, p.161). CASNET focused on causality and temporal sequences of events and, as a result, the model could match treatment plans to patients' current stage in the progression of a disease process (Weiss et al., 1978). This gathered intelligence provided physicians with sufficient knowledge on how to manage and advise patients efficiently. In addition, in the early 1970s, MYCIN, a backward chaining AI system, was developed (Kaul et al., 2020). MYCIN is a lisp software that serves as a consultant on therapy selection for patients suffering from certain infections (Shortliffe, 1977). The initiative was designed to offer a list of bacterial infections with recommended antibiotic treatments based on patient data submitted by clinicians (Kaul et al., 2020). MYCIN provided the framework for the subsequent "EMYCIN", which led to the development of INTERNIST-1 under the same framework to assist with diagnosis (Kaul et al., 2020).

2.3   Facial Recognition Technology

FR, a branch of AI, encompasses several subsections and technologies such as face detection, face position, identity recognition and image processing (Li et al., 2020). FR is a subsection within the field of Pattern Recognition technology which generally incorporates statistical techniques in order to detect and extract patterns from data and match it with patterns that have been stored in databases (Introna & Nissenbaum, 2010). Such databases contain a significant number of photographed faces, along with the accompanying name and other personal information that allows the individual to be identified. FR analyses and measures facial features in an image or video in an attempt to identify a specific human face. FR functions by firstly capturing an individual's face from an image or video. FR software then reads the geometry of the individual's face where the distance between the person' eyes and the distance from their forehead to their chin are important considerations. Next, the software recognises facial landmarks that are important in differentiating the individual's face. As a consequence, the person's facial signature is created. This facial signature, which is a mathematical formula, is then mapped against a database of known faces with a view to matching the person's faceprint to an image in the database.

Other specific characteristics that are observed and measured include the distance between the eyes, the width of the nose and the length of the jaw line. Once measured, these features, that are often referred to as the nodal points, can be translated into templates with unique codes (Hamann & Smith, 2019). One example of FR software includes 'FaceIt', which is developed by Indexit, a developer of FR technology (Thorat et al., 2010, p. 326). A FR software can detect an individual's face in a crowd and match the image to a database of stored photographs by distinguishing a face from the rest of the captured background. The software is capable of recognising 80 nodal points on a human face that serve as defining landmarks or endpoints. These are utilised to quantify characteristics of an individual's face, such as the depth of the eye sockets, the length or width of the nose, and the contour of the cheekbones. The technology operates by collecting data for nodal points on a digital image of a person's face and saving the resulting data as a faceprint. The faceprint is then used to compare data acquired from faces in an image or video. Human faces, on the other hand, have similar configurations and hence provide poor distinctiveness in comparison to other biometrics (Huang et al., 2010). Furthermore, FR technology presents additional issues such as intraclass variations owing to position and facial expressions. More precisely, there is still a great deal of unreliability in relation to 2D FR. However, it has been suggested that the development of 3D technology serves as a solution to the unsolved challenges in 2D recognition, such as the presence of pose and illumination variations (Huang et al., 2010).

2.4   3D Facial Recognition

The majority of FR technology is 2D even though there is ongoing effort and study into the introduction of 3D FR. Such technology is emerging due to the availability of 3D imagining and processes. Unlike 2D FR technology, this algorithm can provide in depth structural information such as "curvature, surface and geodesic distances" which cannot be obtained in 2D processing (Gupta et al., 2010, p.2). 3D FR approaches are classified into three types: hybrid, holistic, and local feature-based techniques (Gupta et al., 2010). To determine an individual's identity, the 3D programme undergoes a sequence of phases, which include Detection, Alignment, Measurement, Representation, and Matching. During the Detection stage, an image can be obtained by digitally scanning an existing 2D photograph or by using a video image to obtain a live image of a 3D subject. Once a face has been detected, the system will then determine the head's position, size and pose in the Alignment stage. Next, during the Measurement phase, the system uses a sub-millimetre scale to measure the curvature of the face and build a template (Thorat et al., 2010). In the Representation stage, the created template is then translated into a code, with the code reflecting the features of a subject's face that is unique to that specific template. During the Matching phase, matching will occur with no changes to the image if the image is 3D and the database holds 3D images. Nevertheless, databases that are still in 2D images are currently encountering. When compared to a flat, stable image, 3D delivers a live, moving varied subject. This issue is being addressed by new technology. Different points are recognised when a 3D image is captured (Thorat et al., 2010).

The holistic matching method operates by analysing the entire face region when feeding data into face catching systems, with Turk and Pentland's (1999) work as cited by Parmar and Mehta (2014) illustrated its first initial success utilising eigenfaces. In the context of FR, an eigenface is a collection of eigenvectors that are obtained from the probability distribution's covariance matrix on vector space of a large set of images representing different human faces. The eigenfaces comprise the initial collection of all images required to build the covariance matrix resulting in the creation of dimension reduction. This is achieved by enabling the smaller collection of initial images to reflect the original training images. Once the eigenfaces have been extracted from the image data using the Principal Component Analysis (PCA) technique, each image will now represent vector of weights and the system is now ready to accept "entering queries". The final stage of an eigenface based recognition system includes comparing the weights of incoming unknown images with the weights of those already found within the system. If the input image's weight is above the assigned threshold, it can be considered unidentified. Identification of an input image is done through finding the image in the database with weight closest to that of the input image and will be returned as a hit to the system user (Parmar & Mehta, 2014). Holistic matching algorisms however pose limitations, one of which being that it requires "accurate normalisation of the faces according to pose, illustration and scale' and such variations in these factors can have effects on the final recognition image produced" (Mian et al., 2008, pp. 1–2).

The other method involved in 3D FR technology is a local feature based technique. Moreover, this feature is often referred to as a feature-based matching method. This is based on identifying similar local features from the face and specific regions of the face such as eyes and nose (Soltanpour et al., 2017). An example of such methods is the region-based 3D matching algorithm. This algorithm works by matching the 3D point clouds of the eyes-forehead and nose regions individually before fusing the results at the score level (Mian et al., 2008). Another example is FR that utilises "booted features" which works to match rectangular sections from facial images at multiple positions, sizes, and orientations (Mian et al., 2008). Local feature extraction methods aim to detect distinctive compact features that are "robust to a set of nuisances" (Soltanpour et al., 2017, p.392). There are three important stages that comprise the local feature-based method including Feature Detector, Feature Descriptor and Feature Descriptor Matching (Lee et al., 2011). Finally, there are hybrid matching FR algorithms that perform recognition by incorporating both holistic and region-based matching (Mian et al., 2008). Moreover, research proposes the concept of hybrid matching schemes which combine global and local features and is argued more accurate in design (Huang et al., 2010).

2.5 Machine Learning

ML is another discipline of AI that seeks to address the question of how to build computers that improve themselves automatically through experience (Jordan & Mitchell, 2015). In its broadest meaning, ML seeks to enable computers to learn without being explicitly programmed (Bi et al., 2019). As a field of study, ML is described as being at the intersection of Computer Science, Statistics, and a range of other fields associated with "automatic improvement over time and interference decision making under uncertainty" (Jordan & Mitchell, 2015, p.256). Examples of related disciplines include, the "psychological study of human learning, the study of evolution, and adaptive control theory" (Jordan & Mitchell, 2015, p.256). Often, after viewing data, we are unable to properly interpret the exact information, and, as a result, ML techniques are used, and data is retrieved (Mahesh, 2020).

ML originates from AI movements of the 1950's era and illustrates practical objectives and applications such as prediction and optimization (Bi et al., 2019). The fundamental concept of ML is to accomplish tasks and learn from experience. Performance is then later measured and continues to improve with experience. ML makes these decisions along with predictions based on the data (Ray, 2019). ML is having a significant impact on many domains of technology and science, as evidenced by its use in robotics and autonomous vehicle control, speech processing, neuroscience, and computer vision (Jordan & Mitchell, 2015). There are three key research fields focusing on the objectives of ML, including Task-Oriented Studies, Cognitive Simulation and Theoretical Analysis (Carbonell et al., 1983b). Task-Oriented Studies illustrate the "development and analysis of learning systems to improve performance in a predetermined set of tasks, often referred to as the 'engineering approach'" (Carbonell et al., 1983a, b, p. 3). Cognitive Simulation concerns the "investigation and computer simulation of human learning processes". Similarly, Theoretical Analysis addresses the "theoretical exploration of the space of possible learning methods and algorithms independent of application domain" (Carbonell et al., 1983a, p. 3-4). ML conveys a capacity to learn and improve through the use of computational algorithms which use large sets of data inputs and outputs that recognise patterns and, as a result, train the machine to make recommendations decisions (Helm et al., 2020). After many iterations of the method, the system has effectively learnt and can take an input and predict an output. To completely assess the algorithm's accuracy, the outputs are afterwards compared with a set of known outcomes, which can then be tweaked to reliably forecast outcomes (Helm et al., 2020).

ML also plays crucial roles in three of the following niches within the software world: Data Mining, difficult to program applications and customised software applications. Data Mining is a process by which historical databases are used to improve subsequent decision making. For instance, banks analyse historical data in order to decide if loan applicants are credit worthy. Furthermore, ML algorithms play a keen part in applications that have been too difficult for traditional manual programming (Mitchell, 1997). An example of such is in FR that has been developed using training examples of face images along with ML (Mitchell, 1997). This is a clear indication of the importance of ML in the development of software. Finally, ML offers the option for allowing software to adapt itself to individual users (Mitchell, 1997). It is unrealistic to manually develop separate systems for each user in terms of personal calendars and online news browsers. Therefore, ML offers a more realistic option (Mitchell,1997). Brownlee (2019) categorises ML algorithms into 14 distinct types as represented in Fig. 5.1. The description of each type is outside of the scope of this chapter. Instead, in the following, the chapter focuses on three main types of ML, namely Supervised, Unsupervised, and

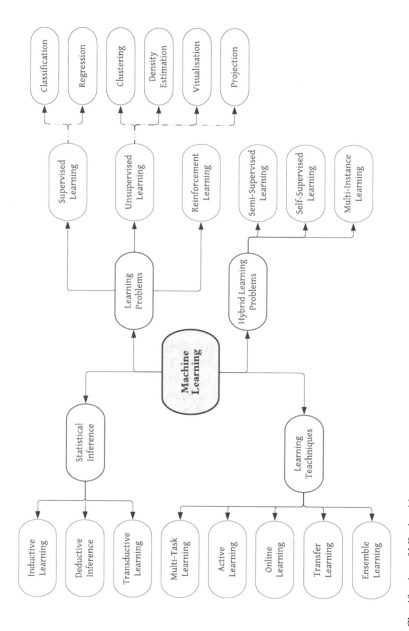

Fig. 5.1 Classification of ML algorithms

Reinforcement Learning. For further information concerning each type of ML, readers are encouraged to consult Brownlee (2019).

2.5.1   Supervised Learning

Supervised learning refers to a type of problem in which a model is used to learn a mapping between input samples and the target variable (Brownlee, 2019). Supervised learning problems are applications in which the training data is made up of instances of input vectors and their matching target vectors (Bishop, 2007). Each instance in Supervised Learning is a pair that is made up of an input (such as a vector) and an output value. The class of each testing instance is determined through combining features and identifying patterns that are commonplace to each category of the training data (Singh et al., 2016). Each data input object has a preassigned class label as the primary function of supervised learning is to learn a model that generates the matching label for the provided data (Dietterich & Kong, 1995). The classification algorithm determines the relationship between the input and output attribute and, as a result, constructs a model which functions as a training process (Dietterich & Kong, 1995).

   Classification occurs in two phases; the first involves the application of a classification algorithm on a training data set, and the second phase involves the extracted model being validated against a labelled test data in order to measure performance and accuracy (Singh et al., 2016). That is, a Supervised Learning algorithm examines the training data and generates an extrapolated function that can be applied to map fresh samples. In an ideal setting, the algorithm will be able to accurately ascertain the class labels for unknown examples. This necessitates that the learning algorithm generalise from the training data to previously unencountered scenarios. The generalisation error is used to assess an algorithm's statistical quality. There exist two primary forms of Supervised Learning problems comprising of classification which concerns predicting a class label and regression which involves forecasting a numerical value. Both classification and regression problems can contain one or more input variables of any data type, such as numerical or categorical data (Brownlee, 2019). The Modified National Institute of Standards and Technology (MNIST) handwritten digits dataset is an instance of a classification in which the inputs are images of handwritten digits and the output is a class label indicating the digit that the image represents (Brownlee, 2019). Similarly, the Boston house prices dataset is an instance of a regression, with the inputs being variables that represent a neighbourhood and the output being a house price in dollars (Brownlee, 2019).

2.5.2   Unsupervised Learning

Unsupervised Learning involves using untagged data to learn patterns. In Unsupervised Learning, the machine will be pushed to develop a compact internal representation of its surroundings through imitation, which is a key way of learning in humans, and then generate inventive content from it. As opposed to Supervised Learning where data is labelled by a ML expert, Unsupervised Learning techniques display self-organisation involving patterns as probability densities or a mixture of neural feature preferences (Hinton & Sejnowski, 1999). In other words, Unsupervised Learning acts just on input data, with no outputs or target variables. As a result, it does not require a ML expert correcting the model. Unsupervised Learning characterises a class of problems in which a model is used to define or extract relationships in data. It involves the use of ML algorithms to analyse and cluster unlabelled datasets (Brownlee, 2019; Goodfellow et al., 2017). These algorithms uncover hidden patterns or data groupings without human involvement. Due to its capacity to detect similarities and contrasts in data, "it is the ideal solution for exploratory data analysis, cross-selling strategies, customer segmentation, and image recognition" (IBM Cloud Education, 2020).

Whilst there exist different type of Unsupervised Learning, the two most common ones consist of Clustering and Density Estimation. Clustering algorithms concerns identifying useful clusters of input data (Russell & Norvig, 2021) whereas Density Estimation involves summarising the distribution of data. An instance of Clustering algorithm is k-Means, in which k is the number of groups to identify in the data. An instance of Density Estimation algorithms is Kernel Density Estimation, which refers to the use of small clusters of associated data samples to approximate the distribution for new points in the data. Clustering and Density Estimation are carried out to discover the patterns in the data (Brownlee, 2019). Other Unsupervised Learning techniques that can be employed include Visualisation and Projection. Visualization refers to creating plots of data in various ways while Projection methods concern the reduction of the dimensionality of the data (Bishop, 2007; Brownlee, 2019). An instance of Visualisation method includes a scatter plot matrix which generates one scatter plot for "each pair of variables in the dataset". An instance of a Projection technique comprises Principal Component Analysis, which concerns summarising a dataset in relation to eigenvalues and eigenvectors without linear dependencies (Bishop, 2007; Brownlee, 2019).

2.5.3 Reinforcement Learning

Together with Supervised Learning and Unsupervised Learning, Reinforcement Learning is one of the three fundamental ML models. Reinforcement Learning focuses on the manner in which intelligent agents must learn to function in a given environment using feedback in order to maximise a numerical reward signal (Sutton et al., 2018). This denotes that there is no predetermined training dataset but, instead, an objective or a set of objectives which an agent must attain, activities that they should undertake and feedback concerning performance toward the objective or a set of objectives (Brownlee, 2019). Analogous to Supervised Learning, Reinforcement Learning receives feedback even though it can be delayed and "statistically noisy", rendering it "difficult for the agent or model to connect cause and effect" (Brownlee, 2019). However, as opposed to Supervised Learning,

Reinforcement Learning does not require labelled input and output pairs, nor does it require sub-optimal measures to be rectified. In various intricate fields, Reinforcement Learning is the only practical approach to train a programme to function at high levels. For instance, in a game play, it is extremely difficult for a ML expert to produce precise and reliable assessments of vast numbers of locations that would be required to train "an evaluation function directly from instances". In lieu of this, the software can be provided with the data about when it has won or lost. The software can then use this knowledge to train an evaluation function that provides reasonably accurate approximations of the probability of winning from any specific position (Russell & Norvig, 2021).

2.6   Support Vector Machine

Support Vector Machine (SVM) was proposed in the 1990's and is arguably considered to be one of the best ML algorithms. SVM is also a form of Supervised ML being commonly used for pattern recognition and pattern classification problems such as image recognition, speech recognition, text categorisation, face detection and faulty card detection (Pradhan, 2012). The concept is based on "VC dimension and structural risk minimisation and is a specific realization for statistical learning theory" (Ding et al., 2017, p.969). SVM can handle both classification and regression problems. When a set of objects are belonging to different classes, A decision plane is required to divide these objects into their various classes. However, kernels are required to divide the objects (which belong to various classes) that "may or may not be linearly separable" and belong to various classes (Ray, 2019, p.37). The algorithm seeks to accurately categorise the objects using examples from the training data sets. SVMs have practical applications in face detection and classification, credit card fraud detection, face detection and classification, handwriting recognition and disease diagnosis (Ray, 2019). When dealing with multi-dimensions and continuous data, SVMs and neural networks frequently perform better. Oftentimes, a large sample size is required for the best prediction accuracy (Kotsiantis et al., 2007). A SVM can provide high accuracy, and, with an appropriate kernel, they can work well even if the data is not "linearly separable in base feature space" (Singh et al., 2016, p. 1311). However, SVMs have some limitations, one of which concerns the fact that its performance decreases with large data set due to the increase in the training time (Ray, 2019).

2.7   Natural Language Processing

The field of NLP, which combines Linguistics and AI, was first studied in the 1950s. Information Retrieval (IR), which NLP initially departs from, has started to merge with NLP (Nadkarni et al., 2011). NLP combines Computational Linguistics,

Computing Science, Cognitive Science and AI. Using a variety of methods, IR powers search engines such as Google and biomedical portals, for instance PubMed, by enabling users to quickly and easily find pertinent information that is present in massive text collections (Chen et al., 2021). NLP examines the use of computers in order to process and understand human languages and perform useful tasks (Deng & Liu, 2018). From a scientific standpoint, NLP aims to "model the cognitive mechanisms underlying the understanding and production of human languages" (Deng & Liu, 2018). Also known as Text Mining, it enables the analysis of unstructured texts and makes them "digestible for human readers". This is accomplished by extracting data from unstructured texts, presenting it in a structured manner suitable for computational analysis, or through transformations such as "summarization or translation" (Chen et al., 2021;4).

Applications of NLP include voice controlled assistants such as Siri and Alexa, Natural Language Generation for Question Answering by customer service chatbots, streamlining and recruiting processes on sites such as LinkedIn, Grammarly and Language models such as autocomplete that are trained to predict the following word in a text. The traditional view of NLP is the idea that the process itself can be broken into a number of stages that mirror the "theoretical linguistic distinction drawn between syntax, semantics and pragmatics" (Indurkhya & Damerau, 2010). Initially, the sentences of a text are analysed in terms of their syntax, which provides them with structure and order. This is followed by a pragmatic analysis stage, which establishes the meaning of the speech, and the discourse makes up the final stage. NLP performs a wide range of tasks, some of which have real world applications whilst others are used as "sub solutions to other problems". In terms of syntax, token generation represents a sequence of characters in a particular document that are processed as a single "semantic unit" (Agarwal & Saxena, 2019, p.2811). Although it can be challenging to divide NLP processing into three discrete boxes, it offers a basic starting point (Indurkhya & Damerau, 2010). The goal of NLP is to create tools and methods that can be designed to comprehend and manipulate natural language and carry out specific activities (Agarwal & Saxena, 2019).

2.8 Big Data

Michael Cox and David Ellsworth were arguably the first to use the term Big Data (BD) and refer to it as a way of using larger volumes of scientific data for visualisation. According to the most widely accepted definition from IBM, BD can be characterised by the five V's, which will be discussed in detail within Chap. 4 (O'Leary, 2013). BD often involves the use of "predictive analytics, user behaviour analytics, or certain other advanced data analytics methods that extract value from data" (Ongsulee et al., 2018, p.1). Due to its complexity and sheer volume, BD cannot be processed by conventional systems or data warehousing methods (Ishwarappa & Anuradha, 2015). The data generated might be structured, semi-structured, or unstructured from a variety of sources. For instance, the demand for BD arises from major corporations such as Google and Facebook, which need to process massive volumes of data in unstructured formats (Ishwarappa & Anuradha, 2015). This data can be difficult to process due to the fact that it contains "billions of records of millions of peoples information thar includes the web social media, images and audio" (Ishwarappa & Anuradha, 2015, p.320). The data however can be produced in structured, unstructured and semi structured forms. Gartner (n.d.) defines BD as "high-volume, high-velocity and/or high-variety information assets that demand cost-effective, innovative forms of information processing that enable enhanced insight, decision making, and process automation" (Gartner, n.d.).

Many organisations incorporate BD to explore challenges and opportunity in their businesses. However, it has been claimed that many businesses lack an understanding of the growing volumes of data, and, as a result, business intelligence and analytics tools deployed by these organisations are typically inadequate to tackle with the complexity of BD (Ohiomah et al., 2017).

BD has five main characteristics including: volume, velocity, variety, veracity and value, which are also known as 5 V's. The first of the 5 V's of BD is volume, that concerns the quantity of data available. Volume can be thought of as the foundation of BD since it is the original size and quantity of gathered data. It is important to note that whilst data that is substantially large can be considered to be BD, this definition of BD is subjective and subject to change depending on the market's supply of computer power (Gillis, 2021). Volume poses the most urgent challenge to traditional IT infrastructures. Velocity can be best described as the increasing speed that data is produced, processed, stored and analysed in addition to the speed at which new data is generated and moves around (Ishwarappa & Anuradha, 2015). Velocity of data continues to increase with both structured and unstructured data especially as the world becomes more developed and global, with an "increasing frequency of data capture and decision making about 'things' as they move through the world" (O'Leary, 2013, p.96). Decisions made using BD can influence the next data that is gathered and analysed and, as a result, add further dimension to velocity (O'Leary, 2013). It is of paramount importance to regulate velocity considering the fact that BD continues to develop into AI in which analytical systems automatically identify patterns in data and employ them to provide insights (Botelho & Bigelow, 2022).

Variety concerns the diversity of data types. Data might be gathered from a wide range of sources, which can have different values. Data might originate both inside and outside of an organisation. The standardisation and distribution of all the data being gathered pose a problem in terms of variety (Gillis, 2021). The fourth of the 5 Vs is veracity, which concerns the statistical quality and trustworthiness of the data. Veracity concerns the degree of confidence in the data that has been collected (Gillis, 2021). Veracity can be impacted by the data's origin, processing methods and trusted infrastructure and facility (Demchenko et al., 2013). This means that data can occasionally become disorganised and challenging to use. Hence, the gathered data can be incomplete, disorganised, erroneous, unable to offer any useful insight, or challenging to use. When the data is incomplete, a vast quantity of it may produce "more confusion than insights" (Gillis, 2021). For instance, in the medical sphere, if the data concerning the medications that a patient is taking is incomplete, the patient's life can be in danger. Therefore, both value and veracity determine the quality and insights derived from data (Gillis, 2021). Finally, value can be considered a newer component of BD and defined as the added-value that collected data brings to a predictive analysis/hypothesis. The value can vary depending on the events or processes they represent "such as stochastic, probabilistic, regular or random" (Demchenko et al., 2013, p.50). It is necessary to be able to extract value from BD because the value of BD greatly depends on the insights that can be obtained from them (Gillis, 2021).

3   RQ 1: The Use of AI by Law Enforcement I

This section aims to address the first research question: "How do law enforcement agencies adopt AI and surveillance technologies to deploy resources efficiently, identify criminal suspects and carry out investigations?"

3.1   *Big Data Predictive Analytics*

Predictive analytics, unlike other business intelligence (BI) technologies is a forward-looking technology that incorporates business intelligence in order to uncover patterns and relationships within large volumes of data to predict various behaviours and events before they occur (Eckerson, 2007). Predictive analytics can often be referred to as data mining in a way to describe the processes involved in predictive methods. It is therefore an inductive method that utilises AI, Statistics, ML, Neural Computing, Robotics, and Computational Mathematics to analyse data (Eckerson, 2007). Moreover, predictive analysis plays a large role in businesses, with the marketing industry being its largest user. Cross-selling, customer acquisition and budgeting forecasts provide just a few of the examples of how businesses adopt predictive analytics (Eckerson, 2007). Police responsibilities are growing beyond traditional enforcement duties, necessitating the implementation of a more proactive crime prevention strategy. As a result, forecasting techniques have been developed to assist in determining when and where crimes are most likely to occur (Fitzpatrick et al., 2019). Additionally, with recent advancements in police data management and gathering combined with forecasting techniques, law enforcement is now better able to deploy resources "to prevent and ultimately lower aggregate levels of crime" (Fitzpatrick et al., 2019, p.474). The phrase used to broadly classify the use of Predictive Analytics is proactive policing, and the police deploy a number of proactive policing tactics. In contrast to traditional reactive policing, proactive policing aims to identify predictable patterns and the casual elements that contribute to crime. It does this by focusing on "underlying forces and phenomena that are casually tied to crime" (Fitzpatrick et al., 2019, p.474).

The 1990's showed successes of crime mapping by police and, as a result, the US National Institute of Justice (NIJ) awarded five grants to study crime forecasting for police use. Accurate short-term crime estimates allowed police to effectively target hotspots, adapt surveillance, and deploy specialised units, such as drug enforcement crackdowns and notifying neighbourhood watch groups of specific offences (Gorr & Harries, 2003). Further success was demonstrated within the United Kingdom (UK) Home Office's first published crime forecasts for police planning and crime reduction policy of 1999 (Gorr & Harries, 2003). Such findings illustrated 3 year ahead projections of property crime in England and Wales with indications of a "strong upward pressure after five full years of falling crime" (Gorr & Harries, 2003, p.557). Supposedly, the pressure had been generated by three key factors, "the number of young men in the general population, the state of the economy and the fact property crime appeared to be below its underlying trend level" (Gorr & Harries, 2003, p.557). These published forecasts informs police and demonstrates success in that police can 'deploy manpower across precincts to manage workloads, shift resources between prevention and enforcement activities and plan budget requests for additional resources' (Gorr & Harries, 2003, p.552). The purpose of police crime forecasts is to directly support law enforcement and crime prevention. However, it can be argued that demands for other parts of the judicial system have not been satisfied and have differing forecast needs. Such examples include the "corrections facility planning of prison capacity based in demographics, predicting impacts of proposed changes in judicial sentencing policies using input/output models, predicting recidivism for prisoner release to parole based on prisoner profiles" (Gorr & Harries, 2003).

3.1.1 PredPol

Supporting research and field trials have shown that predictive mapping software is substantially more effective than traditional intelligence-led techniques at forecasting the location of future crimes (Babuta, 2017). The introduction of intelligence-led policing (ILP) as a result of the 9/11 terrorist attack reinforces increased information sharing and accountability while also encouraging the use of "criminal intelligence in support of collaborative, multijurisdictional approaches to crime prevention; and emphasises the role of analysis and strategic planning" (Beck & McCue, 2009, p.2). An instance of a prediction tool is PredPol,[2] that was developed in 2011 by Santa Clara University in partnership with the Los Angeles Police Department (LAPD) (PredPol, n.d.-a). Although PredPol employs data on crime type, location, and time, it is claimed that the software's algorithms do not use demographic data such as the race and ethnicity criminals when making predictions. PredPol makes forecasts using a ML algorithm. For each new city, historical

---

[2] PredPol, Inc., which is now known as Geolitica, is a Predictive Policing corporation that deploys predictive analytics to forecast property crimes. PredPol is also the name of the corporation's software.

event datasets covering 2–5 years of data are employed to train the algorithm. The algorithm is then updated every day with new events obtained from the department (PredPol, n.d.-b). This ML algorithm is based on seismological models that predict seismic activities. Notably, the Santa Cruz police department demonstrated success in their report of a 14% decrease in burglaries from January to June 2012 in contrast to the previous year, since the deployment of PredPol in July 2011 (Babuta, 2017). More importantly, PredPol claims that their technology is unbiased and non-prejudicial in contrast to the discriminating behaviour that occurs far too frequently with officers (Sandhu & Fussey, 2021).

Similar to other predictive technologies, PredPol is not particularly complex in procedure. PredPol employs only three data points to generate its forecasts, and, as a result, such systems are subject to criticism and scrutiny (Sandhu & Fussey, 2021). The use of the programme has been criticised for its influence on police judgement and questioned as to whether this software's dominance is justified. For instance, Joh 2014 argues the potential cost of reducing "the influence of officers' experimental knowledge in decision making" (Sandhu & Fussey, 2021, p.69). Furthermore, contrary to prior claims, predictive policing is thought to encourage bias by creating hotspots that overrepresent disadvantaged neighbourhoods with racial and ethnic minority residents (Sandhu & Fussey, 2021). In the case of drug crimes, it has also been argued that predictive policing disproportionately overpolices specific communities, with the repercussions including deteriorated mental and physical health owing to increased scrutiny and surveillance. Furthermore, police employ the same (often biased) data to train predictive models, resulting in discriminatory police activity (Lum & Isaac, 2016).

3.1.2   CompStat

Furthermore, the incorporation of data analysis in police practice can be seen in the development of the CompStat system, which served as an internal management tool to increase police accountability (Berk, 2021). CompStat, short for COMPuter STATistics, is a managerial accountability system that was developed and implemented in 1990s by the New York City Police Department (NYPD). Since its inception, CompStat has been employed in police agencies all around the world (Didier, 2018; Vito et al., 2017). CompStat is a quantification program or a "highly focused strategic management system" that aims to reduce crime by "decentralizing decision making to middle managers operating out of districts, by holding these managers accountable for performance, and by increasing the police organization's capacity to identify, understand, and monitor responses to crime problems" (Willis et al., 2010, p.969). CompStat identifies three major components that focus on reducing crime and enhancing community quality of life. These consist of informational technology, operational strategies and managerial accountability (Magers, 2004, p.73). Nonetheless, the reality that prediction methods are dependent on assumptions about crime risk, with social, spatial, and temporal factors, cannot be overlooked (Bennett Moses & Chan, 2018). In terms of data, predictive policing does not provide a complete and accurate portrayal of crime; this is backed by unreported crime, where the disparities between crimes committed and crimes reported are not random, but systemic (Bennett Moses & Chan, 2018). As a result, vulnerable and marginalised groups are excluded from law enforcement decision-making, which only contributes to greater exclusion (Bennett Moses & Chan, 2018).

3.1.3 Person-Based Forecasting

Another prediction-based method incorporated into policing is Person-Based Forecasting (PBF). PBF entails searching for persons who have shown a proclivity for crime through previous crime, gang connection, violent injury, or other risk indicators (Fitzpatrick et al., 2019). PBF is arguably the most controversial due to the fact it targets individual faces. Nevertheless, there has been contributory evidence that provides support for such methods (Hung & Yen, 2020). As an example, the Chicago Police Department's (CPD) strategic subject list (SSL) provides the "highest profile" instance of a PBF program (Fitzpatrick et al., 2019, p.482). The CPD developed a predictive algorithm that was capable of predicting an individual's likelihood of being involved in a shooting or murder, either as a perpetrator or as a victim. This was performed by analysing their previous patterns of criminal activity and interactions with the police (Fitzpatrick et al., 2019). Furthermore, current research that examines the social networks of high-risk individuals suggests that person-based forecasting has the potential to aid in crime prediction and prevention (Fitzpatrick et al., 2019). On the other hand, rights-focused non-governmental organisations (NGOs) strongly oppose the use of PBF technology, claiming that it breaches civil rights. This is supported by recent studies that highlight serious issues of "privacy, inequality, and discrimination" (Fitzpatrick et al., 2019).

3.2 Innovative Surveillance Technology

3.2.1 Hard and Soft Technology

In general, there are two types of technological innovations that can be identified within policing: hard technology and soft technology. Soft technology consists of information-based technologies whereas hard technology refers to material-based technologies. Both technologies have been linked to changes in police organisation, notably in terms of crime prevention (Byrne & Marx, 2011). Examples of hard technology innovations comprise "CCTV cameras, metal detectors in schools, baggage screening at airports, bullet proof teller windows at banks and security systems at homes and businesses" (Byrne & Marx, 2011, p.19). Hard technology also involves the employment of personal protection devices such as tasers, mace, emergency call mechanisms, and ignition interlock systems with alcohol-sensor devices that prevent the vehicle from starting while the driver is intoxicated (Byrne & Marx,

2011). It is, however, difficult to provide an accurate estimate of the extent to which hard technology crime prevention has been adopted. For instance, in 2006, approximately 1 million Closed-Circuit Television (CCTV) cameras were deployed across large US cities such as Boston, New York, Los Angeles, and Chicago, indicating the expansion of video surveillance from private to public spaces. This has now become a police managed and government funded system (Byrne & Marx, 2011).

3.2.2 Closed-Circuit Television

Surveillance technologies such as CCTV and databases enable police to expand their field of vision while simultaneously gathering evidence, boosting crime fighting capabilities and providing a more effective and efficient service to the community. Furthermore, the deployment of surveillance technology has been acclaimed for its financial benefits as it is more cost effective to install such technology than it is to support the equivalent workforce in the long term (Van Brakel & De Hert, 2011). CCTV serves as a deterrent measure, but it is also suggested that CCTV systems as a policing tool serve a dual purpose of monitoring regions where police resources are scarce and clearing cases that would otherwise be difficult to clear without tangible video evidence (Hummer & Byrne, 2017). Furthermore, CCTV can not only police the public but also "police the police". This provides an additional layer of supervision of line officers that monitors behaviour and inhibits certain behaviours in the same way that it would prevent same behaviours in the general population (Hummer & Byrne, 2017). Both advocates and opponents of CCTV believe that closed circuit cameras limit officers' ability to organise policing as well as their working habits and attitudes. Since the 9/11 terrorist attacks, the development of surveillance technology has accelerated, and, with the advancement of storage capacity, BD, and new software, new fundamental criminal justice policies have emerged (Van Brakel & De Hert, 2011). In effect, surveillance technologies have played a significant role and have been legitimised in terms of monitoring counterterrorism (Fussey, 2007).

The CCTV systems are deployed to deter, counter and respond to terrorist attacks. Metropolitans police's 2005 Operation Rainbow demonstrates an instance of how crime control methods deploy surveillance to thwart threats of terrorism through CCTV. This is due to the fact that its primary purpose is to aid in the detection and capture of terrorists operating within the London area (Fussey, 2007). According to the Metropolitan Police, the goal of this operation was to build and maintain a database of CCTV locations in order to produce the possibility for continuous information flows around the capital (Fussey, 2007). The ongoing debate about the need for surveillance technology intensified after the 2005 London bombings. This increased the popularity of camera surveillance and its prominence as a means of preventing counterterrorism, with many countries investing large sums of money in surveillance technology (Stutzer & Zehnder, 2013). The event occurred on the 7th of July and was the largest mass casualty in the UK since World War Two, resulting in 775 casualties and 52 deaths (Brewin et al., 2010). The casualties were caused by three bombs bursting on three underground trains with one device exploding on a bus in central London (Stutzer & Zehnder, 2013). Following the event, the identification of the suspected perpetrator mainly relied on CCTV footage; hence, surveillance technologies played a crucial role. Two weeks following the July 21st attack, four more attacks on London public transportation were launched, but only the detonators of the bombs exploded. The release of CCTV images aided in identifying the perpetrators of the attack, demonstrating the importance of CCTV as a means of identifying and apprehending criminals (Stutzer & Zehnder, 2013). Another instance that changed the usage of CCTV and emphasised its importance was the case of James Bulger on February 12, 1993, when shopping mall CCTV footage captured the toddler's kidnapping and eventual murder (Thomas, 2015).

There are several advantages to the rising body of video surveillance. For example, second-generation CCTV offers "digitalised images" that can be processed and analysed by recognition software. This in turn increases the scope of surveillance whilst lowering monitoring expenses (Stutzer & Zehnder, 2013). The deterrence hypothesis also argues that the dissemination of camera surveillance enhances the control capacities and partially replaces "human capital by technological investments" (Stutzer & Zehnder, 2013, p.2). This in turn leads to more productive and efficient policing. However, this effectiveness can be questioned due to the shifting security priorities and change of threats since the September 11, 2001 attack. For example, antiterrorism policies and legislation are more focused on international threats such as Islamic extremists, which raises further issues of predicting extremist acts on a wider scale with a wider victim base (Fussey, 2007). This emergence of different threats questions the overall sufficiency and elasticity of existing preventative provisions (Fussey, 2007). This is due to the fact that activists are linked more loosely and by ideology as opposed to physical structures, posing a challenge to "policing and intelligence capacities of surveillance and target-hardening strategies" (Fussey, 2007, p.180).

3.2.3   Facial Recognition Technology

The process of FR involves the automated analysis of pictures in a database and video surveillance whereby the visible parts of the cameras, such as CCTV, dash cams or body-worn cameras, capture images of individuals that can later be processed by specific software and matched to existing images (Bromberg et al., 2020). However, FR is only as good as the number of photos in their database, and as a result, many states in the United States (US) contribute to the FBI-supported facial analysis, comparison, and evaluation (FACE) (Bromberg et al., 2020). A notional FR surveillance system can be used within policing to identify and locate targets such as suspected criminals, terrorists, and missing children (Woodward Jr, J. D et al., 2003). The system operates by transmitting video streams over a network to a control room where computers attempt to match the targeted individual with an image in the database by searching for faces in the video. If this is successful and a match is found, the system then alerts an officer with the matched image of the suspect and the image of the individual in the database (Woodward Jr, J. D et al., 2003). To ensure an accurate and valid match has been determined, a verification process is carried out through which a trained officer examines and determines whether the match is a false alarm, and such results are recorded when caught. If the match is confirmed, the alert is forwarded to officers on patrol who are within the regions of the original camera that captured footage of the suspect (Woodward Jr, J. D et al., 2003).

The US National Institute of Standards and Technology as cited in Thomas (2015) reinforces the capabilities of current FR systems by testing an assortment of systems in 2010 and concluding "that the top algorithm properly recognized 92% of unidentified persons from a database of 1.6 million criminal records" (Thomas, 2015, p.55). It is argued that FR technology (FRT) can act as a "force multiplier", extending the scope of limited police resources, and that, when combined with other data-intensive investigative tools, it can improve the accuracy of police practise in addition to addressing the issue of police discretion (Hill et al., 2022). However, the increase of FRTs continue to face scrutiny from civil liberty groups, scholars and the general public on the grounds of ethics and legal concerns (Hill et al., 2022). Firstly, FRT has been heavily criticised for its overall accuracy, with many claiming that the technology involved is far less accurate than other available biometrics when used in real time, such as fingerprinting (Hill et al., 2022). This is because for the technology to be accurate, it has to rely on a number of technological factors such as the "photo quality, lighting, proper thresholds to minimise false positives and negatives, camera position, training sets and physical qualities of the individual (race, glasses, makeup)" (Hill et al., 2022, p.3). In effect, issues with any of the aforementioned factors lead to inaccuracies in the overall results.

Furthermore, there have been numerous legal challenges to the public's legal rights, such as the right to privacy in public spaces (Bragias et al., 2021). Likewise, the House of Lords' 2009 surveillance report 'Surveillance: Citizen and the State' (Parliament. House of Lords, 2009) highlighted additional privacy concerns, citing a number of drawbacks including: the threat to privacy and social relationships, declining trust in the state, and discrimination/security threats associated with storing larger amounts of data (Van Brakel & De Hert, 2011). There is a growing body of legal scholars raising privacy concerns with new surveillance technology, particularly the use of profiling, with some requesting a "ban on automatic profiling or decision making processes that has been laid down in article 15 of the Data protection directive" (Van Brakel & De Hert, 2011, p. 181). Others have highlighted the issues of anti-discrimination and the need to protect minorities in relation to policies profiling practices (Brouwer, 2009). Particularly, in the US, FR has sparked a range of conflicting opinions about Fourth Amendment concerns. On the one hand it can be argued that if an individual's face is open to the public and FRT is used on a short-term basis, it does not violate the Fourth Amendment. However, on the other hand opposing opinion states that warrantless use of FRT allows an individual's movement to be tracked over a long period of time, and thus technology is not available for public use and will in fact violate the Fourth Amendment (Hamann & Smith, 2019). The general consensus on FRT and legal implications is that if law enforcement identifies a suspect and continues to track their movements, a Fourth Amendment issue arises. However, if an individual's movement captured by FRT technology is an isolated event rather than an ongoing procedure over an extended period of time, it can be argued that there is no violation or Fourth amendment concern (Hamann & Smith, 2019).

3.2.4 Body-Worn Cameras

Body-worn cameras can be best described as wearable video cameras that either clip onto police uniform or are worn as a headset (Coudert et al., 2015). Body-worn cameras are intended to serve three primary purposes. The first goal is to increase the transparency of police behaviour by recording events. The second objective is to act as a deterrent against police use of force by exposing both bad and good behaviour within the police. Finally, the deterrent effect overall aims to raise policing standards and re-establish community trust and confidence in the police force (Coudert et al., 2015). Supporting evidence reinforces this, indicating that body-worn cameras have the potential to reduce crime rates, reduce officer complaints, and effectively record and document evidence (Cubitt et al., 2017). With the increased availability of technology, police are frequently confronted with recordings of events from members of the public, which likely undermine police credibility. Thus, body-worn cameras work to offer a solution or, at the very least, limit the amount of police corruption and control the use of excessive force in attempts to improve police accountability (Coudert et al., 2015).

3.2.5 Social Media

In recent years, social media have grown in popularity among LEAs as an important tool for crime detection due to its ability to connect with the general public (Fatih & Bekir, 2015). In addition to communication, social media can be utilised as an intelligence gathering tool and for additional surveillance and monitoring. According to a 2014 vendor online survey of 1200 federal, state, and local law enforcement professionals, 80% of them used social media platforms for the purposes described above (Mateescu et al., 2015). Furthermore, social media help to support crime prevention and community policing efforts through platforms such as Facebook and Twitter, which work to provide a partnership between the community and police. This partnership is facilitated by allowing the community to provide feedback on neighbourhood safety while also making recommendations to improve police efforts via these social media sites (Israni et al., 2017). For instance, in the UK, Manchester police utilise social media to "establish a trusted voice and gather intelligence from the public" (Israni et al., 2017). According to a study of India's Bangalore City Police's Facebook page, the public's contribution is important as it can be used to improve safety and prevent crimes related to fraud, police misconduct, and first information reports (Israni et al., 2017). Law enforcement in England and Wales has faced significant political pressure to maintain this partnership and engage effectively with the general public on the basis of enforcing police accountability. However, it is argued that public trust in the police still remains low, and, thus, more work is required (Crump, 2011). Police also use social media to monitor potential criminal activity, "especially during and post large crisis incidents" through social media analysis, whereby a suspected criminal can be identified and matched across their social media platforms with police records (Domdouzis et al., 2016, p.3). Social media can also be integrated with FRT since matched profile pictures can be taken from images sent or shared by the public through social networking sites (Domdouzis et al., 2016).

4   RQ 2: The Use of AI by Law Enforcement II

BD has increased law enforcements capabilities whilst lowering the overall cost and still deploying effective police strategies to detect criminal behaviour (Joh, 2016). BD tools work by applying computer analytics to large amounts of data in order to identify suspicious activity and the suspected perpetrator committing the act (Joh, 2016). There are three core purposes for the use of BD in terms of policing including the storage of DNA information, mass surveillance and predictive policing (Babuta, 2017). All police forces in the UK have access to the Police National Computer (PNC), a database that holds more than 12.2 million personal records, 62.6 million vehicle records, and 58.5 million driver records as of May 2017. The PNC was introduced to allow officers to search through large amounts of data across various databases (Babuta, 2017). In addition to PNC UK police forces also have access to IDENT1, which is the UK's central national database for storing, searching, and comparing biometric information on individuals who encounter who the police after being detained. Data held on those individuals comprise fingerprints, palm prints, and crime scene marks. IDENT1 contains more than 7 million fingerprint records, and the National DNA Database holds DNA of 5 million members of the public (Babuta, 2017).

When evaluating police tools that assist in decision making, it is important to understand the issue of accountability and determine ways in which police should be held accountable for the decisions they make. Police accountability often refers to the control over police and the requirement to give accounts or explanations about conduct (Bennett Moses & Chan, 2018). Whilst BD might pose threats to liberty and privacy, it simultaneously offers new ways, by means of which police officers can be held accountable for their actions. The remainder of this section aims to address the first research question: "How might the adoption of BDPA assist police in resolving crimes and improving accountability?"

4.1   ML and Data Mining in Policing

Data mining is the process of identifying patterns and extracting information from BD sets using techniques that combine machine learning, statistics, and database systems. Examples of common data mining techniques include: Artificial Neural Networks, Decision Tree, Rule Induction, Nearest Neighbour Method and Genetic Algorithm. These techniques can be utilised in a wide range of fields, but more importantly, they can be employed in criminal investigations (Prabakaran & Mitra, 2018). In policing, a wide range of techniques can be employed for crime analysis, which ultimately aids in identifying a pattern of crime. There exist various data mining techniques that can be applied to different types of crimes in order to forecast and solve the crime more effectively. One instance of this is the use of the Hidden Markov Model (HMM) in fraud detection (Prabakaran & Mitra, 2018). HMM is a statistical model composed of two random variables that modify the state in a sequential manner, allowing the discussion of "both monitored and hidden events". This model is often adopted in the field of Speech Recognition and NLP and consists of three main techniques including likelihood, decoding and learning (Prabakaran & Mitra, 2018, p.3). The application of BD continues to attract LEAs and security intelligence organisations due to its ability to solve complex crimes efficiently.

Considering the technological advancements, the criminal network has continued to expand, with organised crime serving as one example. As a result, authorities must be able to analyse data rapidly and efficiently so that the proper preventative measures can be implemented (Pramanik et al., 2017). BDA has been effective at identifying and extracting the hidden network structures within criminal organisations such as organised crime, and it can assist in identifying, central members and subgroups (Pramanik et al., 2017). AI algorithms have developed learning from data and, as a result, have worked to establish predicting models that can effectively detect "criminal activity, criminal behaviour profiling and clustering of criminal data" (Pramanik et al., 2017, p.2). Link Analysis, also referred to as "affinity analysis or association" is another example of a data mining technique that uncovers relationships amongst data and determines an association rule (Oatley et al., 2006). Since it can correlate large amounts of data in fraud and narcotics cases, the technique can be of a significant value to aid police work. Intelligence analysts can analyse links in criminal networks and establish relationships amongst specific groups of entities in a criminal network such as vehicles, weapons or bank accounts (Oatley et al., 2006). Criminal Link Analysis tools enable police to determine offenders' relationships within groups with the primary objective of depicting who is responsible for what within criminal networks, thereby assisting in resolving these types of crimes (Pramanik et al., 2017). This is just one example of how BD can assist police work. Police rely on alerts generated by BD algorithms, which filter through vast amounts of data and identify suspicious activity and patterns faster and more efficiently than traditional human investigations. Furthermore, these BD tools can detect future and ongoing crimes and threats such as bombs. For instance, the US Department of Homeland Security employs computer analytics to detect suspicious activity by analysing tweets containing words like bomb (Joh, 2016).

4.2 Police Discrimination and Big Data

In recent years, there have been growing concerns about discriminatory policing, particularly during "stop-and-frisk practises". There is also a growing concern about holding those accountable who abuse their policing power to act in a discriminatory manner, and BD can assist with this. Previously, any suspicion of discriminatory motives in police work was dismissed in court, and instead acts/intrusion were viewed as reasonably justified by the Supreme Court. However, the use of BD now works to change that and instead provides compelling proof that would have otherwise been difficult to obtain. (Goel et al., 2017). BD along with algorithmic tools has improved the ability to record and measure data, making it more accessible to those outside of law enforcement and allowing inferences to be made on issues such as discrimination and bias in stop and searches (Goel et al., 2017). The NYPD illustrates an early example whereby they compiled recorded stop and search data. Furthermore, this data is recorded and analysed in order to generate a 'stop level hit rate' which is a measurement of the strength of the evidence supporting the suspicion that a stopped individual has a gun (Goel et al., 2017). This data is recorded on a UF-250 form and allows for police officers to record the factors that caused the officer to stop the suspect (Gelman et al., 2007). While the police are not required to fill out a form for every stop, there are some circumstances in which they must do so (Gelman et al., 2007). SHR analysis is crucial at holding officers accountable and raising policing standards as the analysis reduces the racially disproportionate influence in their practice (Goel et al., 2017).

It can be argued that when BD is combined with statistical techniques such as SHR, it provides "another basis for equal protection challenges to discriminatory stop-and-frisk practices", protecting the most vulnerable members of society (Goel et al., 2017, p.226). Furthermore, the analysis reinforced racial motivators in stop and searches as findings revealed that "blacks and Hispanics were typically stopped on the basis of less evidence than whites" (Goel et al., 2017 , p.226). This type of analysis, however, is not without flaws, and there are limitations in the data collected such as the fact that there is currently no national database on police stops. In addition, SHR is not uniform across all police departments, resulting in variation in how consistent and systematic police departments are in recording stop and search (Goel et al., 2017). On the contrary, BD and Data Mining algorithms have been criticised for being biased and discriminatory, which contradicts the purpose and objectives of statistical techniques. This is owing to the fact that there might be biased data within the algorithmic model that the models learn and replicate in order to make classifications (Favaretto et al., 2019). Schermer (2011) as cited in Favaretto et al. (2019) reinforces this arguing that if "the training data is contaminated with discriminatory or prejudiced cases, the system will assume them as valid examples to learn from and reproduce discrimination in its own outcomes" (Favaretto et al., 2019).

4.3   DNA Databases and Big Data

Due to its ability to merge sources of digital information for preventing and predicting the likelihood of crime, BD is beginning to play a major role in the expansion of criminal DNA in order to support the work of the criminal justice system (Machado & Granja, 2020). It can be argued that BD can expand the current reach of DNA databases and, as a result, improve the status of past cases and current criminal investigations (Neiva et al., 2022). To elaborate, in the context of criminal investigation, BD has the potential to improve "interoperability between genetic and non-genetic data", potentially yielding new types of information (Neiva et al., 2022, p.3). Some argue that BD can be used as an "analytical weapon", analysing data from a variety of sources to create intelligence useful in police investigations. For instance, it can allow professionals in EU police cooperation to link information from distributed databases and other disparate data to derive pertinent information for furthering criminal investigations (Neiva et al., 2022). However, some have expressed concerns about the ethics of DNA databases due to its criteria for collecting and storing data. Furthermore, it has been argued that DNA databases add to "social inequalities", with members of certain minorities being subjected to increased surveillance and monitoring as a result of their DNA databases (Machado & Granja, 2020). Such issues of discrimination and bias undermine its effectiveness, and there is little evidence of improved police accountability. Concerns about using analytical tools and BD technology ethically for law enforcement purposes are a growing trend. The EU General Data Protection Regulation and Directive EU provide a developed guideline to ensure that police officers who are required to handle sensitive and personal data do so in accordance with the standards set forth (Babuta, 2017).

5   Recommendations

5.1   Accountability and Transparency

In terms of police accountability within decision making processes, a promising solution may be to make the "processes of decision making available for scrutiny" so that the fairness of their actions and "validity of their analyses" can be monitored (Vestby & Vestby, 2021, p.2). It is argued that transparency can perhaps work to restore accountability within BD decision making technologies (De Laat, 2017).

More data is now available for analysis, allowing for even more powerful ML. However, the results suffer from significant flaws, such as the fact that almost all aspects of algorithmic decision-making remain opaque (De Laat, 2017, p.2). Many have argued for complete transparency, which would result in "the perfect recipe for restoring accountability for algorithmic systems", with all phases being open to the general public and inviting public opinion and input (De Laat, 2017).

To effectively hold institutions such as law enforcement accountable, all raw data and the processes surrounding it should be made accessible for inspection. Individuals should be informed and made aware when decisions directly affect their informational and privacy rights (De Laat, 2017). Engagement is essential for preserving and enhancing accountability (Vestby & Vestby, 2021). Moreover, a range of actors involved must cogitate and debate implementation and use of ML software both internally, such as in police organisations, and also between "in house or commercial developers; stakeholders and affected populations with police and developers" (Vestby & Vestby, 2021, p.2). This way, an external influence is considered with both specialist and non-specialist opinion on how policing is carried out. While police may not wish their mistakes, misbehaviour, and controversial incidents to be made public, they have a responsibility and duty to do so in order for their choice of strategies to be comprehended, discussed, and rectified as needed (McDaniel & Pease, 2021). Policy involvement should be transparent to the community, with decisions and discussions benefiting both parties (Yen & Hung, 2021). Institutions should arguably work towards becoming more transparent even though complete transparency is almost impossible for a variety of reasons. Instead, institutions must be able to strike a smart balance. The main issue with complete transparency is the risk of sensitive data being leaked; as a result, data should be kept private with some exceptions (De Laat, 2017).

5.2   Bias in ML Algorithms

Algorithms have the ability to be racist, especially when it is programmed and operates in the context of a racially biased criminal justice system (O'Donnell, 2019). Because the data generated by humans are inherently racist, predictive policing algorithms are trained on already discriminatory data, which only perpetuates and reinforces these ideals. As a result, minority populations continue to be disproportionately targeted (O'Donnell, 2019). Many solutions have been proposed in an attempt to combat this issue, one of which is the complete elimination of predictive policing, which is undeniably an unpalatable option for many. An additional resolution is to eliminate bias by removing all information about "protected variables from the data" on "which the models will ultimately be trained" (Johndrow & Lum, 2019, p.1). In doing so, the risk of malicious actors intentionally biasing a model at the expense of protected groups would be decreased and predictions are deemed fairer (Johndrow & Lum, 2019).

Furthermore, a more obvious but contentious solution may be to focus less on the ML bias itself and more on the societal norms that create unjust structures that reinforce biased data in the first place. (Yen & Hung, 2021). It is critical to ensure that the same standards apply universally. However, in terms of support, individuals are undeniably unequal within society due to health and social classes, and applying the same standard may only exacerbate this inequality. Therefore, it should be a priority to fix unjust situations and consider applying different standards to those in society who require it (Yen & Hung, 2021). Furthermore, the proposal of a policy schema may work in order to address the issues of "distrust, efficiency, racism and social equity" (Yen & Hung, 2021). This provides a safety net for predictive policing and includes: forecasting immediate risks and acting on them, identifying individuals who are socially vulnerable and providing them with assistance; and being scrutinised by and communicating with the general public (Yen & Hung, 2021).

5.3   Regulating Surveillance Technology

The final solution aims to address issues of consent and privacy in the context of rapidly evolving digital surveillance technologies. Local governments have a duty to regulate their video systems on an operational level by creating policies and procedures akin to those "that govern many other police practices" (Brown, 2008, p.756). However, this can be challenging considering its pervasiveness and "relative normalisation" as surveillance has now become ingrained in everyday life (Raab, 2012;9). For instance, many criminologists have revealed the extent to which police in the UK utilise automated licence plate readers (Raab, 2012). Furthermore, despite their efforts, many privacy regulators have had great difficulty progressing with the regulation of surveillance. This could be due to the fact that "it is extremely difficult to pinpoint the locus of responsibility for surveillance processes within the invisible world of algorithms, over interoperable systems, between departments of large bureaucracies, and across international boundaries" (Raab, 2012, p.9).

6   Conclusion

To conclude, it is undeniable that traditional policing is evolving to include the incorporation of emerging systems and technologies related to predictive policing and AI (McDaniel & Pease, 2021). Within this period, there have been "two major structural developments": an increase in surveillance technologies and the rise of BD, both of which have aided police practise in both positive and negative ways, as discussed throughout this chapter (Brayne, 2017). Police have effectively used predictive policing as a crime mapping tool to identify where a crime is likely to occur, as well as predictive analytics to identify individuals who are likely to offend (Babuta, 2017). Data-driven policing has received widespread praise for its potential to improve police accountability by requiring law enforcement to respond to discriminatory practices and be held accountable in the process (Brayne, 2017). Furthermore, leading police practice with data-driven decision has the potential to improve "prediction and pre-emption of behaviours by helping law enforcement deploy resources more efficiently" (Brayne, 2017, p.982). This, however, is not entirely accurate, and the adoption of BD and predictive policing raises a number of contentious issues, such as discrimination and bias readings. Furthermore, as these technologies interact and become more integrated into daily life, ethical concerns about privacy and data anonymity rise (Favaretto et al., 2019). Police collect and analyse massive volumes of data, including the location, time, and type of crime committed, which some argue may jeopardise an individual's privacy and security (Ferguson, 2017).

Surveillance technologies are emerging, and cities are being increasingly monitored to ensure public safety and protection by monitoring high crime areas, particularly in the aftermath of the 9/11 terrorist attack, which prompted a public outcry for increased surveillance technologies. However, this influx in surveillance technology such as CCTV and FRT raises concerns about regulatory issues and how to balance police aims and objectives while respecting the general public's privacy and liberties. Nonetheless, police forces can use these new technologies in a way that maximises efficiency while also setting performance and accountability standards, which are reinforced by rules and regulations governing the use of "digital cameras, smartphones, personal computers", and various other technologies (McDaniel & Pease, 2021, p.6). Surveillance technology is ambiguous in that it can cause both exclusion and inclusion within society. However, when used effectively and with respect for individual rights, the technology has great potential in aiding organisational goals (Brayne, 2017). This is reinforced by technologies such as body-worn cameras, which serve not only as an accountability tool but also as an effective means of combating crime and reducing violence (Coudert et al., 2015). Furthermore, law enforcement have embraced the use of social media as an investigative tool.

In conclusion, while it is undeniable that surveillance systems and technologies are rapidly expanding, they are not and will not be completely reliable because there are still widespread issues such as identity diversity and misidentification that undermine and call into question its place in police practise (Wood et al., 2006). Because the adoption of new policing tools has the potential to be harmful to society, effective improvements must be made to regulate their use so that they become an efficient and credible part of police practice.

References

Agarwal, M., & Saxena, A. (2019). An overview of natural language processing. *International Journal for Research in Applied Science and Engineering Technology (IJRASET), 7*, 2811–2813.
Andresen, S. L. (2002). John McCarthy: Father of AI. *IEEE Intelligent Systems, 17*(5), 84–85. https://doi.org/10.1109/MIS.2002.1039837

Babuta, A. (2017). *Big data and policing: An assessment of law enforcement requirements, expectations and priorities*. Royal United Services Institute for Defence and Security Studies.

Beck, C., & McCue, C. (2009). Predictive policing: What can we learn from Wal-Mart and Amazon about fighting crime in a recession? *Police Chief, 76*(11), 18.

Bennett Moses, L., & Chan, J. (2018). Algorithmic prediction in policing: Assumptions, evaluation, and accountability. *Policing and Society, 28*(7), 806–822. https://doi.org/10.1080/1043946 3.2016.1253695

Berk, R. (2021). Artificial intelligence, predictive policing, and risk assessment for law enforcement. *Annual Review Of Criminology, 4*(1), 209–237. https://doi.org/10.1146/annurev-criminol-051520-012342

Bi, Q., Goodman, K. E., Kaminsky, J., & Lessler, J. (2019). What is machine learning? A primer for the epidemiologist. *American Journal of Epidemiology, 188*(12), 2222–2239.

Bishop, C. M. (2007). *Pattern recognition and machine learning (information science and statistics)*. Springer.

Botelho, B., & Bigelow, S. (2022). big data. TechTarget. Available at: https://www.techtarget.com/searchdatamanagement/definition/big-data (Accessed: 13/12/2022).

Bragias, A., Hine, K., & Fleet, R. (2021). 'Only in our best interest, right?' Public perceptions of police use of facial recognition technology. *Police Practice and Research, 22*(6), 1637–1654. https://doi.org/10.1080/15614263.2021.1942873

Brayne, S. (2017). Big data surveillance: The case of policing. *American Sociological Review, 82*(5), 977–1008.

Brewin, C., Fuchkan, N., Huntley, Z., Robertson, M., Thompson, M., Scragg, P., et al. (2010). Outreach and screening following the 2005 London bombings: Usage and outcomes. *Psychological Medicine, 40*(12), 2049–2057. https://doi.org/10.1017/s0033291710000206

Bromberg, D.E., Charbonneau, É., & Smith, A. (2020). Public support for facial recognition via police body-worn cameras: Findings from a list experiment. *Government Information Quarterly, 37*(1), 101415. https://doi.org/10.1016/j.giq.2019.101415

Brouwer, E. (2009). The EU Passenger Name Record (PNR) system and human rights: Transferring passenger data or passenger freedom?. CEPS Working Document, (320).

Brown, J. (2008). Pan, tilt, zoom: Regulating the use of video surveillance of public places. *Berkeley Technology Law Journal, 23*, 755.

Brownlee, J. (2019). *14 Different types of learning in machine learning*. Available at: https://machinelearningmastery.com/types-of-learning-in-machine-learning/ Accessed 21 July 2022.

Byrne, J., & Marx, G. (2011). Technological innovations in crime prevention and policing. A review of the research on implementation and impact. *Journal of Police Studies, 20*(3), 17–40.

Carbonell, J. G., Michalski, R. S., & Mitchell, T. M. (1983a). An overview of machine learning. In R. S. Michalski, J. G. Carbonell, & T. M. Mitchell (Eds.), *Machine Learning: An artificial intelligence approach* (pp. 3–23). Palo Alto.

Carbonell, J. G., Michalski, R. S., & Mitchell, T. M. (1983b). Machine learning: A historical and methodological analysis. *AI Magazine, 4*(3), 69–69.

Chen, Q., Leaman, R., Allot, A., Luo, L., Wei, C. H., Yan, S., & Lu, Z. (2021). Artificial intelligence in action: Addressing the COVID-19 pandemic with natural language processing. *Annual Review of Biomedical Data Science, 4*, 313–339.

Coudert, F., Butin, D., & Le Métayer, D. (2015). Body-worn cameras for police accountability: Opportunities and risks. *Computer Law & Security Review, 31*(6), 749–762.

Crump, J. (2011). What are the police doing on twitter? Social media, the police and the public. *Policy & Internet, 3*(4), 1–27.

Cubitt, T. I., Lesic, R., Myers, G. L., & Corry, R. (2017). Body-worn video: A systematic review of literature. *Australian & New Zealand Journal of Criminology, 50*(3), 379–396.

de Laat, P. B. (2017). Big data and algorithmic decision-making: Can transparency restore accountability? *Acm Sigcas Computers and Society, 47*(3), 39–53.

Demchenko, Y., Grosso, P., De Laat, C., & Membrey, P. (2013). Addressing big data issues in scientific data infrastructure. In *2013 International conference on collaboration technologies and systems (CTS)* (pp. 48–55). IEEE.

Deng, L., & Liu, Y. (Eds.). (2018). *Deep learning in natural language processing.* Springer.

Didier, E. (2018). Globalization of quantitative policing: Between management and Statactivism. *Annual Review of Sociology, 44,* 515–534.

Dietterich, T. G., & Kong, E. B. (1995). *Machine learning bias, statistical bias, and statistical variance of decision tree algorithms* (pp. 0–13). Technical report, Department of Computer Science, Oregon State University.

Ding, S., Zhu, Z., & Zhang, X. (2017). An overview on semi-supervised support vector machine. *Neural Computing and Applications, 28*(5), 969–978. https://doi.org/10.1007/s00521-015-2113-7

Domdouzis, K., Akhgar, B., Andrews, S., Gibson, H., & Hirsch, L. (2016). A social media and crowdsourcing data mining system for crime prevention during and post-crisis situations. *Journal of Systems and Information Technology, 18*(4), 364–382.

Eckerson, W. W. (2007). Predictive analytics. *Extending the value of your data warehousing investment. TDWI Best Practices Report, 1,* 1–36.

Fatih, T., & Bekir, C. (2015). Police use of technology to fight against crime. *European Scientific Journal, 11*(10), 1857–1881.

Favaretto, M., De Clercq, E., & Elger, B. S. (2019). Big data and discrimination: Perils, promises and solutions. A systematic review. *Journal of Big Data, 6*(1), 1–27.

Ferguson, A. (2017). Policing predictive policing. *Washington University Law Review, 94*(5), 1109–1190.

Filimowicz, M. (Ed.). (2022). *Systemic bias: Algorithms and society.* Routledge.

Fitzpatrick, D. J., Gorr, W. L., & Neill, D. B. (2019). Keeping score: Predictive analytics in policing. *Annual Review of Criminology, 2*(1), 473–491.

Fussey, P. (2007). Observing potentiality in the global city: Surveillance and counterterrorism in London. *International Criminal Justice Review, 17*(3), 171–192.

Gartner. (n.d.). Gartner glossary. Gartner. Available at: https://www.gartner.com/en/information-technology/glossary/big-data#:~:text=Big%20data%20is%20high%2Dvolume,decisions%20contributing%20to%20business%20growth Accessed 21 July 2022.

Gelman, A., Fagan, J., & Kiss, A. (2007). An analysis of the new York City police department's "stop-and-frisk" policy in the context of claims of racial bias. *Journal of the American Statistical Association, 102*(479), 813–823.

Gillis, A.S. (2021). 5 V's of big data. TechTarget.. Available at: https://www.techtarget.com/searchdatamanagement/definition/5-Vs-of-big-data Accessed 23 July 2022.

Goel, S., Perelman, M., Shroff, R., & Sklansky, D. A. (2017). Combatting police discrimination in the age of big data. *New Criminal Law Review, 20*(2), 181–232.

Goodfellow, I., Bengio, Y., Courville, A., & Bach, F. (2017). *Deep learning (Adaptive computation and machine learning series).* MIT Press.

Gorr, W., & Harries, R. (2003). Introduction to crime forecasting. *International Journal of Forecasting, 19*(4), 551–555. https://doi.org/10.1016/s0169-2070(03)00089-x

Gupta, S., Markey, M., & Bovik, A. (2010). Anthropometric 3D face recognition. *International Journal of Computer Vision, 90*(3), 331–349.

Haenlein, M., & Kaplan, A. (2019). A brief history of artificial intelligence: On the past, present, and future of artificial intelligence. *California Management Review, 61*(4), 5–14. https://doi.org/10.1177/0008125619864925

Hamann, K., & Smith, R. (2019). Facial recognition technology. *CRIM. JUST, 9.*

Helm, J., Swiergosz, A., Haeberle, H., Karnuta, J., Schaffer, J., Krebs, V., et al. (2020). Machine learning and artificial intelligence: Definitions, applications, and future directions. *Current Reviews in Musculoskeletal Medicine, 13*(1), 69–76. https://doi.org/10.1007/s12178-020-09600-8

Hill, D., O'Connor, C. D., & Slane, A. (2022). Police use of facial recognition technology: The potential for engaging the public through co-constructed policy-making. *International Journal of Police Science & Management, 14613557221089558.*

Hinton, G., & Sejnowski, T. J. (Eds.). (1999). *Unsupervised learning: Foundations of neural computation.* MIT press.

Huang, D., Zhang, G., Ardabilian, M., Wang, Y., & Chen, L. (2010). 3D face recognition using distinctiveness enhanced facial representations and local feature hybrid matching. In *2010 Fourth IEEE International Conference on Biometrics: Theory, Applications and Systems (BTAS)* (pp. 1–7). IEEE.

Hummer, D., & Byrne, J. (2017). Technology, innovation and twenty-first-century policing. In *The Routledge handbook of technology, crime and justice* (pp. 375–389). Routledge.

Hung, T., & Yen, C. (2020). On the person-based predictive policing of AI. *Ethics and Information Technology, 23*(3), 165–176. https://doi.org/10.1007/s10676-020-09539-x

IBM Cloud Education. (2020). *Unsupervised learning.* IBM. Available at: https://www.ibm.com/cloud/learn/unsupervised-learning Accessed 21 July 2022.

Indurkhya, N., & Damerau, F. J. (Eds.). (2010). *Handbook of natural language processing.* CRC Press LLC..

Introna, L., & Nissenbaum, H. (2010). *Facial recognition technology a survey of policy and implementation issues.* Lancaster Universit.

Ishwarappa, & Anuradha, J. (2015). A brief introduction on big data 5Vs characteristics and Hadoop technology. *Procedia Computer Science, 48*(1), 319–324. https://doi.org/10.1016/j.procs.2015.04.188

Israni, A., Erete, S., & Smith, C. L. (2017, February). Snitches, trolls, and social norms: Unpacking perceptions of social media use for crime prevention. In *Proceedings of the 2017 ACM conference on computer supported cooperative work and social computing* (pp. 1193–1209).

Joh, E. E. (2016). The new surveillance discretion: Automated suspicion, big data, and policing. *Harvard Law & Policy Review, 10*, 15.

Johndrow, J. E., & Lum, K. (2019). An algorithm for removing sensitive information: Application to race-independent recidivism prediction. *The Annals of Applied Statistics, 13*(1), 189–220.

Jordan, M., & Mitchell, T. (2015). Machine learning: Trends, perspectives, and prospects. *Science, 349*(6245), 255–260. https://doi.org/10.1126/science.aaa8415

Kaul, V., Enslin, S., & Gross, S. A. (2020). History of artificial intelligence in medicine. *Gastrointestinal Endoscopy, 92*(4), 807–812.

Kotsiantis, S. B., Zaharakis, I., & Pintelas, P. (2007). Supervised machine learning: A review of classification techniques. *Emerging Artificial Intelligence Applications in Computer Engineering, 160*(1), 3–24.

Lee, Y., Song, H., Yang, U., Shin, H., & Sohn, K. (2011). Local feature based 3D face recognition. *Lecture Notes in Computer Science, 3546*, 909–918. https://doi.org/10.1007/11527923_95

Li, L., Mu, X., Li, S., & Peng, H. (2020). A review of face recognition technology. IEEE access, 8, 139110-139120.

Lum, K., & Isaac, W. (2016). To predict and serve?. *Significance, 13*(5), 14–19.

Machado, H., & Granja, R. (2020). DNA databases and big data. In *Forensic genetics in the governance of crime* (pp. 57–70). Palgrave Pivot,.

Magers, J. S. (2004). Compstat: A New Paradigm for Policing or a Repudiation of Community Policing? *Journal of Contemporary Criminal Justice, 20*(1), 70–79. https://doi.org/10.1177/1043986203262312

Mahesh, B. (2020). Machine learning algorithms-a review. *International Journal of Science and Research (IJSR).[Internet], 9*, 381–386.

Mateescu, A., Brunton, D., Rosenblat, A., Patton, D., Gold, Z., & Boyd, D. (2015). Social media surveillance and law enforcement. *Data Civ Rights, 27*, 2015–2027.

McDaniel, J. L. M., & Pease, K. G. (Eds.). (2021). *Predictive policing and artificial intelligence* (1st ed.). Routledge. https://doi.org/10.4324/9780429265365

Meijer, A., & Wessels, M. (2019). Predictive policing: Review of benefits and drawbacks. *International Journal of Public Administration, 42*(12), 1031–1039. https://doi.org/10.108 0/01900692.2019.1575664

Mian, A., Bennamoun, M., & Owens, R. (2008). Keypoint detection and local feature matching for textured 3D face recognition. *International Journal of Computer Vision, 79*(1), 1–12. https://doi.org/10.1007/s11263-007-0085-5

Mitchell, T. (1997). *Machine Learning.* McGraw Hill

Nadikattu, R. R. (2016). The emerging role of artificial intelligence in modern society. *International Journal of Creative Research Thoughts., 4*(4), 906–911.

Nadimpalli, M. (2017). Artificial intelligence–consumers and industry impact. *International Journal of Economics & Management Sciences, 6*(03), 4–6.

Nadkarni, P. M., Ohno-Machado, L., & Chapman, W. W. (2011). Natural language processing: An introduction. *Journal of the American Medical Informatics Association, 18*(5), 544–551.

Neiva, L., Granja, R., & Machado, H. (2022). Big data applied to criminal investigations: Expectations of professionals of police cooperation in the European Union. *Policing and Society,* 1–13.

O'Donnell, R. M. (2019). Challenging racist predictive policing algorithms under the equal protection clause. *The New York University Law Review, 94*, 544.

O'Leary, D. E. (2013). Artificial intelligence and big data. *IEEE Intelligent Systems, 28*(2), 96–99.

Oatley, G., Ewart, B., & Zeleznikow, J. (2006). Decision support systems for police: Lessons from the application of data mining techniques to "soft" forensic evidence. *Artificial Intelligence and Law, 14*(1), 35–100.

Ohiomah, A., Andreev, P., & Benyoucef, M. (2017). *A Review of Big Data Predictive Analytics in Information Systems Research.* In Proceedings of the Conference on Information Systems Applied Research ISSN (Vol. 2167, p. 1508).

Ongsulee, P., Chotchaung, V., Bamrungsi, E., & Rodcheewit, T. (2018). Big data, predictive analytics and machine learning. In *2018 16ᵗʰ international conference on ICT and knowledge engineering* pp. 1–6. doi:https://doi.org/10.1109/ICTKE.2018.8612393.

Parliament House of Lords. (2009). *Surveillance: Citizens and the state: 2nd report of session 2008–09.* (HL Paper 18–I). The Stationery Office Limited.

Parmar, D. N., & Mehta, B. B. (2014). Face recognition methods & applications. *arXiv preprint arXiv:1403.0485.*

Prabakaran, S., & Mitra, S. (2018, April). Survey of analysis of crime detection techniques using data mining and machine learning. In *Journal of physics: Conference series* (Vol. 1000, No. 1, p. 012046). IOP Publishing.

Pradhan, A. (2012). Support vector machine-a survey. *International Journal of Emerging Technology and Advanced Engineering, 2*(8), 82–85.

Pramanik, M. I., Lau, R. Y., Yue, W. T., Ye, Y., & Li, C. (2017). Big data analytics for security and criminal investigations. *Wiley Interdisciplinary Reviews: Data Mining and Knowledge Discovery, 7*(4), e1208.

PredPol. (n.d.-a). Overview. *PredPol.* Available at: https://www.predpol.com/about/. Accessed 23 July 2022.

PredPol. (n.d.-b). Predictive Policing: Guidance on Where and When to Patrol. *PredPol.* Available at: https://www.predpol.com/how-predictive-policing-works/#:~:text=PredPol%20uses%20 a%20machine%2Dlearning,are%20received%20from%20the%20department. Accessed 23 July 2022.

Pruijt, H. (2006). Social interaction with computers: An interpretation of Weizenbaum's ELIZA and her heritage. *Social Science Computer Review, 24*(4), 516–523.

Raab, C. D. (2012). Regulating surveillance: The importance of principles. In *Routledge handbook of surveillance studies* (pp. 377–385). Routledge.

Rajaraman, V. (2014). JohnMcCarthy: Father of artificial intelligence. *Resonance, 19*(3), 198–207.

Ray, S. (2019, February). A quick review of machine learning algorithms. In *2019 international conference on machine learning, big data, cloud and parallel computing (COMITCon)* (pp. 35–39). IEEE.

Russell, S. & Norvig, P. (2021). Artificial intelligence: A modern approach, *Global Edition*. (4th ed.). Pearson.

Sandhu, A., & Fussey, P. (2021). The 'uberization of policing'? How police negotiate and operationalise predictive policing technology. *Policing and Society, 31*(1), 66–81.

Shah, H., Warwick, K., Vallverdú, J., & Wu, D. (2016). Can machines talk? Comparison of Eliza with modern dialogue systems. *Computers in Human Behavior, 58,* 278–295.

Shortliffe E. H. (1977). Mycin: A knowledge-based computer program applied to infectious diseases. In *Proceedings of the Annual Symposium on Computer Application in Medical Care* (pp. 66–69). Institute of Electrical and Electronics Engineers

Singh, A., Thakur, N., & Sharma, A. (2016). A review of supervised machine learning algorithms. In *2016 3rd international conference on computing for sustainable global development (INDIACom)* (pp. 1310–1315). IEEE.

Soltanpour, S., Boufama, B., & Wu, Q. J. (2017). A survey of local feature methods for 3D face recognition. *Pattern Recognition, 72,* 391–406.

Stutzer, A., & Zehnder, M. (2013). Is camera surveillance an effective measure of counterterrorism? *Defence and Peace Economics, 24*(1), 1–14. https://doi.org/10.1080/10242694.2011.650481

Sutton, R. S., Barto, A. G., & Bach, F. (2018). *Reinforcement learning: An introduction (adaptive computation and machine learning series)* (2nd ed.). MIT Press.

Switzky, L. (2020). ELIZA effects: Pygmalion and the early development of artificial intelligence. *Shaw, 40*(1), 50–68. https://doi.org/10.5325/shaw.40.1.0050

Thorat, S. B., Nayak, S. K., & Dandale, J. P. (2010). Facial recognition technology: An analysis with scope in India. *International Journal Of Computer Science and Information Security, 8*(1), 326.

Thomas, M. J. (2015). Combining Facial Recognition, Automatic License Plate Readers and Closed Circuit Television to Create an Interstate Identification System for Wanted Subjects. Naval Postgraduate School Monterey United States.

Van Brakel, R., & De Hert, P. (2011). Policing, surveillance and law in a pre-crime society: Understanding the consequences of technology based strategies. *Technology Led Policing, 20,* 165–192.

Vestby, A., & Vestby, J. (2021). Machine learning and the police: Asking the right questions. *Policing: A Journal of Policy and Practice, 15*(1), 44–58.

Vito, G. F., Reed, J. C., & Walsh, W. F. (2017). Police executives' and managers' perspectives on Compstat. *Police Practice and Research, 18*(1), 15–25. https://doi.org/10.1080/1561426 3.2016.1205986

Weiss, S., Kulikowski, C., Amarel, S., & Safir, A. (1978). A model-based method for computer-aided medical decision-making. *Artificial Intelligence, 11*(1–2), 145–172. https://doi.org/10.1016/0004-3702(78)90015-2

Willis, J. J., Mastrofski, S. D., & Kochel, T. R. (2010). The co-implementation of Compstat and community policing. *Journal of Criminal Justice, 38*(5), 969–980.

Wood, D. M., Ball, K., Lyon, D., Norris, C., & Raab, C. (2006). A report on the surveillance society. Surveillance Studies Network, UK, 1-98.

Woodward Jr, J. D., Horn, C., Gatune, J., & Thomas, A. (2003). Biometrics: A look at facial recognition. RAND CORP SANTA MONICA CA.

Yen, C., & Hung, T. (2021). Achieving equity with predictive policing algorithms: A social safety net perspective. *Science and Engineering Ethics, 27*(3). https://doi.org/10.1007/s11948-021-00312-x

Chapter 6
The Potential Impacts of the National Security Uses of Big Data Predictive Analytics on Human Rights

1 Introduction

All across the globe, there has been what is referred to as a "mass digitisation of information" (Brayne, 2017: p.977) in which computers and technology are increasingly being tasked with the analysis of large and varied data sets. This is often called Big Data (BD). This relatively novel concept of Big Data Analytics (BDA) has continued to spread across a multitude of fields and is beginning to creep further into the sphere of policing. Against the backdrop of crime analysis and policing, BD refers to the vast amount of crime data available and is what crime trends are based on (Hardyns & Rummens, 2018). More recently, this has given power to the concept of predictive policing, which utilises statistical methods to produce new insights, giving police the potential to predict crime trends and events (Ibid.). Whilst there is literature available for the use of BD in other social domains, there appears to be a gap within which the effects of Predictive Big Data Policing (PBDP) have not been thoroughly researched (van Brakel, 2016). If this is to be the way in which BD is to be used in the future, fuelling the transition of reactive to preventative and predictive policing, then it is of paramount importance that the consequences of this are fully researched. Furthermore, any challenges that come to light must be mitigated, to ensure ethics and the protection of society is at the heart of any changes.

Considering the foregoing discussion, this Chapter aims to investigate the potential impacts of the use of Big Data Predictive Analytics (BDPA) in policing, focusing on how it can threaten the individual liberty of citizens. Following this, ways in which a balance can be found between the use of predictive policing whilst ensuring the preservation of civil liberties will be investigated. Additionally, the chapter will analyse how automated operations carried out by LEAs can result in the heavy surveillance and over policing of minority populations. To address the research aim, the following research objectives have been developed:

© The Author(s), under exclusive license to Springer Nature Switzerland AG 2023
R. Montasari, *Countering Cyberterrorism*, Advances in Information Security
101, https://doi.org/10.1007/978-3-031-21920-7_6

– Provide a critical analysis of how BDPA is used in policing.
– Examine potential implications of BDPA for individual freedom and ways in which these can be sufficiently addressed without compromising on national security.
– Explore the ramifications of automated operations on minority groups.

Likewise, to achieve the stated research objectives, the following research questions will be addressed:

RQ1. What are the potential impacts of BDPA in policing on individual liberty, and what steps can be taken to create a smart balance between conducting predictive policing and preserving civil liberties?

RQ2. What are the impacts of the law enforcement's automated operations on the minority populations such as being entangled in a web of surveillance and punishment?

These will be endeavoured through a comprehensive and extensive review of available literature in an effort to ascertain a nuanced and well-rounded understanding of this topic to answer the research questions by which this chapter is guided. The remainder of this chapter is structured as follows: Section 6.2 provides background information covering important concepts that will aid the understanding of this topic. These will include: what BDPAs are, what automated and predictive policing is and how it works, and the importance of civil liberties and their conservation. Sections 6.3 and 6.4 address the first and second research questions respectively. Section 6.5 offers a set of recommendations concerning amendments to policy and practice. Finally the Chapter is concluded in Sect. 6.6, which will aim to capture the main elements of the chapter highlighting the main points of interest from the research.

2   Background

2.1   Big Data Predictive Analytics

BD can be explained as the evolution of new datasets with extremely large volume that change at an exponential pace. BD are very complex and "exceed the reach of the analytical capabilities of commonly used hardware environments and software tools for data management" (Panneerselvam et al., 2015: p. 3). Essentially, it is sets of data that are too large and intricate that generally used data processing application software are not able to cope with (Ongsulee et al., 2018). As a result of technological advancements in many areas, the sources that produce data are constantly increasing, particularly from electronic communications due to day-to-day human activities. Examples of such production of data include emails, mobile communications, social media, health care records and systems, from companies such as retail, transport, utilities, and from real-time data like sensors or satellites (Panneerselvam et al., 2015).

BD may be categorised as either structured, unstructured or semi-structured. Structured data is characterised by its organised and easily understandable nature meaning it is easily stored. This constitutes the majority of data found in traditional databases (Ibid.). Unstructured data, however, is very complex and does not possess a predetermined data format which makes it increasingly difficult to investigate and analyse. Around 80% of data generated is considered unstructured (Ibid.). Semi-structured data can be seen as a merge between structured and unstructured data, in which some of the contents are organised but not to the extent of the former (Ibid.). Whilst it is disputed as to how many there are, the key and most notable characteristics of BD are often referred to as the five V's (Ishwarappa Anuradha, 2015) as represented in Fig. 6.1. These include Volume, Velocity, Variety, Veracity and Value. Volume refers to the large amount of data, Velocity regards the increasing speed of the production of the data, Variety concerns what forms the data comes in (structured, unstructured or semi-structured), Veracity refers to the quality of the data and whether it is trustworthy and finally, the Value of the data is regarding its usefulness and what the data can be turned into (Ibid.). BD is used and processed by many companies and organisations. The analysis of BD can help to improve operations and provide better services and the general use of the data to make faster and more informed decisions in a business context. This has now been extended to apply to more specific contexts such as the government use of BD for the purpose of crime prevention, which as mentioned previously is key to this chapter (Botelho & Bigelow, 2022).

Predictive Analytics can be used to mean the analysis and use of historical data to identify patterns and make predictions about future outcomes (IBM, 2022). Unlike traditional analytics, predictive analytics is not limited to the amount and type of data that can be processed. Instead, it has the ability to deal with

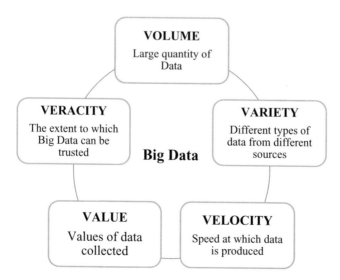

Fig. 6.1 The most notable characteristics of BD, i.e. the 5Vs

unprocessed, large scale and complex types of data (Ogunleye, 2014). Therefore, the use of predictive analytics technology is crucial to the understanding and making sense of BD (Ibid.). The fact that this discipline is able to bring together a variety of knowledge such as quantitative research methods and analysis, risk management and decision-making theory, operation research, computer science and more indicates that it can be applied and used in a multitude of different contexts (Ibid.). Having separately reviewed what BD and Predictive Analytics are, the following definition can now be used to combine the two and to understand what BDPAs are:

> Big data predictive analytics is the use of iterative and methodical techniques that collect, analyze, and interpret high volume, variety, velocity, veracity and value data to reveal trends, relationships and patterns within data to identify problems and opportunities, predict future events, and guide decision making in a wide range of application contexts, including individual, group, and social behaviors and actions (Ohiomah et al., 2017: p.4).

The driving factors for use of such technologies is that it has the potential to improve accountability and effectiveness; in the case of policing, it can enhance the prediction and anticipation of behaviours by aiding law enforcement in the efficient deployment of resources, which can subsequently prevent and obstruct criminal activity (Brayne, 2017). In terms of accountability, the use of BDPAs in policing could arguably have the potential to act as a response to discriminatory practices because of the decreased reliance on discretionary decision making (Ibid.). The reality of this will be investigated further in the chapter.

2.2   The Application of Predictive Policing

The use of BDPAs and analytical techniques by law enforcement to identify accurate targets for police intervention and to prevent crime from occurring is often referred to as predictive policing (Perry et al., 2013). Whilst there is no universal definition of predictive policing, one that encompasses the main elements has been put forward by Meijer and Wessels (2019: p. 1033). According to this definition, predictive policing is.

> the collection and analysis of data about previous crimes for identification and statistical prediction of individuals or geospatial areas with an increased probability of criminal activity to help developing policing intervention and prevention strategies and tactics (ibid).

Thus, the main aim of predictive policing is to contribute to the reduction of crime levels (Hardyns & Rummens, 2018). The notion of intelligence-led policing is not a new concept and has been developing since the 1990s in Europe and the USA. The addition of experiments investigating the geography of crime (Ferguson, 2017) and an increasing interest regarding situational crime prevention theories has led to the development of hotspot analysis and then prospective hotspot analysis. These aimed to use previous crime data to determine areas that may be at risk of crime as a result (Bowers et al., 2004). During the twentieth century a change could be observed from wall maps displaying daily crimes to digital maps of all recorded crimes. The introduction of professional crime analysts to decipher the data meant that suggestions could be made about the deployment of officers and resources (Ferguson, 2017). This developed into the first instances of predictive policing where crime statistics and automated mapping technology such as CompStat ('Computer Statistics') was used in New York by the Police Department in 1995 (Bachner, 2013).

CompStat was initially used for reactive policing in which it relied on the collection and review of previous crime data whereas predictive policing involves the application of computer analysis of such data. Therefore, it can be noted that the novel aspect of predictive policing is the use of Artificial Intelligence (AI) and its application to relevant data (Joh, 2014). The first predictive policing application developed in the UK was known as ProMap. Other types of software have also been utilised such as PredPol ('Predictive Policing'), which has been deployed in the United States (US) too (van Brakel, 2016). These new predictive, data-focused techniques were seen as objective and applicable for other jurisdictions due to its concern of correlations rather than causations (Ferguson, 2017). By virtue of the economic recession faced in 2008 which placed economic restrictions on police departments, the appeal of predictive policing was emphasised and was highlighted as a cost-effective solution to crime. As a result, it gained many investments and attention (Ibid.).

One of the epistemologies of predictive policing employs ML, a sub-branch of AI, which makes use of data and algorithms and learns from it to improve its accuracy and performance (IBM Cloud Education, 2020). This process is influenced by human cognition and is sometimes also referred to as inductive learning for problem solving (Halterlein, 2021). ML algorithms are able to learn from experience by analysing the training data to create likely hypotheses. The training data in the context of predictive policing could be historical crime data fed into the algorithm (Ibid.). By linking input data to the outputs, the algorithm is able to identify the 'best' hypothesis and create a predictive model that can generate these predictions (Moses & Chan, 2014). However, various other types of input data are also collected and used including commercial data and social networks (Selbst, 2017).

Although ML is directed by algorithms, it is important to note that it is not without the interference of humans, their input and assumptions. It is humans who set up the ML algorithms and select the type of ML to use, the datasets that are included and the volume of the data sets, the extent to which the data is processed, the types of hypothesis to include and how validation is sought (Ibid.). Examples of different types of ML types include Regression Analysis, Artificial Neural Networks (ANN), and Bayesian Learning, amongst others (Halterlein, 2021). However, the most widely used ML technique is Decision Trees. In this method, the predictive model that is learned from the training data assumes the form of a Decision Tree (similar to the form of a visual tree structure). This Decision Tree illustrates the established rules that lead to an outcome to be predicted (Ibid.).

There are two main types of predictive policing, the first form is location based (Brayne et al., 2015). This is because the model of predictive policing relies on well-founded premises regarding the spatial distribution of criminal activity and how it tends to occur in specific and confined areas rather than being randomly scattered (Joh, 2014). For example, in an investigation of the spatial distribution of crime in Seattle over a fourteen-year time frame, around 50 percent of crime was found to have taken place within 4.5 percent of the street segments (Weisburd et al., 2004). Thus, it is acknowledged that crime can be circumstantiated by specific environmental factors that create vulnerabilities for victims at certain times (Ferguson, 2012). Appertaining to this connection between crime and place, computer models adopt different approaches towards the prediction of crime (Joh, 2014). The second type of predictive policing can be thought of as predictive identification, in which the crime analysis takes place at an individual or group level in order to predict potential offenders, their identities, criminal behaviour and even likely victims of crime (van Brakel, 2016). These techniques are much less developed but have given rise to applications that aim to predict who is most likely to offend, order a list of suspects, and even suggest a specific rehabilitation program based on an offender's personal characteristics (Miro-Llinares, 2020).

In both types of predictive policing processes there have been four identified stages consisting of collection of data, data analysis, police intervention and the target response. The first stage, collection of data, includes basic crime data (i.e., the location and times of historical crimes) to more intricate environmental data such as seasonality, neighbourhood construction, and even risk factors (e.g., cash machines, empty car parks) (Brayne et al., 2015). The second stage is concerned with data analysis which serves to produce predictions about future crimes. It is at this point that law enforcement should review the type of crime they are targeting and the resources available to determine which predictive method to use (Ibid.). The third stage is regarding police intervention; typically, this consists of the distribution of crime forecasts to commanders who will decide on the deployment of officers based on this (Ibid.). Patrol officers may be given reports to notify where they should be on shift and when they are not responding to service calls. The focus is placed on surveilling the locations and people predicted to be involved in crime (Ibid.). The fourth stage, the target response, exemplifies that the predictive cycle continues to become progressively complex as law enforcement must take into consideration individual responses to police interventions. This is because interventions may deter crime, prevent it from occurring or alternatively lead to the displacement of crimes to a different area (Ibid.).

2.3   Civil Liberties and National Security

It is also necessary to be reminded of the civil liberties and rights that citizens are entitled to, which are specifically relevant to the context of policing. Furthermore, it is vital to discuss why it is paramount that individuals' civil liberties and rights be protected despite potential changes to policing operations. Additionally, prior to engaging with the research questions, it is important briefly to examine the conflict between the protection of civil liberties and national security interests and how law enforcement is becoming more involved in the latter. One of the major challenges faced when adopting an intelligence-led policing model is the certification that citizen's civil liberties are safeguarded and protected (Jackson & Brown, 2007). It has been noted that as science and technology improve, powers afforded to the police to assist them in carrying out their duties have simultaneously increased, as has their potential to invade citizens' personal lives and impair their individual civil liberties (Murdoch & Roche, 2013).

Should predictive policing tools be used in a disproportionate or unjustified manner, there are certain rights that may be at risk and must be protected by all member states that are signatory to the Charter of Fundamental Rights of the European Union (CFREU) (European Union, 2012). These rights include: the right to physical and mental integrity (CFREU, article. 3), the right to liberty and security (CFREU, article. 6), the right to respect for private and family life (CFREU, article. 7), the right to protection of personal data (CFREU, article. 8), the right to equality before the law (CFREU, article. 20) and the right to non-discrimination (CRFEU, article. 21). The likelihood of impairing these risks increases when predictive policing is used to target individuals as suspects as opposed to places where crime might occur (Castets-Renard, 2021). Similarly, in the US, predictive policing has the potential to threaten some of the key fundamental rights featured in the US Constitution. The most prominent amendments associated with the context of this chapter include the Fourth, the Fifth and the Fourteenth Amendment. The Fourth Amendment is intended to protect civilians from any unreasonable search and seizure without a warrant that is based on a probable cause. The Fifth Amendment safeguards the citizen's right to due process, and the Fourteenth Amendment entitles all individuals to equal protection of the law (Ibid.).

These rights and freedoms serve to protect individuals from the power of the state and ensure that the government does not interfere with or challenge the notion of liberty, limiting the circumstances in which a government may act against its citizens (Martin, 2004). It appears that there does not exist any domestic intelligence agency that is explicitly free of foul play which includes a range of actions that not only endanger individual rights but also the operation of democratic governments (Ibid.). This is why now more than before the importance of citizens civil liberties must be recognised and shielded with the prospect of new modes of practice on the horizon. However, it is important to recognise that within the practice of predictive policing and the acquisition of intelligence by law enforcement is the inherent risk to civil liberties (Ibid.). This is owing to the fact that gathering intelligence must be discrete and secretive, making it difficult to hold actions to account and maintain transparency so as to eliminate the potential for abuses of power (Ibid.).

Therefore, the greatest obstacle to the complete protection of civil liberties by law enforcement and intelligence agencies is perhaps the apparent overriding concern of national security (Ibid.). Additionally, law enforcement agencies have continued to play an increasing role in protecting national security, coupled with their standard objectives of countering and disrupting crime (O'Brien, 2009). This means that the organisations typically tasked with national security work (the Special Branches in the United Kingdom (UK), and the Federal Bureau of Investigation

(FBI) in the US) are being joined by mainstream police (Ibid.). As a result, police officers can now be seen to be tasked with a dual role in ascertaining public safety and security along with producing intelligence on possible threats from domestic communities (Ibid.).

3   RQ 1: The Use of AI by Law Enforcement I

This section aims to address the first research question: "What are the potential impacts of BDPA in policing on individual liberty, and what steps can be taken to create a smart balance between conducting predictive policing and preserving civil liberties?" However, prior to engaging with the question, it will be of value to provide a brief overview of the main benefits of using BDPA in policing. Perhaps, the most convincing argument for the use of BDPA in policing is its stated claim to be able to provide information to help with the effective and accurate deployment of resources and officers to specific locations at specific times (Meijer & Wessels, 2019). Predictive policing tools are used to identify high risk areas by using both historical crime data and a wider range of data. For example, complex hot spot identification models and risk terrain analysis can be applied to predict where criminal activity is likely to take place (Ibid). In this geospatial analysis, both criminal data and data collected through data mining are important. Even data that has no immediate or obvious relevance can be used to potentially help to prevent and forecast crime when it is connected and linked to other pieces of data (Andrejevic, 2017).

Furthermore, through spatiotemporal analysis by using the same types of data, estimates can be made about when crime is likely to take place. This is due to the fact that these models are designed to predict when criminal activity in a specific zone is at its peak (Meijer & Wessels, 2019). Approaches such as the near-repeat method, which is based on the idea that future crimes will occur in close proximity in place and time to previous crimes, have been studied along with others (Perry et al., 2013). Evidence of how the analysis of space and time can provide the foundation to the efficient deployment of resources can be found in the work of Camacho-Collados and Liberatore (2015). The authors claim to have been able to develop a tool to assist with the distribution of available patrols across geographical areas. This was evaluated by using the model to predict property crimes occurring in Madrid. It was subsequently demonstrated that the tool was able to accurately predict crimes and also calculate an economical and effective distribution of police officers in the area (Ibid.). It is important to note that although this method appears fruitful, it needs to be applied to other areas and other types of crime to be able to understand its actual value.

Another positive application of predictive policing is the claim that it is able to identify individuals that have the potential to be involved in crime, as either a perpetrator or a victim (Meijer & Wessels, 2019). Through the use of inductive policing, individuals who have the potential to offend in the future can be identified. This is where known characteristics of the criminal population are given percentages to indicate how likely an individual with these characteristics is to offend in the future (Van Brakel & De Hert, 2011). In this way, those individuals that appear to have attributes associated with a higher likelihood of offending can be monitored in attempts to prevent crime. This type of profiling can consist of both demographic characteristics and behavioural patterns (Ibid.). For instance evidence suggests that sex crimes are most likely to occur in places that are frequently visited by the offender (Downs, 2016). However, whilst these technologies have their advantages, full evaluations of their effectiveness in the available literature tend to be inconclusive and ambiguous due to their novel nature and the limitations of their studies (Van Brakel, 2016). This includes small samples and minimal longevity, lack of recognition for other variables and broader crime trends. Therefore, it is vital to conduct proper evaluations of predictive technologies to be able to determine their true effectiveness (Ibid.). Apart from the effectiveness aspect of these technologies, the nature of predictive policing and its reliance on BD collection and processing raises many other questions. These include both privacy-related risks as well as the threats that these technologies could pose to individual liberty (Mantelero, 2018). This is the focal point of the analysis in this section.

3.1 Civil Liberties and National Security

At present, because predictive policing is still being trialled and tested in many police departments, there is still arguably a complete lack of transparency at all levels of predictive policing (Ferguson, 2017). There is currently little information available on how law enforcement is actually employing these technologies and how they serve the general public. Therefore, there is a great deal of uncertainty and scepticism surrounding the concept of predictive policing (Miro-Llinares, 2020). It is often unclear and difficult to establish who or what has provided the input information and who is accountable for deciding on the categories that form the basis of the predictive algorithm (Van Brakel, 2016). Other questions raised surround the types and quantity of data gathered, the context in which the data is acquired, and the specific purpose for data collection (Hardyns & Rummens, 2018).

In situations where the police are dealing with vast quantities of data pertaining to a large number of people and their actions, there is a need for transparency and accountability mechanisms (Joh, 2016). This evident lack of transparency has been highlighted by a coalition of organisations who have voiced their concerns regarding the impact of predictive policing on civil rights (ACLU, 2016). It has been pointed out that a lack of openness obstructs the chance for a well-informed public discourse (Ibid.) and is undemocratic in the sense that it does not allow those who are affected to participate responsibly (Miro-Llinares, 2020). However, it has been recognised that complete transparency is unlikely to be attainable. For instance, software used may be subject to commercial-in-confidence terms, or certain components of the algorithm utilised must not be disclosed (Moses & Chan, 2018). Whilst full transparency cannot be attained in order to hold law enforcement to account, alternatives suited for practice must be sought. This will be discussed in the Recommendation Section of this chapter.

3.2 Chilling Effect, Privacy Rights and Freedom of Speech

Another potential impact of the mass data collection required for predictive policing is the risk of producing a 'chilling effect', which occurs when there is a persistent sense of being observed. This can lead to a feeling of mistrust towards government and other authorities, resulting in an intentional change of behaviour and self-censorship (Schlehahn et al., 2015). This consequentially activates Articles 10 and 11 of the European Convention on Human Rights (ECHR), the right to freedom of expression and the right to freedom of assembly and association (Oswald & Babuta, 2019). Additionally, the integration of data from independent, non-police organisations can increase surveillance across previously institutional confines, inadvertently forcing individuals to avoid those institutions and interacting with them in order to avoid leaving a digital trace (Brayne, 2017).

Brayne (2014) coined the term "system avoidance", which refers to the practise of avoiding institutions such as hospitals, banks, and employment that retain formal records, that increases the likelihood of being watched and apprehended by authorities. Furthermore, the combination of the ever-growing amount of data available with advances in data mining can illicit an urge to obtain as much data, or 'data haystacks' as possible (Schlehahn et al., 2015). As a consequence of 'data haystacking', the effects of violating individual privacy begin to be undervalued and the idea that people may wish to keep some information private is ignored. This is founded on the belief that "if you have done nothing wrong, you have nothing to hide." (Ibid.). Thus, it must not be forgotten that privacy is a vital element of civilian lives and a nuanced and context-specific notion. Therefore, the long-term ramifications of such 'chilling effects' should not be ignored or underestimated (Ibid.).

3.3 The Fourth Amendment and Stop and Search

The use of BDPA in policing can also threaten the Fourth Amendment because the predictions generated might be used to justify stop and searches under its existing parameters (Brayne et al., 2015). The Fourth Amendment protects the "right of the people to be secure in their persons, houses, papers and effects, against unreasonable searches and seizures" and continues to explain that "no warrants shall issue, but upon probable cause" (US Constitution: Amendment IV). Therefore, this protection seeks to protect personal property including homes and cars and the seizure of an individual for a brief investigatory stop against unreasonable searches carried out by law enforcement. One exception to this protection is the 'Terry stop', which states that officers are permitted to carry out a brief investigatory stop and search on an individual if they have a reasonable belief or suspicion that criminal activity may be occurring and that the individual they have stopped is believed to be armed or dangerous (*Terry v. Ohio*, [1968] 1 U.S. 392).

This exception, combined with the development of predictive analytic techniques in policing, makes it easier for police officers to justify reasonable suspicion, resulting in increased stop and searches (Lau, 2020). Ferguson (2018) offers an example to explain the dilemma. If predictive policing technology directs officers to a certain place at a specific time to search for a particular crime and the officers spot something that could be suggestive of that crime, does this amount to reasonable suspicion? However, research into the limits of the Fourth Amendment have concluded that these predictions alone cannot amount to reasonable suspicion. Instead, they have the potential to change the balance of suspicion in the predicted areas (Ferguson, 2012). If there are no defined limits and thresholds in place to limit police discretion when utilising BDPA in policing, it can substantially damage citizens' Fourth Amendment rights, especially in high-crime regions. This could lead to law enforcement being able to conduct suspicion-less stops on innocent citizens (McGehee, 2021).

3.4 Striking a Smart Balance

One of the ways in which a smart balance can be created between the potential impacts of BDPA in policing and the protection of individual liberties could be through the concept of purpose limitation (Schlehahn et al., 2015). Purpose limitation seeks to disprove the widely held belief that law enforcement obtains, stores, and analyses all available information. It means that data collection would be limited to only what is required for analysis and what is needed to produce predictions. By imposing constraints on data collection and processing that are aligned with the predetermined purpose, more types of data would be protected from unauthorised access. This could help to strengthen privacy rights for civilians (Ibid.). However, some (Fantin & Vogiatzoglou, 2020) have argued that, in its current form, purpose limitation does not appear to be effective enough in the context of predictive policing. This is due to the broad mandate that LEAs have for combating crime, the rising capabilities of BDPA technologies that they can utilise, and other components that enable an overlap between the law enforcement and intelligence services, which also broadens the amount of data that police have access to. Although it is not a completely developed solution, specification and purpose compatibility should be built into technology at the design level (Ibid.). This would require the algorithm developers and LEAs to determine the logical data needed to suit the specific purpose of the technology. Such measures would help to improve transparency and reduce the risk of unnecessary data collection and processing by restricting the technology and the user to utilising the system only for its initial intended purpose (Ibid.).

Another potential method to conduct predictive policing while simultaneously protecting civil liberties would be to include provisions for regular audits of data collection, analysis, software used, and how the algorithm manipulates the data (Ferguson, 2017). An audit should consist of an "independent evaluation of conformance of software products and processes to applicable regulations, standard, guidelines, plans, specifications, and procedures" (IEEE, 2008: p. 30). This means that there should also be regulations and standards for best practice in place that must be followed (Ferguson, 2012). In order for audits to be possible, secure and accurate logging of all system actions must be practiced, allowing for evaluations to be made about the effectiveness and appropriateness of such actions (Schlehahn et al., 2015). Audits must be performed by competent data analysts who are familiar with predictive systems and are able to determine whether predictive policing systems are operating within the parameters of the set guidelines and whether they are supporting their stated objectives (Ferguson, 2017). One of the main goals of AI audits is to transform ethical concepts into practical methods for fair AI. Furthermore, there is evidence that audits are capable of detecting and exposing algorithmic harms (Ugwudike, 2022). Additionally, audit results must be stored so that they can be publicised when it is judged appropriate (Ferguson, 2017). In this way, it can provide quality reassurance and boost public confidence through means of transparency and accountability (Ugwudike, 2022).

A further proposal to strike a balance between capitalising from the benefits of predictive policing and ensuring the protection of individual liberties is to utilise Model-Driven Security to implement a policy-based approach towards predictive policing. As a result, this can help to define and enforce necessary data protection regulations (Schlehahn et al., 2015). This requires the human conceptualisation of all applicable data protection concepts including: the purpose, data type and information flow, and codification of them into a human readable, Domain Specific Language (DSL) metamodel (Ibid.). Through the use of the DSL, usable polices for data protection, privacy and security can be composed. Then, as previously stated, these developed policies can use model transformations to be translated into simple machine-enforced rules and settings for the purpose of data protection and security measures (Ibid.). In this way, Model-Driven Security can improve and simplify management of policies allowing for sophisticated access control. It can also promote the debate within society around cementing policies, enabling a strong sense of democracy and transparency and allowing citizens to be a part of the process and to voice their opinions and concerns about the policies that are intended to protect them (Ibid.).

The foregoing discussion presented in this Section reveals that there is no simple remedy for protecting and preserving individual liberties whilst deploying BDPAs in policing to try to forecast and prevent crime. However, there are certain legal and technical mechanisms that can be implemented to help mitigate some of the key challenges associated with the stated issues (Schlehahn et al., 2015). This can result in maximising the promise of predictive technologies while avoiding the negative consequences of compromising critical civil rights and liberties.

4   RQ 2: The Use of AI by Law Enforcement II

This section aims to answer the second research question, "What are the impacts of the law enforcement's automated operations on the minority populations such as being entangled in a web of surveillance and punishment?" It has been argued that the use of BDPA for predictive policing can be a means through which the effects of bias and inequalities in traditional policing can be mitigated. This is because data and algorithms can be programmed to replace inaccurate suspicion of racial and ethnic minorities and human exaggeration of trends, with less biased predictions (Brayne, 2017). However, it has been pointed out that this is not so straightforward, and that struggles between law enforcement, civilians, and information technology companies play a significant part in determining whether BD policing will reduce or increase inequality (Ibid.). There are also other variables affecting the data that can influence the predictions made, and it is crucial to realise that algorithms are only as accurate as the data with which they are working (Barocas & Selbst, 2016). The first is that the training data, itself, used by the algorithm may be biased, resulting in biased predictions. (Yang, 2019). Oftentimes, the data used by algorithms include information that is influenced by social, cultural, and economic factors. (Zavrsnik, 2021). Whilst this may be unintentional, it can be explained as a result of institutional discrimination that already exists in traditional policing. Therefore, if the training data contains examples in which prejudice has played a role, the ML component of the algorithm will ignore this and use it as an example to learn from. This will result in the reproduction of the prejudice and discrimination that was involved in the previous cases (Barocas & Selbst, 2016).

Another reason why the data utilised for policing purposes can provide discriminating and biased predictions is due to the data set and the manner in which it is obtained. The predictions generated are primarily based on data from historical crimes. However, due to their incomplete nature, these data sets are notoriously inaccurate (Ferguson, 2017). Therefore, the training data does not provide an accurate representation of criminal activity and is severely limited by what citizens report and what police officers observe, and what law enforcement subsequently record (Moses & Chan, 2018). Similarly, if there is insufficient data, or if the data is irrelevant, inaccurate, old or of poor quality, the predictions will most likely reflect this (Gstrein et al., 2019). For instance, some crimes, such as murder, burglary, and vehicle theft, are routinely recorded, whereas others, such as sexual assault, domestic violence, and fraud, are notoriously underreported (Ferguson, 2017). As a result of the incomplete data used as the basis for the predictions, it is questionable whether the predictions will be accurate or credible. Furthermore, there could be discrepancies in the training data labelling process. Sometimes data is prelabelled; however, in some cases, this must be done manually by the data miners (Barocas & Selbst, 2016). This process can be arduous, time-consuming and unavoidably subjective, skewing projections since these labels will characterise all future cases that appear to be similar (Ibid.). However, it should be noted that, whilst biases do not always imply discrimination, they are extremely essential (Hung & Yen, 2020).

4.1   Overpolicing of Certain Areas

One impact of the use of place based predictive policing is the over policing of high crime areas. This occurs when there are high levels of reported crime fed into the algorithm which subsequently causes the predictive technology to suggest the same hot spot area to be monitored by law enforcement patrols (Zavrsnik, 2021). Empirical research pertaining to predictive policing technology has discovered that such technologies can be susceptible to runaway feedback loops, in which police are constantly sent back to patrol certain locations irrespective of the area's real crime rate (Ensign et al., 2018; Richardson et al., 2019). Through this runaway feedback loop, there can be unintentional repercussions that disproportionately affect minority individuals and communities (Brayne, 2017). This is because the high crime label is usually given to hyper-segregated, low income, minority areas (Koss, 2015). This bias can be attributed in part to the practise of policing prior to the development of predictive technologies. For instance, there has been much criticism of American law enforcement and its disproportionate enforcement and unequal treatment of specific communities and individuals based on race and other factors (Yang, 2019).

One of the consequences of over policing these low-income, minority communities is that a disproportionate percentage of people of colour are stopped and searched under the Terry exception as discussed previously (Koss, 2015). Furthermore, this has fuelled a culture of mass incarceration, has disparately impacted specific areas with low income, minority citizens (Ibid.), and has increased the surveillance of those that are already considered suspicious by law enforcement (Brayne, 2017). Baradaran (2013) argues the full effects of this process with reference to black communities. As police forces direct more time and resources towards policing black people in urban neighbourhoods, the population of those arrested deviates further from the actual offending population and grows to disproportionately represent black citizens. Furthermore, it is widely accepted that criminal records make it more difficult to re-enter society and access employment or education, resulting in individuals becoming trapped in a cycle of crime. Furthermore, the distribution of more punitive punishments for repeat offenders leads to more black people being incarcerated for longer sentences, and increased supervision in probation decisions, skewing the representation of black people in the criminal justice system. This not only perpetuates the predictive feedback loop but can also contribute to the exaggerated perception held by some members of the public and police that black people commit more crime, creating significant animosity between the police and these communities (Koss, 2015). This can also act to confirm the association between being black and being a criminal, which is extremely harmful (Baradaran, 2013).

4.2 *Focus on Crimes of the Poor*

A further bias identified is the disproportionate targeting of automated operations on those that are on lower incomes and live in poorer areas. This is due to the fact that some types of crime, 'crimes of the poor', are more likely to be prosecuted than others. This shows a clear disregard for the central principle of legality which encompasses the requirement that all crimes are to be ex officio, rather than on the basis of opportunity (Zavrsnik, 2021). As law enforcement focus on types of high impact crimes that are generally more likely to be committed by the poor, such as assault and robbery, there is less surveillance of those committing crimes that are typically perpetrated by the rich or by corporations, such as white collar crimes (van Brakel, 2016). As a result, those that commit the former types of crime are more likely to receive criminal records and be put under further surveillance. The subsequent crime data that is available will place more attention on the crimes of the poor, causing predictive policing operation to follow suit and further entrench the bias towards high impact crimes (Ibid.). Other scholars agree that data fed into predictive policing algorithms may fail to incorporate pertinent information due to police practises and policies that fail to notice certain crimes and criminals (Richardson et al., 2019).

Despite the fact that they are more likely to occur, white collar crimes are underinvestigated and overlooked in crime reporting, with a higher emphasis on property, violent, street, and quality of life offences (Ibid.). Furthermore, analysed reports found on an unsecure server containing crime forecasts by PredPol from all across the US revealed consistent patterns indicating that predictive police patrols were more likely to be placed in locations where low-income families qualified for the federal free and reduced lunch programme (Sankin et al., 2021). On multiple occasions, the software suggested daily patrols in and around public and subsidised housing neighbourhoods, targeting the poorest of the poor. This pattern was observed in every jurisdiction assessed, including Michigan, Alabama, Los Angeles, Boston, and Illinois (Ibid.). On the other hand, crimes of the powerful, which are more likely to be perpetrated by middle and upper class citizens, are more likely to go unnoticed by the criminal justice system. To deflect them, they "often become 're-labeled' as 'political scandals' or merely occupational 'risk'" (Zavrsnik, 2021: p. 636). As also noted by Baradaran (2013), this overrepresentation of the poor can lead them to the same destiny faced by black people, further marginalising individuals with less financial capital whist preserving the rich and widening the gap between the rich and the poor.

4.3 *System Avoidance*

Aside from being entangled in a web of punishment and surveillance as explored thus far, another impact that can be experienced by minorities is the social stratification of individuals who choose system avoidance as a mechanism to lessen the possibility of coming into contact with the criminal justice system (Brayne, 2014). Due to the integration of external, non-police data into the law enforcement sphere, police can increase their surveillance across other institutions. This can result in a 'chilling effect' (Brayne, 2017), as detailed in the previous section. Therefore, those who have had any type of interaction with the criminal justice system, "granting them an illegal or semilegal status", might have a subsequent deep rooted fear of becoming involved with the criminal system again. Hence, as a result of the increasing levels of surveillance, they become suspicious of all those around them and begin either to act with a sense of unpredictability or completely to avoid any kind of institution, location or relationship they previously relied upon (Goffman, 2009: p340). As previously noted, system avoidance refers to the practice of avoiding institutions such as healthcare, employment, or banks, among others, in order to avoid any formal records that make an individual traceable or able to be captured by surveillance, and therefore more readily apprehensible by law enforcement (Brayne, 2014).

Although this might appear to be a favourable approach, the effect of system avoidance can result in a lack of employment and healthcare, among other necessities, implying that this minority group possess an extremely low capital in all aspects. (Lerman, 2013). System avoidance can thus be viewed as a means by which these individuals become even more marginalised from society as a result of being excluded from BD sets. Further implications of this can pose challenges in economic opportunity, democratic opportunity, and social mobility (Ibid.). Specific negative repercussions of system avoidance include a lack of access to healthcare, which can have destructive consequences since it is associated with the early detection of illnesses and health conditions and lower rates of mortality. Individuals who are unable to open a bank account may become vulnerable to predatory loan services and lose their ability to generate income (Brayne, 2014). Furthermore, having connections to educational and employment institutions is critical in shaping outcomes during the transition from childhood to adulthood. It appears that individuals without connections are at a severe disadvantage. Additionally, the importance of having connections to education and employment institutions are important in shaping outcomes through the transition from childhood to adulthood, and can leave those with no connections at a severe disadvantage. Thus, predictive policing can potentially "create a new kind of voicelessness, where certain groups' preferences and behaviors receive little or no consideration when powerful actors decide how to distribute goods and services and how to reform public and private institutions" (Lerman, 2013: p. 59).

5   Recommendations

As previously mentioned, there are benefits to using BDPA in policing to make predictions and seek to prevent crime, but there are also many concerns (Gstrein et al., 2019). The issues and complexities that predictive policing introduce into law enforcement can arguably be viewed as an advantage as it allows for an opportunity to reflect and evaluate policing processes and functions (Ibid.). If the purpose of using predictive policing remains to benefit civilians and do good for society as a whole, then predictive policing has the potential to improve the work of LEAs and to be a valuable asset (Ibid.). However, this is not on the horizon just yet as there is still a significant amount of research and development to be made. Therefore, the purpose of this section is to offer a number of recommendations for reaping the benefits of predictive technologies whist simultaneously ensuring the protection of minority communities and individual liberties that every human being is entitled to.

Arguably one of the most important aspects that needs to be addressed is the lack of transparency of law enforcement use of BDPA in policing. Whilst it is understood that complete transparency is not attainable due to the nature of the data involved, there are many ways through which this can be addressed. There should be easy to understand reports produced by academics, think tanks, and oversight bodies in order to enable citizens understand how they are being policed. This should include a method of mapping the technologies that are being used to develop a complete picture of Europe. (Williams & Kind, 2019). If this discipline is kept under a cover of secrecy, it can further alienate the public from the police and exacerbate relations between the public and the police. This is owing to the fact that policing is not a technological enterprise but a democratic institution with the aim of protecting the public (Joh, 2016). Furthermore, a holistic and transparent approach to community policing is critical to really understanding the interests at stake, which will result in a higher possibility of averting individuals who might become involved in crime (Miro-Llinares, 2020). In order to ensure the necessary level of transparency, predictive policing methods and tools must be clearly identified as either internally developed or external commercial solutions (Egbert & Leese, 2021). Additionally, there should be greater transparency concerning how and when personal data is to be exchanged between jurisdictions, particularly when institutions within the criminal justice system gain access to data from other external institutions (Brayne, 2014).

Another recommendation aimed at improving accountability and transparency in predictive policing and ensuring the fair and responsible use of predictive technology could be the establishment of a neutral and independent third-party oversight, as well as a set of mandatory uniform standards to be followed (Koss, 2015). A longer-term recommendation would be to incorporate these professional standards into primary legislation, clearly setting out how the police intend to use algorithms while also outlining the revised role and function of law enforcement to ensure the legitimacy of their powers in public protection and preventative functions (Oswald & Babuta, 2019).

Another recommendation is to ensure that the data fed into the algorithm is reliable considering the fact that data is critical in developing high-quality and accurate crime predictions (Hardyns & Rummens, 2018). Furthermore, it can be useful to carry out evaluations on the data collection process and the overall data quality within a law enforcement unit to ensure that the use of predictive policing is optimised (Ibid.). Similarly, evaluations can be carried out to test how variations in data quality will impact the performance of predictions produced by the technology

(Ibid.). Data origins and authentication can also be considered in that there should be measures in place to track where data originates, how it is processed and labelled, and whether the labelling was carried out automatically or manually (Schlehahn et al., 2015). This means that self-checking data can be encouraged, and questionable data can be easily identified and removed if necessary to minimise the skew of predictions (Ibid.). An additional suggestion concerns the power between predictions and human interference in that in no circumstance should there be full automation of analytical processes. Instead, human analysts should always remain in control over system functions and be aware of what is occurring (Egbert & Leese, 2021). This also includes the premise that no information should be withheld from analysts by the algorithmic system and that the system should in no circumstance perform any functions without user approval (Ibid.). In the event that automated bias may occur, algorithmic recommendations should be reviewed and engaged, and the right to override the algorithm should always be available and supported by the law enforcement institute (Ibid.). Furthermore, it is of paramount importance that the capabilities and limitations of predictive policing be fully assessed and understood. Hence, it is important to note that automated operations should be utilised in conjunction with policing and should not be used to replace any long-term programmes aimed at addressing the root causes of crime (Ibid.).

An overreliance on data to make decisions concerning complex social, political and economic issues can pose serious threats to fairness and justice (Richardson et al., 2019). In particular, if biased data is used to inform delicate concepts such as public safety, the risks can be detrimental to individuals and have long-term consequences that can ripple through the criminal justice system and wider society (Ibid.). In order to implement the aforementioned recommendations, it is critical that scientific methodological research be conducted to gain a clear understanding of the potential of law enforcement use of predictive policing (Hardyns & Rummens, 2018). This research must also be able to ascertain whether predictive policing has any advantages over current policing methods. Similarly, such research must be able to offer transparent means by which the implementation of traditional policing methods and new predictive ones can be compared (Ibid.). In addition, the reliability of predictive technology needs to be tested to determine if the tool can be used across different jurisdictions with different police units (Ibid.).

There are other ways in which BD can be utilised to prevent crime and provide further assistance to disadvantaged individuals in society. For instance, BD applications could be concurrently deployed by police, social workers, neighbourhood workers, schools, civil society organisations and city planners to determine which sections of a city require more attention and address specific problems (Van Brakel, 2016). Data drawn upon could encompass, among others, average incomes, crime rates, unemployment levels and school quality measures. Furthermore, safeguards must be implemented to protect those practicing system avoidance in fear of coming into contact with law enforcement. Such safeguards could help minimise the further marginalisation of these individuals, enabling them to feel protected enough to interact with institutions and use essential services without subjecting themselves to danger or vulnerability to apprehension by law enforcement (Brayne, 2014). In the same vein, the adoption of data-sharing firewalls could allow parents to take their child to the hospital for medical treatment without exposing themselves to possible contact with law enforcement (Ibid.).

6 Conclusion

This chapter started by providing a brief overview of predictive policing and the manner in which LEAs were beginning to advance and deploy BDPA to forecast and prevent crime. It was discussed that the use of BDPA was the resultant of the ever-growing availability of data that could be utilised. Next, the chapter explored in more detail how algorithms and ML tools were used to analyse and process vast data sets. The chapter proceeded to examine the relevant civil liberties that were threatened by the blurring of lines due to new predictive policing techniques. The chapter continued to address the first research question and delve deeper into how predictive policing can infringe on individual liberty. It was identified that such breaches occurred through a lack of transparency preventing a well-informed public debate about policing operations. In an attempt to provide a comprehensive answer to the question, the chapter also explored how predictive technologies could lead to chilling effects and place limits on the right to freedom of expression, and how it could pose threats to the Fourth Amendment. The answer also encompassed an investigation into the ways in which it might be possible to strike a balance between police use of BDPA in their operations and the adequate protection of individual liberties. To this end, the concept of purpose limitation was explored, the introduction of standardised and independent audits was suggested and the adoption of a policy-based approach towards predictive policing was discussed.

Subsequently, the chapter addressed the second research question by investigating in detail the ways in which automated operations could further marginalise and disproportionately target minority groups, such as ethnic minorities, those that have previously been in contact with the criminal justice system, and the poorer communities. These effects were considered to be the result of over policing of specific areas and communities, intentional practice of system avoidance and the focus of police operations on crimes of the poor. System avoidance, and a focus of police operations on poor crime. Finally, several recommendations were offered in order to influence further research in relation to the practice of predictive policing. These, amongst others, consisted of the introduction of measures to increase transparency, the introduction of audits and uniform standards for practice, the importance of reliable data collection, and alternative ways in which BD could be utilised within the community to prevent crime. Overall, this chapter placed an emphasis on uncovering the ways in which BDPA could restrict freedoms and create disparities, as well as promoting awareness of the limitations and challenges associated with BDPA. This was to assist with improving the use of BDPA and maximising its potential for its future use in within the criminal justice sphere.

References

ACLU. (2016). Predictive Policing Today: A Shared Statement Of Civil Rights Concerns. *American Civil Liberties Union.*

Andrejevic, M. (2017). To preempt a thief. *International Journal of Communication, 11*, 879–896. https://ijoc.org/index.php/ijoc/article/viewFile/6308/1936

Bachner, J. (2013). Predictive policing: Preventing crime with data and analytics. IBM Center for The Business of Government. https://www.businessofgovernment.org/sites/default/files/Management%20Predictive%20Policing.pdf

Baradaran, S. (2013). Race, prediction, and discretion. *George Washington Law Review, 81*(1), 157–222. https://heinonline.org/HOL/P?h=hein.journals/gwlr81&i=171

Barocas, S., & Selbst, A. D. (2016). Big data's disparate impact. *California Law Review, 104*(3), 671–732. https://doi.org/10.15779/Z38BG31

Botelho, B., & Bigelow, S. J. (2022, January 1). *Big Data.* SearchDataManagement. https://www.techtarget.com/searchdatamanagement/definition/big-data#:~:text=Big%20data%20comes%20from%20myriad,mobile%20apps%20and%20social%20networks

Bowers, K. J., Johnson, S. D., & Pease, K. (2004). Prospective hot-spotting. *British Journal of Criminology, 44*, 641–658. https://doi.org/10.1093/bjc/azh036

Brayne, S. (2014). Surveillance and system avoidance: Criminal justice contact and institutional attachment. *American Sociological Review, 79*(3), 367–391. https://doi.org/10.1177/0003122414530398

Brayne, S. (2017). Big data surveillance: The case of policing. *American Sociological Review, 82*(5), 977–1008. https://doi.org/10.1177/0003122417725865

Brayne, S., Rosenblat, A., & Boyd, D. (2015). Predictive policing. Data Civil Rights. http://www.datacivilrights.org/pubs/2015-1027/Predictive_Policing.pdf

Camacho-Collados, M., & Liberatore, F. (2015). A decision support system for predictive police patrolling. *Decision Support Systems, 75*, 25–37. https://doi.org/10.1016/j.dss.2015.04.012

Castets-Renard, C. (2021). Human rights and algorithmic impact assessment for predictive policing. In *Constitutional challenges in the algorithmic society* (pp. 93–110). Cambridge University Press. https://doi.org/10.1017/9781108914857.007

Downs, J. A. (2016). Mapping sex offender activity spaces relative to crime using time-geographic methods. *Annals of GIS, 22*(2), 141–150. https://doi.org/10.1080/19475683.2016.1147495

Egbert, S., & Leese, M. (2021). *Criminal futures: Predictive policing and everyday police work.* Routledge. https://library.oapen.org/bitstream/handle/20.500.12657/42895/9781000281729.pdf?sequence=1

Ensign, D., Friedler, S. A., Neville, S., Scheidegger, C., & Venkatasubramanian, S. (2018). Runaway feedback loops in predictive policing. In *Conference on fairness, accountability and transparency* (pp. 160–171). PMLR.

European Union. (2012). Charter of fundamental rights of the European Union. *Official Journal of the European Union.* https://eur-lex.europa.eu/eli/treaty/char_2012/oj

Fantin, S., & Vogiatzoglou, P. (2020). Purpose limitation by design as a counter to function creep and system insecurity in police artificial intelligence. United Nations Interregional Crime and Justice Research Institute (UNICRI), UNICRI Special Collection on AI. https://papers.ssrn.com/sol3/papers.cfm?abstract_id=3679850

Ferguson, A. G. (2012). Predictive policing and reasonable suspicion. *Emory Law Journal, 62*(2), 259–325. https://scholarlycommons.law.emory.edu/elj/vol62/iss2/1

Ferguson, A. G. (2017). Policing predictive policing. *Washington University Law Review, 94*(5), 1109–1189. https://openscholarship.wustl.edu/law_lawreview/vol94/iss5/5

Ferguson, A. G. (2018). The legal risks of big data policing. *Criminal Justice, 33*(2), 4–7. https://www.courts.wa.gov/subsite/mjc/docs/2019/Legal%20Risks%20of%20Big%20Data%20Policing.pdf

Goffman, A. (2009). On the run: Wanted men in a Philadelphia ghetto. *American Sociological Review, 74*(3), 339–357. https://doi.org/10.1177/000312240907400301

Gstrein, O. J., Bunnik, A., & Zwitter, A. (2019). Ethical, legal and social challenges of predictive policing. *Catolica Law Review, 3*(3), 77–98. https://ssrn.com/abstract=3447158

Halterlein, J. (2021). Epistemologies of predictive policing: Mathematical social science, social physics and machine learning. *Big Data and Society, 8*(1), 1–13. https://doi.org/10.1177/20539517211003118

Hardyns, W., & Rummens, A. (2018). Predictive policing as a new tool for law enforcement? Recent developments and challenges. *European Journal on Criminal Policy and Research, 24*, 201–218. https://doi.org/10.1007/s10610-017-9361-2

Hung, T., & Yen, C. (2020). On the person-based predictive policing of AI. *Ethics and Information Technology, 23*, 165–176. https://doi.org/10.1007/s10676-020-09539-x

IBM. (2022, May 12). *Predictive analytics.* https://www.ibm.com/analytics/predictive-analytics

IBM Cloud Education. (2020, July 15). Machine Learning. https://www.ibm.com/cloud/learn/machine-learning

IEEE. (2008). IEEE standard for software reviews and audits. *IEEE Std, 1028-2008*, 1–53. https://doi.org/10.1109/IEEESTD.2008.4601584

Ishwarappa Anuradha, J. (2015). A brief introduction on big data 5Vs characteristics and Hadoop technology. *Procedia Computer Science, 48*, 319–324. https://doi.org/10.1016/j.procs.2015.04.188

Jackson, A. L., & Brown, M. (2007). Ensuring efficiency, interagency cooperation, and the protection of civil liberties: Shifting from a tradition al model of policing to an intelligence-led policing (ILP) paradigm. *Criminal Justice Studies, 20*(2), 111–129. https://doi.org/10.1080/14786010701396855

Joh, E. E. (2014). Policing by numbers: Big data and the fourth amendment. *Washington Law Review, 89*(1), 35–68. https://heinonline.org/HOL/P?h=hein.journals/washlr89&i=42

Joh, E. E. (2016). The new surveillance discretion: Automated suspicion, big data, and policing. *Harvard Law and Policy Review, 10*(1), 15–42. https://harvardlpr.com/wp-content/uploads/sites/20/2016/02/10.1_3_Joh.pdf

Koss, K. K. (2015). Leveraging predictive policing algorithms to restore fourth amendment protections in high-crime areas in a post-Wardlow world. *Chicago-Kent Law Review, 90*(1), 301–334. https://scholarship.kentlaw.iit.edu/cgi/viewcontent.cgi?article=4066&context=cklawreview

Lau, T. (2020). Predictive policing explained. Brennan Center for Justice. https://www.brennancenter.org/our-work/research-reports/predictive-policing-explained

Lerman, J. (2013). Big data and its exclusions. *Stanford Law Review Online, 66*, 55–64. https://doi.org/10.2139/ssrn.2293765

Mantelero, A. (2018). AI and big data: A blueprint for a human rights, social and ethical impact assessment. *Computer Law and Security Review, 34*(4), 754–772. https://doi.org/10.1016/j.clsr.2018.05.017

Martin, K. (2004). Domestic intelligence and civil liberties. *The SAIS Review of International Affairs, 24*(1), 7–21. https://doi.org/10.1353/sais.2004.0016

McGehee, M. (2021). Predictive policing technology: Fourth amendment and public policy concerns. University of Cincinnati Law Review Blog, https://uclawreview.org/2021/02/17/predictive-policing-technology-fourth-amendment-and-public-policy-concerns/#_ftn27

Meijer, A., & Wessels, M. (2019). Predictive policing: Review of benefits and drawbacks. *International Journal of Public Administration, 42*(12), 1031–1039. https://doi.org/10.1080/01900692.2019.1575664

Miro-Llinares, F. (2020). Predictive policing: Utopia or dystopia? On attitudes towards the use of big data algorithms for law enforcement. https://doi.org/10.31235/osf.io/a7juk.

Moses, L. B., & Chan, J. (2014). Using big data for legal and law enforcement decisions: Testing the new tools. *University of New South Wales Law Journal, 37*(2), 634–678. https://doi.org/10.3316/informit.613165001799453

Moses, L. B., & Chan, J. (2018). Algorithmic prediction in policing: Assumptions, evaluation, and accountability. *Policing and Society, 28*(7), 806–822. https://doi.org/10.1080/10439463.2016.1253695

Murdoch, J., & Roche, R. (2013). The European convention on human rights and policing. Council of Europe. https://www.echr.coe.int/documents/handbook_european_convention_police_eng.pdf

O'Brien, K. A. (2009). Managing national security and law enforcement intelligence in a globalised world. *Review of International Studies, 35*(4), 903–915. https://doi.org/10.1017/S0260210509990349

Ogunleye, J. (2014). The concepts of predictive analytics. *International Journal of Knowledge, Innovation and Entrepreneurship, 2*(2), 82–90. http://www.ijkie.org/IJKIE_December2014_JAMES%20OGUNLEYE.pdf

Ohiomah, A., Andreev, P., & Benyoucef, M. (2017). A review of big data predictive analytics in information systems research. *Journal of Information Systems Applied Research, 10*, 1–23. https://proc.conisar.org/2017/pdf/4512.pdf

Ongsulee, P., Chotchaung, V., Bamrungsi, E., & Rodcheewit, T. (2018). Big data, predictive analytics and machine learning. In *2018 16ᵗʰ international conference on ICT and knowledge engineering* (pp. 1–6). https://doi.org/10.1109/ICTKE.2018.8612393

Oswald, M., & Babuta, A. (2019). Machine learning predictive algorithms and the policing of future crimes: Governance and oversight. In J. L. M. McDaniel & K. Pease (Eds.), *Policing and artificial intelligence (pp. 1–19)*. Routledge. https://ssrn.com/abstract=3479081

Panneerselvam, J., Liu, L., & Hill, R. (2015). An introduction to big data. In B. Akhgar, G. B. Saathoff, H. R. Arabnia, R. Hill, A. Staniforth, & S. Bayerl (Eds.), *Application of big data for National Security: A Practitioner's guide to emerging technologies* (pp. 3–13). Butterworth-Heinemann. https://doi.org/10.1016/B978-0-12-801967-2.00001-X

Perry, W. L., McInnis, B., Price, C. C., Smith, S. C., & Hollywood, J. S. (2013). *Predictive policing: The role of crime forecasting in law enforcement operations*. RAND Corporation. https://www.rand.org/content/dam/rand/pubs/research_reports/RR200/RR233/RAND_RR233.pdf

Richardson, R., Schultz, J. M., & Crawford, K. (2019). Dirty data, bad predictions: How civil rights violations impact police data, predictive policing systems, and justice. *New York University Law Review Online, 94*, 15–55. https://heinonline.org/HOL/P?h=hein.journals/nyulro94&i=15

Sankin, A., Mehrotra, D., Mattu, S., Cameron, D., Gilbertson, A., Lempres, D., & Lash, J. (2021). *Crime prediction software promised to be free of biases*. New Data Shows It Perpetuates Them. https://gizmodo.com/crime-prediction-software-promised-to-be-free-of-biases-1848138977

Schlehahn, E., Aichroth, P., Mann, S., Schreiner, R., Lang, U., Shepherd, I. D. H., & Wong, W. B. L. (2015). Benefits and pitfalls of predictive policing. *European Intelligence and Security Informatics Conference*. https://doi.org/10.1109/EISIC.2015.29

Selbst, A. D. (2017). Disparate impact in big data policing. *Georgia Law Review, 52*(1), 109–196. https://heinonline.org/HOL/P?h=hein.journals/geolr52&i=125

Ugwudike, P. (2022). AI audits for assessing design logics and building ethical systems: The case of predictive policing algorithms. *AI Ethics, 2*, 199–208. https://doi.org/10.1007/s43681-021-00117-5

Van Brakel, R. (2016). Pre-Emptive big data surveillance and its (dis)empowering consequences: The case of predictive policing. In B. van der Sloot et al. (Eds.), *Exploring the boundaries of big data* (pp. 117–141). Amsterdam University Press. https://doi.org/10.2139/ssrn.2772469

Van Brakel, R., & De Hert, P. (2011). Policing surveillance and law in a pre-crime society: Understanding the consequences of technology based strategies. *Journal of Police Studies, 20*, 163–192. https://www.researchgate.net/publication/233831922_Policing_surveillance_and_law_in_a_pre-crime_society_Understanding_the_consequences_of_technology_based_strategies

Weisburd, D., Bushway, S., Lum, C., & Yang, S. (2004). Trajectories of crime at places: A longitudinal study of street segments in the city of Seattle. *Criminology, 42*(2), 283–322. https://heinonline.org/HOL/P?h=hein.journals/crim42&i=295

Williams, P., & Kind, E. (2019). *Data-driven policing: The hardwiring of discriminatory policing practices across Europe*. European Network Against Racism. https://e-space.mmu.ac.uk/624446/1/data-driven-profiling-web-final.pdf

Yang, F. (2019). Predictive policing. *Oxford Research Encyclopedia of Criminology.* https://doi. org/10.1093/acrefore/9780190264079.013.508

Zavrsnik, A. (2021). Algorithmic justice: Algorithms and big data in criminal justice settings. *European Journal of Criminology, 18*(5), 623–642. https://doi.org/10.1177/1477370819876762

Chapter 7
National Artificial Intelligence Strategies: A Comparison of the UK, EU and US Approaches with those Adopted by State Adversaries

1 Introduction

AI is central to the debate over technological rivalry and breakthroughs, particularly in relation to international competitiveness. Many in the AI community have reason to suggest that an AI revolution is already among us (Horowitz, 2018), and that this could possibly bring about far-reaching implications. There is an abundance of literature focusing on AI and its place in the modern world. However, there appears to be less academic work comparing and critically analysing the reports and systems put in place by community leaders. This chapter attempts to help fill the gap by cross-examining the first proper AI strategies put forward by the United States (US), United Kingdom (UK) and European Union (EU), and comparing them with those set forth by the likes of other international competitors such as China and Russia.

As is the case with many new technological advancements, there is a lack of concise definitions for AI terminology. Hence, understanding precisely what these terms mean is critical for assessing how AI might impact the international security environment and the future of international competition. By investigating and assessing a variety of national AI policies, one may begin to understand why, internationally, governments have started integrating AI and the associated technologies into every aspect of society. It is through such an assessment that one could also start to understand the risks that may subsequently arise as a result. The increased usage of AI presents a plethora of legal, ethical, economic and societal challenges. In view of this, many countries have decided to release preliminary reports detailing their preparation for a future led by AI technologies, beginning with Canada in 2017. These reports have tended to focus on the challenges presented by AI, both present and predicted future challenges. Each report proposes a plan not only to deal with the problems but also to decrease the chances of significant economic impact. Each strategy has taken a distinct approach to the national development of AI. Furthermore, each has its own set of unique challenges to overcome owing to

© The Author(s), under exclusive license to Springer Nature Switzerland AG 2023
R. Montasari, *Countering Cyberterrorism*, Advances in Information Security 101, https://doi.org/10.1007/978-3-031-21920-7_7

the diverse array of socio-political foundations upon which the future of AI must be built. Often, governments are continuing to build upon their initial strategy, releasing reports and research papers that supplement their initial proposals.

With regards to defining AI, The Engineering and Physical Science Research Council states, "Artificial Intelligence technologies aim to reproduce or surpass abilities (in computational systems) that would require 'intelligence' if humans were to perform them." Thus, this chapter shall refer to AI as such. Truly understanding what AI is in relation to how it is used and implemented on a global scale is critical to determining how it will likely effect the international security environment and the future of international competitiveness. AI was first recognised in the 1950s, with American computer scientist John McCarthy coining the term "Artificial Intelligence" at the Dartmouth Conference in 1956 (Smith et al., 2006). Enthusiasm for AI began to skyrocket, but by the 1970s, government support for such technologies began to waver, resulting in the inevitable 'AI winter' of the 1980s, when enthusiasm for the subject began to fall (Smith et al., 2006).

The definitions of AI and its surrounding concepts are constantly evolving due to the ever-changing classification of the term 'intelligence' – what determined a machine to be 'intelligent' 60 years ago may not hold such weight nowadays. This 'AI Effect' is considered to be a significant contributor to the decline of AI research in the US – the pioneer of early AI research - in the 1980s. Throughout this time, most firms in the US benefitted from expert systems either as a user or as a researcher (Toosi et al., 2021). As a consequence of applying expert systems to real-world issues, a broad variety of representations and reasoning tools have been developed. In Europe and Japan, the Prolog programming language became more popular, whilst the Planner programming language family grew in prominence in the US. By spending more than $1.3 billion on intelligent systems within the 1980s, Japan intended to keep up with the US on the development of new forms of 'intelligent' technology.

AI research was revived in 1982 when the U.S. government established the Microelectronics and Computer Technology Corporation, and thus began funding chip design, hardware development, and software research. Funds for Machine Learning (ML) capabilities that had previously been reduced due to a lack of interest were reassigned as a result of a surge in interest in AI technology throughout the developed world. During the 1980s, AI went through a phase of so-called "summer", in which vast amounts of funding was allocated towards the development and progression of AI, and ultimately a wide range of businesses arose, from expert systems developers to domain-specific hardware, computer vision, and robotic systems (Toosi et al., 2021). Investment and interest in AI boomed in the first decades of the twenty-first century when ML was successfully applied to many problems in academia and industry due to new methods, the application of powerful computer hardware, and the collection of immense data sets (Hall & Pesenti, 2017). Increased public interest and increased efficiency when incorporated into workplace settings has resulted in AI, robotics, and ML being integrated into almost all sectors of society. This means that countries must now decide what regulations they wish to impose both on external and internal sources of AI as well as on the related software.

In view of the foregoing discussions, the aim of this chapter is threefold. First, the chapter seeks to analyse and critique the national AI strategies proposed by the US, UK and EU in order to identify their strengths, shortcomings and gaps. Second, it intends to compare the aforementioned states' AI approaches with those adopted by state adversaries, namely China and Russia. Third, following the analyses, the chapter intends to propose a set of recommendations that could be implemented by the governments to ensure that they leverage the beneficial elements of AI, whilst mitigating its potential risks to their national security. To this end, the remainder of the chapter is structured as follows. Section 7.2 discusses the main factors and problems encountered in a world where the use of AI is rapidly increasing, as well as the methodologies employed to conduct research in this chapter. Section 7.3 examines the strategies put forward by the UK, EU, and US. Section 7.4 analyses AI approaches adopted by state adversaries, namely China and Russia, and compares them with the ideas put forward in the previous Section. Section 7.5 examines the strategies in greater depth, focusing on their shortcomings in relation to one another and making a number of recommendations. Finally, the chapter is concluded in Sect. 5.

2 AI Strategies of the UK, EU and US

2.1 The UK AI Strategy

The UK's National AI strategy prioritises innovation in its approach to AI. The strategy begins by claiming that the United Kingdom is a "global AI superpower". Although the UK has tremendous potential in the AI sector, it can also be argued that they are on the verge of falling behind if their strategy does not take immediate shape and does not deliver on all of its promises in the coming years. The UK has a credible lead over other top countries in the field, such as Canada and South Korea, but it falls short of China and the US, which are measured above the rest of the competition (Calhoun, 2021). Brexit has allowed the UK to take a much more US-centric approach to its framework, focusing on the economic outcomes of its strategies. However, this has raised questions as to whether this is a step in the right direction and whether following in the footsteps of the US is a sensible approach for data protection rights in the UK. The UK is an appealing destination for AI investment, having benefited from £2.3 billion in Government investment since 2014 (Stephens, 2021). However, the foundations laid out by the Government and related organisations must be built upon in order for the UK to fully maximise their potential, while also taking into account the ethical and moral implications that the modernisation of AI technologies can bring about.

Three pillars support the UK AI Strategy: investment and planning, supporting the transition to incorporate AI across the whole economy, and ensuring regulatory and governance frameworks are followed in order to promote responsible AI development (Keeling, 2021). The first pillar discusses the notion that AI innovation in

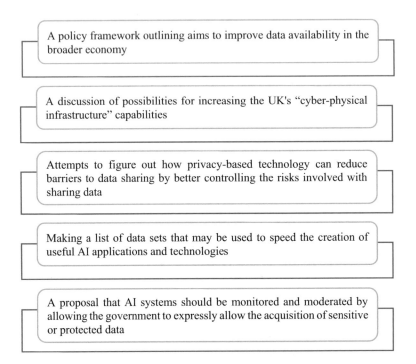

A policy framework outlining aims to improve data availability in the broader economy

A discussion of possibilities for increasing the UK's "cyber-physical infrastructure" capabilities

Attempts to figure out how privacy-based technology can reduce barriers to data sharing by better controlling the risks involved with sharing data

Making a list of data sets that may be used to speed the creation of useful AI applications and technologies

A proposal that AI systems should be monitored and moderated by allowing the government to expressly allow the acquisition of sensitive or protected data

Fig. 7.1 Separate items emphasising access and availability of data

the UK may be improved by strengthening the nation's human capital and enhancing its access to resources. Access and availability of data is emphasised in a number of separate items (Weinberg, 2022) as demonstrated in Fig. 7.1.

The UK is currently ranked third in the world in terms of private venture capital investment into AI companies (Stephens, 2021), and this first pillar aims to ensure that this growth continues by ensuring that this investment is sustained in the long-term. By launching a National AI Research and Innovation Programme, collaboration between UK-based researchers can be enhanced while increasing industry and government use of AI technologies and their capacity to commercialise them. By collaborating with UK Research & Innovation (UKRI) on a report on the availability and capacity of computing power for UK researchers and organisations, the Government are able to take into account the broader, long-term considerations for the commercialisation of AI, especially in business settings, which includes AI's environmental impacts and further hazards. Likewise, by increasing ease of access to AI education, and closing the skills gap through education courses in AI and data sciences and providing access to specialist courses for students from a wide range of backgrounds, the UK can expand the talent pool, and decrease the need for reliance on overseas expertise.

The second pillar is also intended to assist the government in the widespread use of AI throughout the economy. One of the objectives of this pillar is to ensure that the benefits of AI innovation are distributed across all financial aspects of government and the workforce. This pillar is concerned with providing businesses with the ability to commercialise their AI intellectual property (IP) rights. The UK's Intellectual Property Office (IPO) have previously launched a consultation on AI and IP, and the government plans to do so in the near future. This will enable businesses to identify and understand their AI-related intellectual assets, as well as to ensure that their rights in AI technology are protected and eventually enforced. Furthermore, the second pillar of action includes new information surrounding the idea of constructing a new AI Defence Centre in addition to ways to strengthen ties between defence and industry. This will be released soon by the Ministry of Defence's AI plan, which will describe how the UK might gain a technological advantage in defence (Kazim et al., 2021).

A separate national strategy on AI in relation to its place within the health and social care sector is expected to be released later this year. The National Health Service (NHS) AI Lab is developing the plan in collaboration with the UK government, with the goal of adopting safe and ethical AI-driven technologies and incorporating them into the healthcare system - streamlining regulation and assisting the health and care workforce in understanding the benefits of AI and developing the skills to use it. AI-driven management systems will be used to increase efficiency throughout hospitals and care facilities, with predictive AI technologies being employed to gain a better understanding of patients' and communities' health needs (NHS AI Lab, 2022). In addition, the second pillar intends to examine how climate technology has the potential to assist the UK in meeting its net-zero targets. Funding will be allocated to boost local innovation ecosystems in emerging AI countries, allowing for international collaborations to fully address global climate concerns as well as larger global issues such as poverty reduction and disaster response efforts (Department for Business, Energy, & Industrial Strategy, 2021).

According to the second pillar, there should be a greater emphasis on ensuring that AI benefits all sectors and regions (Kazim et al., 2021). At the moment, the leading AI sectors are based solely in London and the South-East of England (Barclays business, 2021). The UK strategy seeks to level out this imbalance by increasing investment, research, and development in areas that are currently less affected by AI technologies, such as agricultural communities. Introducing innovative software into labour-intensive practises can help to optimise production and effectively manage resources. Such examples can be found in Agricultural Technology (AgriTech) firms such as Gardin, a London-headquartered start-up that aims to optimise food production by using ML and remote optical sensors to provide intricate data feedback to help determine plant health (PYMNTS, 2021). According to the United Nation's (UN) estimates, a 150 percent increase in agricultural production is required to meet the increase in global food demands by 2050 (Barclays business, 2021). Additionally, the emergence of new technologies in the ML and robotics sectors can help to underpin some of the most fundamental changes in agriculture in order to kickstart the growth in development that the sector so desperately requires. Furthermore, 51% of UK farmers have invested or plan to invest in emerging AgriTech to increase productivity, providing critical insight into the potential that AI integration may have for modern agricultural businesses and industries (Barclays business, 2021). The third and final pillar establishes a framework for government regulation and oversight. This section addresses the harms and risks that an increase in AI usage poses to all sectors of society, but cautions that cross-sectoral legislation may result in overlaps and inconsistencies in regulating the use of AI (Cooper et al., 2021). This pillar focuses on what steps should be undertaken to ensure that AI systems are not abused and that fairness, transparency, and ethics are maintained during the implementation of new AI strategies. The Office for AI plans to release a white paper on AI regulation later this year, which will outline the potential dangers and shortcomings of AI and recommend ways to mitigate them.

The government has also included a Digital Regulation Strategy Proposal in order to establish a new direction for data protection. UK legislators refer to the scope of coverage and draw on the need for such regulation in the UK now that EU regulators are less involved (Department for Business, Energy, & Industrial Strategy, 2021). The strategy highlights the need to remove regulatory burdens that are creating unnecessary barriers to innovation, implying that the UK is eager to follow a lighter regulatory approach in order to encourage progress. Defence and security are referenced continuously throughout the strategy, in two distinct forms: Utilisation and Governance (Kazim et al., 2021). The defence strategy published by the Ministry of Defence (MoD) can be seen as somewhat of a short term intention. However, this does not imply that the incorporation of AI into national defence is something to be taken lightly, especially since the Government's ability to advance defence strategies while using AI transparently, ethically, and ultimately for the 'public good' is understood to be a long-term consideration in the use of AI.

The National Security and Investment Act (NSI) is a new legal framework that provides British Ministers with broad authority to prevent foreign takeovers of domestic businesses. It went into effect on January 4, 2022, and gives the government the authority to vet and monitor takeovers by anyone, including companies and investors, that may be deemed harmful to the UK and its citizens (Davies, 2022). Although there are already powers in place which allow Members of Parliament (MPs) to intervene in cases foreign-led takeovers could threaten economic stability and national security, the Act introduces oversight to 17 new areas of the economy including AI, robotics, and military technology. This has been seen by observers as the government's attempt to prevent a Chinese takeover of strategically important technology companies (Milligan & Gemmell, 2022). An example of this concerns the recent decision by UK regulators to prevent US software company Nvidia from acquiring the world's largest chip maker 'Arm', a Japanese-owned semi-conductor chip design company based in Cambridge, UK. In 2016, Arm was sold to the Japanese tech giant 'SoftBank', a move that was criticised by those who believe that the UK are losing 'technological sovereignty' (Shead, 2022). Furthermore, in July 2021, the UK government launched an investigation into technology company Nexperia's acquisition of the UK's largest semiconductor factory, Newport Wafer Fab. Nexperia is a Dutch company that is entirely owned by the Chinese firm WingTech. The Competition and Markets Authority (CMA) stated in its report that the combined business entity would have the ability and incentive to harm Nvidia's competitors by limiting access to ARM's IP used by companies that compete with Nvidia in the manufacture of semiconductor chips and related products (Clark, 2022).

2.2   The EU AI Strategy

The majority of EU nations have their own national policies for AI regulation, though they are mostly quite similar, with no significant differences in their structure or long or short term goals (NíFhaoláin et al., 2020). The EU is guided by a European Strategy on AI, which is supported by a High-Level Expert Group on AI (Smuhana, 2018; Andraško et al., 2021). In April 2019, the European Commission published its Ethics Guidelines for Trustworthy AI, followed by Policy and Investment Proposals for Trustworthy Artificial Intelligence in June (EU Commission, 2018). The European Commission further produced a 'Coordinated Plan on Artificial Intelligence', which outlines the commitments and actions that have been discussed and agreed upon by several EU member states, as well as Switzerland and Norway, in order to ultimately build upon the fast-growing AI Talent pool. It should be noted that AI talent across EU regions tends to remain concentrated in certain developing industries and has not yet been dispersed more effectively across the economy (LinkedIn, 2019). This is set to be improved upon by emphasising the importance of public-private partnerships, creating European-only data spaces, and developing strict ethics principles in order to align with the pre-established principles of AI development within EU spaces (Zhang et al., 2021).

Central to the EU's AI strategies is the ability to cultivate and produce "home-grown AI talent and technology". Although this is directly comparable to the strategies produced by other international competitors such as China and the US, the EU are undoubtedly much more focused on the human effects of AI, as well as the ethical, social, and legal risks associated with rapidly integrating AI and robotics technology into business and society (Sheehan, 2022). Arguably, this is insufficient to qualify the EU as a top global leader in AI; therefore, growth within European technological development is needed. To achieve this growth, the EU states must work together as a cohesive EU State to ensure that the vast amount of resources and funding is met in order to keep up with the competitive nature of modern technological development on a global scale. The EU has been slightly more receptive to international AI investment than the likes of the US in order to cement themselves as a modern global competitor. They have an avid interest in collaborating globally to further AI research. For instance, there have been efforts to establish pan-European research networks, such as the Confederation of Laboratories for Artificial Intelligence Research in Europe (CLAIRE) (2018), which has the support of the European Association for Artificial Intelligence, and the AI4EU consortium, backed by the European Commission's Horizon 2020 programme (AI4Europe, n.d .AI4). The white paper on AI, published in 2020, outlined prospects for increased collaboration among member states in order to capitalise on each other's assets while fully utilising the benefits of cross-border and sectoral networks of excellence, which could help Europe maximise its current AI potential (Sheehan, 2022).

Under the new strategy, AI systems that are deemed by the EU as "high-risk" in that they pose "significant risks to the health and safety or fundamental rights of persons" (Del Castillo, 2021) are subject to an assessment to determine their threat. According to the European Commission, regulatory and safety risks are being assessed and determined in order to maintain the concept of AI as a public good. When examining the approaches taken by other leading countries such as the US, ignoring the problems associated with the most high-risk forms of AI is something that is considered an issue, and the EU ensure that they are staying away from this type of attitude within their strategy. Overall, the EU strategy takes an innovative approach to the legality of new AI systems, owing to pre-existing technology legislation such as the General Data Protection Regulation (GDPR), putting the EU measures ahead of China and Russia in terms of the ethical and legal challenges posed by AI. However, due to a significant lack of funding in comparison to their competitors, as well as a need for technological development across all regions to even out the geographical imbalance, the EU strategy will need to be implemented strictly and quickly in order for the EU to be considered a frontrunner in AI development and application.

2.3   The US AI Strategy

The US report on AI, entitled "Preparing for the Future of Artificial Intelligence" (National Science and Technology Council (US), 2016a), was issued on October 12th, 2016 by the White House Office of Science and Technology Policy (OSTP) amid the National Science and Technology Council (NSTC). This was released alongside an accompanying document titled "National Artificial Intelligence Research and Development Strategic Plan" (National Science and Technology Council (US), 2016b), which lays out a strategic plan for Federally-funded research and development in AI. The initial report was developed following a series of workshops, the results of which were produced as the AI report (National Science and Technology Council (US), 2016a). The main purpose of the report is to conclude that government regulations should not impede AI development but that relevant agencies should "remain mindful of the fundamental purposes and goals of regulation to safeguard the public good, while creating space for innovation and growth in AI". The purpose of this strategy was to provide a high-level framework for identifying AI's scientific and technology requirements over the following 5 to 15 years, whilst specifically outlining the Government's role as merely a coordinator, in order to allow the relevant agencies take a more proactive position (Parker, 2018).

The most important authorities in the US with regards to AI promotion comprise the Department of Commerce, the Energy Department, the Department of Defence, the National Science Foundation (NSF), and the Intelligence Advanced Research Projects Activity (IARPA), a research organisation created to support the intelligence services. Leaders from these institutions have been appointed to an AI committee to improve coordination and advise the White House, as announced at the May 2018 AI Summit (Select Committee on AI of the National Science and Technology Council, 2019). In comparison with other nations, the US has been relatively slow to implement a national AI policy. Given the competitive nature of technological advances seen between the US and nations such as China and Russia, this may come as a surprise. Nonetheless, this does not imply that AI growth has slowed or that it is significantly lagging behind other countries considering that several notable advancements have been made in recent years, with no signs of slowing down. The US will be able to be at the forefront for establishing guidelines and principles in order to allow the positives of AI to outweigh the ever-growing list of negatives. This can be achieved by becoming more proactive in developing strategies to address the need to compete in a climate in which the US is viewed as a dominating AI superpower.

Under the Trump administration, it was made clear that his government would no longer prioritise ethical issues concerning AI. This was in contrast to the previous government under the Obama administration, which had taken a more EU-based approach. The summit and resulting report produced under the Obama administration included criteria for more openness in AI-assisted decision-making processes. It also contained recommendations for ethical governance designs such as a two-stage monitoring architecture for operational and ethical and legal evaluations of AI applications (National Science and Technology Council (US), 2016a). These were subsequently removed from the May 2018 summit. In comparison to the EU strategy, the US strategy places a greater emphasis on the importance of workplace needs. This highlights the dangers of AI in the workplace and the ways in which low-wage and middle-income workers are most likely to suffer as a result of AI integration (National Science and Technology Council (US), 2016a; Growth et al., 2019). It also demonstrates that the government should enact policies to mitigate the effects of economic inequality on the American workforce (Cath et al., 2017).

As will be discussed later in the Chapter, the EU approach has largely disregarded the impact that AI might have on workers, and thus the US strategy has covered an important ground in terms of the human impact of AI. The US has always been at the forefront of technological development due to their vast amounts of funding and a colossal talent pool from which many important AI software foundations have emerged. This, combined with the US's massive industry focused on semi-conductor chips, indicates that they are unlikely to be surpassed as a global AI superpower in the near future. However, the malleability of the US's socio-political sphere means that the future of AI development is never quite certain, and therefore the US will need to take a bipartisan approach to ensure that AI and its related technologies are prioritised in future technological proposals.

3   AI Strategies of Russia and China

3.1   The Chinese AI Strategy

As represented in Table 7.1, since 2016, China has published several national documents, detailing their intention to develop and deploy AI across a variety of sectors. A state-led 10-year plan entitled "Made in China 2025" was launched in 2015; however, this was not taken seriously by international competitors. Being aware of this, the Chinese stated that the plan was merely "aspirational and unofficial" (McBride & Chatzky, 2019). In August 2016, the 13th Five-Year National Science and Technology Innovation Plan was published with the intention of establishing their plans to overtake all competitors in the international technology community. China also launched fifteen "2030 megaprojects", covering developments in robotics, big data, and manufacturing (Kania, 2018; Webster et al., 2017). However, there was a noticeable lack of attention paid towards the AI sector despite being included in previous plans such as the "Internet Plus" and "AI Three Year Implementation Plan (2016 - 2018)", released in May of 2016. In order to fill this gap, the Chinese Ministry of Science and Technology (MoST) added "Artificial Intelligence 2.0" to the list of mega-projects. In 2017, the Chinese technology sector released the "New Generation Artificial Intelligence Development Plan (AIDP)", which they viewed as one of their most important projects (Kania, 2018; Webster et al., 2017).

The aspirational strategy outlined China's ambitions to become the world leader in AI by 2030, breaking away from the competition put forward by the US in the recent years, which has resulted in a contentious rivalry between the first and second- placed superpowers (Allen, 2019). It is comprehensive to a certain degree and encompasses research and development (R&D), industrialisation, talent development, education and skills acquisition, standard setting and regulations, "ethical standards", and security efforts and objectives. According to the AIDP's three distinct approaches, China's AI sector will be on par with competitors by 2020, "world-leading" in several AI disciplines by 2025, and the "primary" hub for AI innovation by 2030 (Kania, 2018; Webster et al., 2017). They aim to develop a 1 trillion Yuan AI sector by 2030, with connected industries worth more than 10 trillion Yuan (Jain, 2019). Furthermore, the Chinese government intends to use education to attract and recruit the world's top AI professionals, improve AI training for domestic workforce, and establish global standards for laws, regulations, and ethical standards, demonstrating its desire to lead in global AI governance.

3.2   The Russian AI Strategy

In April 2016, Sberbank, a Russian majority-owned bank (the largest in Russia and Eastern Europe) (The Banker, 2014), established the first venture capital fund in Russia to focus solely on financial technology and artificial intelligence. Only two

Table 7.1 National documents published by China concerning AI

Document Title	Date	Key Elements	Importance
Made in China 2025	05.2015	Identified smart manufacturing as a major element of China's future as a global manufacturing superpower (He, 2017) Mentions and highlights the importance of robotics and AI	10-year plan to establish China as a global competitor in high-tech manufacturing
"Internet plus" and AI three year implementation plan	05.2016 (−2018)	More focused on AI emerging industry, intellectual products, IT intelligent terminal Continuation of internet plus policy	Identified AI as one of 11 priority areas to implement government strategy to accelerate the use of ICT
13th five year plan for developing National Strategic and emerging industries	08.2016 (−2020)	Launched a series of 15 "science and Technology Innovation 2030 Megaprojects" Did not explicitly include AI as a priority	Implements AI into the current five-year plan Recognised AI's strategic value to national development
Robotics industry development plan	2016	Intended to boost per capita labour productivity to a 38% increase over 5 years	First strategy to focus strongly on productivity
Artificial intelligence 2.0″	02.2017	The first mega-policy to include a focus on AI Added to the previously published 15 mega-policies	Establishes AI as a focal point of developing technology by promoting it to 'mega-project' status, brings with it funding and an ability to further cultivate the AI talent pool
Three-Year Action Plan for Promoting Development of a New Generation Artificial Intelligence Industry (2018–2020)	12.2017 (2018–2020)	More focused on industry and applications ICT and manufacturing technology deeply integrated Multiple detailed specification requirements Highlights the basic foundations needed to create a favourable environment for AI development (Ding, 2018))	More focus on individual details than other previous plans Integrates AI with other developing technologies, and proposes how this is to be done
New generation artificial intelligence development plan (AIDP)	2017	Proposed China as the world AI leader by 2030 Puts emphasis on R&D, industry, education development, and ethics	The first proper long-term plan proposed by China Demonstrates their determination to be measures above the US in AI development and use

years later, in March 2018, was the first major Russian government AI statement proposed (Ministry of Defence of the Russian Federation, 2018). The 10-point AI development proposal brought together the government sectors of the Ministry of Defence, the Ministry of Education and Science, and the Russian Academy of Sciences to direct funding and resources into developing Russian AI technologies, utilising the best education, governmental, and industrial professionals and organisations. This proposal emphasised the importance of government-led advancements in order to truly influence and modernise Russia's technological climate. Later that year, Russian President Vladimir Putin issued his "May Decrees", which aimed to accelerate national development in a number of sectors. The Digital Economy National Project, for example, proposed two separate initiatives centred on AI development. This was the first time that the Russian government had chosen to produce projects that specifically mentioned AI development, and it was a promising start for progress within the sector.

The first initiative, The Digital Technologies Federal Project, aimed to develop AI, wireless communications, virtual reality (VR), robotics, and modernise manufacturing technologies. The second initiative, The National Strategy for AI Development also known as the AI Federal Project, had a primary emphasis on AI. Both projects emphasised the importance of relying on the private sector to develop such programmes and ideas, and thus marked the beginning of the Russian government's withdrawal from further AI development. Sberbank was tasked with being the main figurehead in drafting the "Roadmap for Artificial Intelligence", which was finalised and published in October 2019 (Ministry of Digital Development, Communications, and Mass Media, 2019), demonstrating that the Russian Government was not interested in a completely state-led AI Strategy. In addition to producing strategic policy papers such as the AI Roadmap and AI Federal Project, the Russian government have explored numerous avenues for developing Russia's AI ecosystem. For innovations covered by the Digital Technologies Federal Project, the so-called "regulatory sandboxes" or experimental legal regimes were made available from January 2021. It has been proposed that regulatory sandboxes will improve Russia's investment environment by making it easier to create and test ideas by relaxing regulations that firms claim stifle innovation (Rukinov, 2021).

According to the Russian Ministry of Economic Development, eight initiatives have already been selected for inclusion in Russia's regulatory "sandboxes". Among these are the projects comprising Mobile TeleSystems, one of the country's largest mobile carriers, which include a staffless "smart hotel", the ability to sign contracts for services over the phone without a physical presence, autonomous transportation, and telemedicine (Ministry of Economic Development, 2020). Considering the fact that these development platforms are used outside of the finance market, it can be argued that the Russian approach to the development of these sandboxes differs from the approach typically seen in other countries using this in practice. In December 2020, President Vladmir Putin attended the Artificial Intelligence Journey Conference, where he presented four ideas for AI policies. These consisted of establishing experimental legal frameworks for the use of AI, developing practical measures to introduce AI algorithms, providing neural network developers with competitive access to Big Data, and boosting private investment in domestic AI industries. Whilst Russia is eager to be considered a world leader in technological modernisation, this appears unlikely in the near future considering their lack of funding and resources to make their future plans a reality.

4 Shortcomings and Recommendations

4.1 Shortcomings of the UK AI Strategy

One of the main criticisms that can be arguably levelled against the UK AI national strategy is that, while it is presented as a National Strategy for Artificial Intelligence, the majority of its contents focus on the future plans for the economy, geopolitical climate, and the manner in which AI can assist their development. Other strategies such as the EU's appear to focus primarily on their plans to develop innovative, ethical, and well-governed AI systems and technologies, as well as ways in which these can be efficiently and transparently integrated into a modern environment. However, the UK strategy appears to fall short of this standard. If ethical innovation is to be truly realised, it will necessitate both multidisciplinary subject intelligence and global diplomacy. Furthermore, if the UK intends to build alternative data custody systems, the boundaries beyond which it will not cross must be more explicitly specified. New approaches to AI development and data security are available, but adequate documentation and development of ethical AI innovation will require extensive research and funding (West & Allen, 2018). A second criticism that can be perhaps made against the legal and ethical implications of the UK strategy is that it has yet to be determined who will be held responsible and liable for any AI regulations. Currently, there does not appear to exist a clear methodology for developing such regulations or rules. Nor does it appear to exist any statement/s clarifying how stakeholders will be involved in the process (Cooper et al., 2021). Thus this will require improvement if the UK is to compete with the likes of the EU in terms of ethically proficient AI integration.

According to the National AI Strategy, the government have invested over £2.3 billion in AI initiatives since 2014. However, Shrier (n.d.), as cited by Weinberg (2022), argues that approximately three times the levels of investment discussed are required. The October budget promised £23 million for AI and data science tracking, but he proclaims that a figure closer to £100 million would be more efficient considering the UK's global competition. Shrier also claims that the government's £2.3 billion investment is dwarfed by China's contribution last year, when $52 billion were directed towards AI development, with private sector companies promising billions more. Although funding is obviously not the sole factor in determining who will be at the forefront of the AI technological race, the UK are likely to struggle until they catch up with the likes of China and the US. Similar to the EU's approach, discussed further in Sect. 4.2, students and businesses will need to equip themselves with appropriate skills in order to leverage future developments in AI (Weinberg, 2022). Christopher Philp,[1] the former UK's Minister for Tech and The Digital Economy at the Department for Digital Culture, Media, and Sport, as cited by (Pickup, 2021), states, "ensuring that business' staff have access to suitable training and development opportunities" is a great way to ensure that those working alongside AI are technologically-literate, adding that the government's online list of skills bootcamps is an excellent place to start (Pickup, 2021).

Considering the fact that the UK lags behind in terms of infrastructure (19th) and development (11th) (Weinberg, 2022), it appears that it is still a long way to catch up with countries such as the US and China. The strategy fails to emphasise the legality of AI systems, which is critical especially when competing with a country such as China, whose ethics surrounding technological advancements have been deemed questionable at best. Although the discussion presented in the focuses primarily on 'review' and 'revision', it should be asked whether data protection rights are likely to be less stringent, given that the EU's strict data protection rights were an important factor used in arguing for Brexit back in 2016. Historically, data protection laws in the UK have followed those set out in EU law (e.g., UK GDPR), and the EU has consistently attempted to balance AI performance with transparency. This could mean that, while AI technologies might not reach their full potential with the funding and resources available, citizens' rights and values are met, which is of greater importance.

The UK strategy appears to prioritise technology performance and innovation in the future, which can be interpreted as a step away from allowing full transparency of systems and data protection. This begs the question of whether the National AI Strategy is simply pro-innovation or a step back in terms of data protection rights. To answer this question, it appears that the definitions of 'innovation' must be internationally aligned - enabling standards and regulations are what the EU appears to consider innovative, but this does not appear to align with the UK strategy. To be able to address this question properly, it appears that the definition of 'innovation' must be internationally aligned as enabling standards and regulations are what the EU appear to consider innovative whereas this does not appear to align with the UK strategy.

Overall, while this strategy provides important signals for fostering and encouraging creativity, achieving ethical innovation is a more complex task that will require a carefully established framework constructed with more investment into AI implementation, as well as more considerations into the legal ramifications of modern use of AI technology on UK citizens and workers. The transparency and clarity of such practises, as emphasised in the EU strategy, should also be improved. Furthermore, the UK will need to focus even more on avoiding foreign-based takeovers of UK AI start-ups and software companies in order to keep AI technologies 'homegrown,' preventing the UK from falling even further behind in the race to become a global AI superpower.

---

[1] A member of the British Conservative Party who held the position of Parliamentary Under-Secretary of State for Tech and the Digital Economy from 2021 to 2022.

4.2   Shortcomings of the EU AI Strategy

AI has become one of the most misused terms in modern technology (Vincent, 2019). According to a study carried out by London-based investment firm MMC Ventures, as cited in Ram (2019), 40 percent (two-fifths) of Europe's 2830 AI start-ups across 13 EU nations that are classified as AI companies do not truly employ AI programs in their products in a manner that is significant to their businesses. In spite of this, the companies are frequently described as AI-focused. This is due in part to the ambiguous definition of AI, which means that businesses that believe they are using technology with ML capabilities are actually not. On the other hand, given the current enthusiasm for AI and the resulting investment surrounding those involved in the subject, some organisations attempt to profit from this uncertainty by exploiting terms such as AI, ML, and Deep Learning (DL). To prevent companies misusing such concepts, it is critical to define these terms more precisely in relation to other related ideas and to specify what they share and what they do not share.

Several EU policies, such as the Copyright Directive, were enacted with the intention of improving certain human rights but have instead had the opposite effect. The right to free speech and expression is a contentious issue in light of the increasing popularity of technology, and EU initiatives to combat misinformation may potentially grant corporations the authority to censor material online (Nielsen, 2021). Meanwhile, the EU also desire to promote innovation even though it is increasing costs for innovators through regulations such as the GDPR, which requires corporations to explain AI algorithms if an individual believes an algorithm was used discriminatorily (Brattberg et al., 2020). In essence, the EU wishes for AI to contribute to Europe's economic prosperity while also attempting to ensure that it serves the general population for the greater good. Similar to the US, the EU strive to combine public expectations for regulation with the need to innovate (Engler, 2022).

One immediately noticeable shortcoming of the EU strategy is that the Commission takes a noticeably constrained risk-based approach to their legislation. Thus, this leaves many areas unaccounted for such as the issue of liability if risks occur as a consequence of the use of AI, worker-protection legislation, and the numerous grey-areas that emerge due to the use of regulatory sandboxes when testing new business models (Pierides & Roxon, 2021). One suggestion for addressing these issues could be to enact a directive that focuses on employment-based AI risks, thereby protecting workers and businesses to a higher standard and allowing them to hold and express their rights on an individual or group basis. By holding employers to a higher standard in their implementation and use of AI technologies, just as they are expected to uphold regulatory health and safety standards, AI can be more tightly regulated, allowing the EU to avoid issues such as data protection scandals and AI misuse observed in other countries (Del Castillo, 2021). Transparency is a major issue in all sectors of AI use, and the EU strategy does not account for employers being required to provide complete transparency with their employees when implementing AI into their practises. This is an obvious flaw in a strategy that takes pride in enforcing strict regulations in order to provide AI in ways that uphold its values, have positive effects, and work alongside its citizens.

Ensuring that employees' data protection rights are upheld is a separate matter. While the GDPR laws have facilitated employees' data protection rights in the workplace, this does not cover all applicable bases, especially with the growing popularity of AI technology across a wide range of areas. Furthermore, AI technologies can effortlessly collect data on workers. These issues, when combined, result in a significant gap in AI implementation within the workplace. This gap is further exacerbated by many AI users who do not simply understand the purpose of newly introduced algorithms and the potential dangers that they can introduce into the workplace. With the proposed directive, employees subject to EU regulations should be required to consult their employees as opposed to simply informing them when new algorithms are possibly being introduced (Del Castillo, 2021). This is due to the fact that this might assist them in fully understanding the weight and technology with which they are working. As it is the case with the implementation of AI across all sectors of society, technology should not play the last part in any process. It is imperative to ensure that AI and related technologies are not provided with the ability to make final decisions, or decisions that might impact the employees, clients and related individuals. Due to the complexity of modernising technology and integrating it into workplaces, IT consultants and related employees must be involved in all processes in order to protect employees' rights across all technological fields (Del Castillo, 2021). This is not explicitly mentioned as a regulation in the EU strategy, and can thus be viewed as a flaw in the proposal.

Preserving EU citizens' fundamental right to life must be a primary consideration in the debate over the use of military technology while simultaneously ensuring that the EU's key foundational ideals are upheld. This ensures that developing nuclear weapons and modern military-grade technology in the same way as the US, China or Russia would not be possible. The EU should focus on developing values-based, morally sound military technology with no negative consequences. The same can be stated about AI developed by the EU: although it can be the most outstanding AI globally, it must adhere to the EU rules and principles. Furthermore, needless to say, it should be designed to convey a stern warning to any government that employs malevolent AI and fails to adhere to these ethical standards (Del Castillo, 2021).

4.3 Shortcomings of the US AI Strategy

When the Trump administration took office in 2016, there were concerns about the viability of international relationships, particularly in the technology community. Trump's strict views on non-American citizens were controversial for a variety of reasons. While his emphasis on 'homegrown talent' drew a large number of patriotic Conservatives who truly believed that the country's reliance on international trade was a hindrance to progress, there was a significant risk to the country's emerging technology talent pool. By restricting work and student visas, the already limited number of AI researchers based in the US was further reduced. In May 2019, the White House OSTP proposed a subcommittee on Research Security "to protect America's researchers from undue foreign influence without compromising our values or our ability to maintain the openness and integrity of our innovation ecosystem." Researchers and universities were caught between a rock and a hard place, having to choose between U.S. and international investment (Aaronson, 2020).

Although this appeared to be an ingenious approach by the US to promote home-grown talent while removing the risks associated with outside competitors, the move was somewhat counterintuitive. This was perceived by China as a threat to bilateral technological relations. Arguably, by continuing down the path of increasing competitiveness, the US under the Trump administration was only alienating itself from any viable and meaningful collaborations and partnerships with other AI powers. Hence, the US did not appear to be in a position to sustain this for their long-term AI goals (Aaronson, 2020). This sparked a pressing conversation about the history of AI and its application for public good. Had the US indeed cut ties with countries such as China, it would have been unclear whether the US intended to preserve openness and integrity of its innovation ecosystem or whether there were other factors at play.

However, reducing their association with Chinese AI firms can also be considered a positive step towards taking a decisive stance against China's human rights abuses on an international scale. This is owing to the Chinese Government's insistence on violating the human rights of minorities within their country, and those who wish to report on the atrocities being committed. It can be argued that a more efficient strategy could have been adopted by the US, such as working with their allies on a unified strategy to overcome such obstacles. By severing ties with Chinese companies, US firms might suffer losses to their competitors. Whilst this is somewhat beneficial, it can also mean that the US's customer base will be likely to decline. Instead of collaborating with US allies on a unified strategy, the Trump administration blacklisted companies in October 2019 that allegedly used AI services to monitor Uighurs within China. Among the companies blacklisted were Megvii, an image recognition software developer; iFlytek, a voice recognition specialist; Hikvision, one of the world's largest Closed-Circuit Television (CCTV) system manufacturers; and Yitu, a developer of machine imaging and voice recognition software. These firms rely on US-based knowledge and expertise, but as previously stated, US firms rely on these companies as customers and competitors. These companies are reliant on US-based knowledge and expertise, and some US's firms, in turn, depend on these companies both as customers and as competitors.

By adopting this approach, the US became the first country to punish Chinese firms for misusing AI technologies, reiterating its commitment to condemning human rights violations (Aaronson, 2020). However, by doing so, the US also signalled that it was unwilling to encourage and possibly allow international collaboration on AI variants based on Facial Recognition (FR) software despite the potential benefits of such technologies. The move could possibly inspire China to devote more resources to separating its companies from U.S. firms, researchers, and capital, which can have a global impact given that almost every data giant has an AI research lab in China (Vincent, 2017). Many of these companies not only collaborate on research with US universities but also rely on advanced US chips. Pursuant to Aaronson (2020), "In the long term, the move could spell an end to partnerships with U.S. companies and institutions that go back years and limit access to top overseas talent." Instead of cutting ties and shutting down partnerships, the new US Government under President Biden and other successive US administrations could place a closer focus on integrating national security strategies with AI's. This will once again enable the US to work constructively with overseas AI firms. Both of these issues are highly complex, and the integration of both sectors might present its own set of uniquely challenging issues. However, the US's stance, that it can and will be the only leader, on their future AI and technology development has been somewhat counterintuitive in recent years following the presidency of Donald Trump. The foregoing discussion must not be construed as the fact that the US should be expected to overlook the atrocities being committed by the Chinese government. However, AI will only reach its full potential if a balance can be struck between progressing AI as a global public good and allowing AI research collaboration from other technology leaders to take place. This must be based on the understanding that there is no threat to National Security in the specific areas that are being worked on.

Another notable shortcoming of the US's approach to AI could be its inability to regulate false and dangerous information disseminated online via AI systems. Section 230 of the Communications Decency Act states that content providers' protection should be upheld to the highest possible standards. This might mean that the public face harm as a consequence of their protection being deemed less important than the content being pushed out by providers. Furthermore, the Trump administration formally refused to sign the "Christchurch Call to Action Summit" also known as "Christchurch Call",[2] a declaration signed by 17 other governments to commit to taking steps to ensure the eradication of terrorist and violent extremist content online (Aaronson, 2020). This has been seen by some observers as a significant shortcoming of the US's AI usage and strategies.

Modern AI can be ingeniously used to positively shape the future of public Internet use, and social media platforms such as Facebook must be held to high standard when advocating the use of AI to advance the eradication of dangerous materials online. Some have argued that the US government appear to be disregarding this application of AI for lawful purposes, instead prioritising business ventures with online content providers over the need for restrictions on harmful content. One factor that may contribute to this might be the absence of a unified federal data protection law in the US (Fischer et al., 2021). Current cybersecurity and data protection laws vary from state to state, which has proven to be somewhat ineffective, leading companies to exploit loopholes around non-federal laws and, ultimately, jeopardise citizens' personal data protection. Consequently, while the US is far

---

[2] A political summit convened by New Zealand Prime Minister Jacinda Ardern on May 15, 2019 in Paris, France

from lacking a comprehensive AI strategy aimed at advancing the next generation of AI technology on a national and international scale, it must be asked whether this is ultimately undermining the concept of AI as a public good (Aaronson, 2020).

Furthermore, despite the fact that US emphasises the importance of transparency in the future of AI, it does not specify how this might be enforced. In contrast, the third pillar of the UK's national AI strategy openly states their objectives and processes in order to introduce a transparent and ethically proficient future of AI. According to the US's strategy, in order to increase transparency, more research will be conducted. However, this research indicates that there is an increasing need for transparency within the US technology sector, thereby potentially making this suggestion ineffective (National Science and Technology Council (US), 2016a). To develop the talent required to implement its national AI goals, the US must drastically revitalise its STEM[3] education system whereby it compels an emphasis on Computer Science education in schools and early childhood. Failure to invest in STEM technology could potentially risk relegating the US as a serious competitor in the field of AI (Vincent, 2017).

4.4   Shortcomings of the Chinese AI Strategy

The Chinese strategy has several flaws, one of which is its reliance on globally produced AI systems. AI systems are frequently developed from pre-existing programmes developed by others in the field and shared to a data library, saving time and resources that can instead be focused on the systems' specific requirements. The majority of the most popular ML software frameworks are developed in Western countries, most notably the US, resulting in a significant shortfall in Chinese AI development (Allen, 2019). However, because China has access to vast amounts of global technology research and markets, this does not have a direct impact on their levels of AI development in the short term. For instance, in the consumer drones market, where the leading Chinese company DJI holds 74% of the global market share, the US owns 35% of the materials in each drone, owing primarily to the US' central role in the manufacturing of semi-conductors. Due to its critical role in ML and AI technologies, semiconductor technology is regarded as critical for the rapidly developing digital economy (Calhoun, 2021).

Semiconductor manufacturing and construction are a key part of China's future plans as they intend to rely less on foreign imports of such critical technological components and more on domestic technology to maintain their status as a manufacturing superpower. China's concerns are not unfounded, as evidenced by the fact that one of the country's largest electronics manufacturers, ZTE, faced bankruptcy after the US imposed export restrictions on critical products such as semiconductors

---

[3]A broad term used to categorise four different academic disciplines comprising Science, Technology, Engineering and Mathematics (STEM)

(Allen, 2019). As stated in China's New Generation AIDP, homegrown talent and manufacturing power will be developed in the coming years. As also highlighted, this should be at the forefront of any development plans that China draw up, ultimately reducing their reliance on international collaborations, imports, and software foundations. Currently, there do not exist laws in China that allow for clear data ownership. While there are some specific restrictions on data collection, processing, and storage (Ning & Wu, 2022), implementing these is intricate considering the ambiguity of data ownership rules. More emphasis should be placed on this when developing future AI and data ownership proposals.

When examining China's expansive and ever-growing AI initiatives, it is arduous to distinguish between their Intelligence advancements for technological purposes and their need for mass surveillance techniques. According to Sheehan (2022), "it's tempting to view these initiatives as little more than a fig leaf to cover widespread buses of human rights." However, China's AI ecosystem has had an impact on global AI development, owing to its technological development over the last few decades. Furthermore, when comparing Chinese AI strategies to those of their leading international competitors, their regulations, that allow for a path to immense human rights violations, must not be overlooked. It would be an easy solution to simply discuss the technological impact of all of the aforementioned strategies on global advancements in the field. However, many mitigating legal and ethical factors must not be overlooked particularly when examining advancements made in President Putin's Russia or under the Chinese Communist party.

Surveillance is simply a new way of life for Chinese citizens, ushering in a new wave of "techno-authoritarianism" (Wang, 2021). This authoritarianism must be countered by other AI superpowers to prevent the Chinese government from adopting even more extreme approaches concerning its surveillance and control procedures. With the world's largest population and growth that show no signs of slowing, the Chinese government claim that their use of vast surveillance techniques is simply allowing them to meet the modern needs of a developing global superpower. Because China lacks the rules that allow holding companies accountable for any violations they commit, certain "shortcuts" can be used when developing intelligence technologies. It is unlikely that any significant changes will be made to the future of human rights laws in China, especially under the current government. Instead, legislations such as The Global Magnitsky Act sanctions, which allow US policymakers to impose sanctions on companies that violate human rights (Wang, 2021), could be useful in preventing countries and their associated organisations from collaborating with states such as China, engaged with human rights abuses. This potentially enables these entities to readjust their actions in order to avoid being sanctioned.

4.5   *Shortcomings of the Russian AI Strategy*

In light of the recent invasion of Ukraine by Russian forces, multiple North Atlantic Treaty Organization (NATO) countries have imposed a wide range of sanctions on Russian-owned businesses and corporations. Due to economic restrictions preventing new investment in Russia, this has had significant implications for Russian technological developments. Organizations worldwide are making the decision to comply with these sanctions and, in some cases, are entirely withdrawing from the Russian market (Lichfield et al., 2022). The economic consequences of the Russian invasion of Ukraine will undoubtedly have a devastating impact on Russian AI development. Since announcing in 2017, "AI is the future, not only for Russia, but for all of humanity" (West & Karsten, 2019), Russian President Vladimir Putin has pushed for Russia to eventually become a world leader in AI technologies. However, developments in this sector have been slowed due to a recent need for increased military spending and a lack of access to international resources.

Although Russia is considered to be one of the top AI players such as the UK, it has always lagged behind the US in the majority of key AI benchmarks (Vanian, 2022). Margarita Konaev, an Associate Director of Analysis and Research Fellow at Georgetown University's Centre for Security and Emerging Technology, as cited in Vanian (2022), points to the fact that Russia is primarily interested in researching AI for autonomous drones and surveillance systems. However, she argues that recent economic restrictions, such as those barring Russia from importing computer chips, might jeopardise the country's ability to actually build the technology (Vanian, 2022). Furthermore, the Russian Association of Electronic Communications advocacy organisation estimates that between 50,000 and 70,000 Russian IT employees have fled the country as a result of the sanctions, which have cut off access to technologies required for their work (Metz & Satariano, 2022). AI is becoming increasingly important in discussions surrounding terms concerning modern conflicts. AI can not only understand and translate documents from Russian, which is critical for lawyers and organisations involved in enacting and enforcing ever-increasing sanctions, but can also help to anticipate future changes in standards and regulations by adapting as social customs or laws shift (Weaver, 2022). Russian businesses' and associated stakeholder groups' potential lack of compliance with such sanctions could have disastrous moral and ethical consequences for their futures.

More businesses will need to fully utilise AI systems and technologies to remain compliant with the unprecedented volume of legal documentation that will need to be reviewed and which is frequently stored inefficiently across different environments. This is necessary to keep up with the changes in laws and regulations. AI is capable of partially understanding the documents, allowing a large number of them to be rapidly processed and key information to be extracted and subsequently acted upon. This comprehensive view of an organization's entire contractual environment, regardless of the number, complexity, or language of the papers, makes AI indispensable to attorneys in the midst of what are arguably the most rapid and irreversible sanctions ever imposed on a major economy. AI will help appropriate organisations respond to even the most unexpected events and regulatory upheavals, assisting with contractual interpretations and freeing up legal teams to deal with the other consequences of these developments (Weaver, 2022).

Furthermore, the funding that Russia had to support their AI research and development appears to have been depleted as a result of their main contributor, Sberbank, recently declaring bankruptcy due to international sanctions. Sberbank invested 45 percent of its funds in the AI Roadmap. Therefore, so the economic implications of fulfilling the objectives outlined in the Russian AI strategy are likely to be severe. In addition, the 2019 Roadmap outlined the Kremlin's overall strategy for increasing Russia's share of the global AI market from 0.2 percent in 2018 to 1.8 percent in 2024 by expanding scientific research into AI, increasing data availability, and implementing a new digital regulatory structure. The strategy, however, was imprecise and lacked critical financial details. It was asserted that the Kremlin would dominate AI research in Russia while the government was concurrently outsourcing AI implementation and some financing to state-owned companies, such Sberbank, as part of the Digital Technologies Federal Project (Petrella et al., 2021). The Russian government's AI strategy was seen as highly aspirational at the time of its release, perhaps owing to its inability to truly cement itself as a genuine AI superpower. However, there was no doubt that their rapid development across other sectors in the twenty-first century has proven that they might be able to achieve such goals even though the recent sanctions against it have cast serious doubts on this ability.

5   Conclusion

As demonstrated in this chapter, each national AI strategy presents its own set of unique challenges in terms of the legal, ethical, economic, and overall societal impact of AI and related technologies. This brings with it an array of issues and shortcomings that must be addressed in order to truly comprehend how the society can coexist peacefully with intelligent technology. Advances in AI are transforming many aspects of human existence, and, with ML already being used in fields such as the military, it's difficult not to wonder whether coexisting with machines that can almost think for themselves will be more of a gift than a burden. Ensuring that the ethical ramifications of this are regulated is of utmost importance and should therefore be prioritised in any future strategies developed by any of the aforementioned countries. Competitiveness is the driving force behind the majority of national developments and strategies. However, collaboration should arguably be the next step in ensuring that we have complete control over the technology we utilise in our daily lives. AI is already a potentially dangerous entity; hence, governments will need to ensure that they collaborate to the best of their abilities in order to fully capitalise on the potential that AI and ML have to offer.

References

Aaronson, S. A.. (2020). America's uneven approach to AI and its consequences, *Institute for International Economic Policy Working Paper Series* AI4EU Consortium, (2021), About the Project, https://www.ai4eu.eu/about-project

AI4Europe. (n.d.). Europe's AI-on-Demand Platform. Available at: https://www.ai4europe.eu/. (Accessed: 14/12/2022).

Allen, G. C. (2019). Understanding China's AI strategy: Clues to Chinese strategic thinking on artificial intelligence and National Security. https://www.cnas.org/publications/reports/understanding-chinas-ai-strategy

Andraško, J., Mesarčík, M., & Hamuľák, O. (2021). The regulatory intersections between artificial intelligence, data protection and cyber security: challenges and opportunities for the EU legal framework. *AI & SOCIETY, 36*(2), 623–636. https://doi.org/10.1007/s00146-020-01125-5

Barclays Business. (2021). Insight to AI in UK AgriTech. *Barclays.*. https://www.barclays.co.uk/content/dam/documents/business/business-insight/Insights_AI_in_Agriculture.pdf

Brattberg, E., Csernatoni, R., & Rugova, V. (2020). *Europe and AI: Leading, lagging behind, or carving its own way?* Carnegie Endowment for International Peace [Online].

Calhoun, G. (2021). The U.S. still dominates in semiconductors; China is vulnerable (Pt 2). https://www.forbes.com/sites/georgecalhoun/2021/10/11/the-us-still-dominates-in-semiconductors-china-is-vulnerable-pt-2/?sh=59bd140670f7

Cath, C., Wachter, S., Mittelstadt, B., Mariarosaria, T., & Luciano, F. (2017). Artificial intelligence and the 'good society': The US, EU, and UK approach. *Science and Engineering Ethics.*

Clark, J. (2022). The UK government gives itself the power to prevent foreign takeovers of domestic companies in 17 areas, including artificial intelligence, robotics, chips, transport and nuclear power. *Aviation Analysis.* https://www.aviationanalysis.net/the-uk-government-gives-itself-the-power-to-prevent-foreign-takeovers-of-domestic-companies-in-17-areas-including-artificial-intelligence-robotics-chips-transport-and-nuclear-power/

Confederation of Laboratories for Artificial Intelligence Research in Europe (CLAIRE). (2018). A Brief History of CLAIRE, https://claire-ai.org/about/

Cooper, D., Hansen, M., Peets, L., Young, M., Reilly, T., Jungyun, C., Drake, M., & Ong, J. (2021). The UK government publishes its AI strategy. *Art Intelligence.*

Davies, R. (2022). UK government extends powers to intervene in foreign takeovers. *The Guardian [online].*. https://www.theguardian.com/business/2022/jan/04/uk-government-extends-powers-to-intervene-in-foreign-takeovers

Del Castillo, A. (2021). The missing link in Europe's AI strategy. *Project syndicate,* https://www.project-syndicate.org/commentary/eu-artificial-intelligence-regulation-must-protect-worker-rights-by-aida-ponce-del-castillo-2021-08

Dep. For Business, Energy & Industrial Strategy. (2021). *UK innovation strategy.* National Archives.

Ding, J. (2018). *Deciphering China's AI dream.* Centre for the Governance of AI.

Engler, A. (2022). The EU and U.S. are starting to align on AI regulation. *TechTank.*

EU Commission. (2018). *Communication artificial intelligence for europe, shaping Europe's digital future.* European Commission.

Fischer, S., Leung, J., Anderljung, M., O'Keefe, C., Torges, S., Khan, S. M., Garfinkel, B., & Dafoe, A. (2021). *AI policy levers: A review of the U.S.* Government's Tools to Shape AI Research, Development, and Deployment.

Growth, O., Nitzberg, M., & Zehr, D. (2019). Comparison of National Strategies to promote artificial intelligence. *Konrad Adenauer Stiftung.* https://www.kas.de/documents/252038/4521287/Comparison+of+National+Strategies+to+Promote+Artificial+Intelligence+Part+1.pdf/397fb700-0c6f-88b6-46be-2d50d7942b83?version=1.1&t=1560500570070

Hall, W., & Pesenti, J. (2017). *Growing the artificial intelligence industry in the UK.* UK. https://www.gov.uk/government/publications/growing-the-artificial-intelligence-industry-in-the-uk

He, Y. (2017). How China is preparing for an AI-powered future. *Wilson Centre*. https://www.wilsoncenter.org/sites/default/files/media/documents/publication/how_china_is_preparing_for_ai_powered_future.pdf

Horowitz, M. C. (2018). Artificial intelligence, international competition, and the balance of power. *Texas National Security Review, 1*, 3. https://doi.org/10.15781/T2639KP49

Jain, A. (2019). *AI policy analysis: AIDP of China vs.* India's NITI Aayog AI policy paper. https://www.orfonline.org/expert-speak/ai-policy-analysis-aidp-of-china-vs-indias-niti-aayog-ai-policy-paper-52935/

Kania, E. (2018). China's AI agenda advances. *The Diplomat Online*. https://thediplomat.com/2018/02/chinas-ai-agenda-advances/

Kazim, E., Almeida, D., Kingsman, N., Kerrigan, C., Koshiyama, A., Lomas, E., & Hilliard, A. (2021). Innovation and opportunity: Review of the UK's national AI strategy. *Discov Artif Intell*. https://doi.org/10.1007/s44163-021-00014-0

Keeling, E. (2021). The UK's national AI strategy: Setting a 10-year agenda to make the UK a global AI superpower. *Allen & Overy [online]*. https://www.allenovery.com/en-gb/global/blogs/digital-hub/the-uks-national-ai-strategy%2D%2D-setting-a-10-year-agenda-to-make-the-uk-a-global-ai-superpower

Lichfield, C., Nikoladze, M., & Busch, S., (2022), Global sanctions dashboard: Russia and beyond, *Atlantic council [online]*,

LinkedIn. (2019). AI Talent in the European Labour Market. https://economicgraph.linkedin.com/content/dam/me/economicgraph/en-us/reference-cards/research/2019/LinkedIn-AI-Talent-in-the-European-Labour-Market.pdf

McBride, J., & Chatzky, A. (2019). Is 'made in China 2025' a threat to global trade? *Council on Foreign Relations*. https://www.cfr.org/backgrounder/made-china-2025-threat-global-trade

Metz, C., & Satariano, A. (2022). Russian tech industry faces 'brain drain' as workers flee. *The New York Times Online*.

Milligan, E., & Gemmell, K. (2022). UK flexes its new National Security Powers to intervene on deals. *Bloomberg Online*. https://www.bloomberg.com/news/articles/2022-05-27/uk-flexes-its-new-national-security-powers-to-intervene-on-deals

Ministry of Defense of the Russian Federation. (2018). Artificial intelligence: Problems and solutions [conference]. http://mil.ru/conferences/is-intellekt.htm

Ministry of Digital Development, Communications, and Mass Media. (2019). Roadmap for the Development of 'end-to-end' digital technologies. *Neurotechnology and artificial intelligence*, https://digital.gov.ru/ru/documents/6658/.

Ministry of Economic Development. (2020). Passport of the AI Federal Project. https://www.tadviser.ru/images/5/5b/2_5373326957167511384.pdf.

National Science and Technology Council (US). (2016a). Committee on Technology. Subcommittee on Machine Learning and Artificial Intelligence. Preparing for the Future of Artificial Intelligence. Executive Office of the President of the United States.

National Science and Technology Council (US). (2016b). Networking and Information Technology. Research and Development Subcommittee. The National Artificial Intelligence Research and Development Strategic Plan. Executive Office of the President of the United States.

Networking and Information Technology Research and Development Subcommittee. (2016). The national artificial intelligence research and development strategic plan, *14*, 26.

NHS AI Lab. (2022). Our national AI strategy ambitions [online]. https://www.nhsx.nhs.uk/ai-lab/ai-lab-programmes/the-national-strategy-for-ai-in-health-and-social-care/our-national-strategy-ambitions/

Nielsen, R. K. (2021). How to respond to disinformation while protecting free speech. *Reuters Institute [Online]*.

NíFhaoláin, L., Hines, A., & Nallur, V. (2020). *Assessing the Appetite for Trustworthiness and the Regulation of Artificial Intelligence in Europe* (pp. 1–12). Technological University Dublin, School of Computer Science, Dublin.

Ning, S. X., & Wu, H., (2022), China's techno-authoritarianism has gone global, *Global legal insights,* https://www.globallegalinsights.com/practice-areas/ai-machine-lear, ning-and-big-data-laws-and-regulations/china

Parker, L. E. (2018). Creation of the National Artificial Intelligence Research and development strategic plan. *Association for the Advancement of Artificial Intelligence.*

Petrella, S., Miller, C., & Cooper, B. (2021). Russia's artificial intelligence strategy: The role of state-owned firms. *Orbis.* https://www.sciencedirect.com/science/article/abs/pii/S0030438720300648

Pickup, O. (2021). Will the new national strategy make the UK an AI superpower? *RACONTEUR.* https://www.raconteur.net/technology/will-the-new-national-strategy-make-the-uk-an-ai-superpower/

Pierides, M., & Roxon, C. (2021). *Legislative approaches to AI: European Union v.* United Kingdom. https://www.jdsupra.com/legalnews/legislative-approaches-to-ai-european-7749490/

PYMNTS. (2021). *UK AgTech Firms Use AI.* New Technology to Reduce Labor Costs.

Ram, A. (2019). Europe's AI start-ups often do not use AI, study finds. *Financial Times..* Available at: https://www.ft.com/content/21b19010-3e9f-11e9-b896-fe36ec32aece (Accessed August 6, 2022)

Rukinov, M. (2021). Russia's regulatory sandbox and the implementation of blockchain tech. https://cointelegraph.com/news/russia-s-regulatory-sandbox-and-the-implementation-of-blockchain-tech

Select Committee on AI of the National Science and Technology Council. (2019). The National Artificial Intelligence Research and development strategic plan: 2019 update, https://www.nitrd.gov/pubs/National-AI-RD-Strategy-2019.pdf

Shead, S. (2022). French billionaire's stake in BT probed under Britain's tough new security law. *CNBC [online].* https://www.cnbc.com/2022/05/26/bt-and-newport-wafer-fab-deals-probed-by-britains-new-security-act.html (Accessed: 14/12/2022).

Sheehan, M. (2022). China's new AI governance initiatives Shouldn't be ignored. *Carnegie Endowment Online.* https://carnegieendowment.org/2022/01/04/china-s-new-ai-governance-initiatives-shouldn-t-be-ignored-pub-86127

Smith, C., McGuire, B., Huang, T., & Yang, G. (2006). The history of artificial intelligence. *University of Washington.* https://courses.cs.washington.edu/courses/csep590/06au/projects/history-ai.pdf

Smuhana. (2018). High-Level Expert Group on Artificial Intelligence. In *Shaping Europe's digital future.* European Commission.

Stephens, K., (2021), The UK as a Global Superpower, *Bird & Bird [Online],* https://www.two-birds.com/en/insights/2021/uk/the-uk-as-a-global-ai-superpower#:~:text=On%2022%20September%202021%2C%20during,boosting%20business%20use%20of%20AI.

The Banker. (2014). Top 1000 world banks – Sales bring changes in CEE but Russia still rules.

Toosi, A., Bottino, A., Saboury, B., & Siegel Rahmim, A.. (2021). A brief history of AI: how to prevent another winter (a critical review).

Vanian, J. (2022). Invading Ukraine has upended Russia's a.I. ambitions—And not even China may be able to help. *Fortune Online.* https://fortune.com/2022/03/25/russia-ai-sanctions-ukraine-china/

Vincent, J. (2017). China and the US are battling to become the world's first AI superpower, *the verge [online]*

Vincent, J. (2019). Forty percent of 'AI startups' in Europe don't actually use AI, claims report, *the verge online,* https://www.theverge.com/2019/3/5/18251326/ai-startups-europe-fake-40-percent-mmc-report

Wang, M. (2021). China's techno-authoritarianism has gone global. *Foreign Affairs.*

Weaver, E. (2022). Using AI to navigate compliance with Russian sanctions. https://aibusiness.com/document.asp?doc_id=776878&

Webster, G., Creemers, R., Triolo, P., & Kania, E. (2017). China's 'New generation artificial intelligence development plan. *New America.* https://www.newamerica.org/cybersecurity-initiative/

digichina/blog/full-translation-chinas-new-generation-artificial-intelligence-development-plan-2017/

Weinberg, J. (2022). Building an AI superpower: Does the UK stand a chance? *ITPro.*. Available at: https://www.itpro.co.uk/technology/artificial-intelligence-ai/362082/building-an-ai-superpower-does-the-uk-stand-a-chance (Accessed August 4, 2022).

West, D M., Allen, J R., (2018), How artificial intelligence is transforming the world, .

West, D., & Karsten, J. (2019). It's time to start thinking about governance of autonomous weapons, *TechTank –* .

Zhang, D., Mishra, S., Brynjolfsson, E., Etchemendy, J., Ganguli, D., Grosz, B., ... & Perrault, R. (2021). The AI Index 2021 Annual Report. AI Index Steering Committee, Human-Centered AI Institute, Stanford University, Stanford, CA.

Printed in the United States
by Baker & Taylor Publisher Services